The Kids' Catalog Collection

The Kids'

A SELECTIVE GUIDE
TO MORE THAN 500
CATALOGS JAM-PACKED
WITH TOYS, BOOKS, CLOTHES,

Catalog

SPORTING GOODS,
PARTY SUPPLIES,
AND EVERYTHING ELSE
KIDS WANT
AND NEED

Collection

• JANE SMOLIK •

The Globe Pequot Press

Chester, Connecticut

Library of Congress Cataloging–in–Publication Data

Smolik, Jane.
   The kids' catalog collection / by Jane Smolik. — 1st ed.
     p.   cm.
   Includes index.
   ISBN 0-87106-433-2
   1. Children's paraphernalia—Catalogs—Directories. 2. Mail-order business—Directories. 3. Catalogs, Commercial—Directories.
   I. Title.
HD9970.5.C482S66   1990
670'.29'4—dc20   90-42796
                                            CIP

Illustrations by David Reau Johnson

Manufactured in the United States of America
First Edition/First Printing

Table of Contents

■

■ Dear Reader,

The idea for this book came about one day when, to my delight, I found an inexpensive source of tights for my four-year-old daughter. Libby easily goes through tights, and I was paying between $4.00 and $7.00 a pair. After trying all the local discount stores, I discovered a catalog called Showcase of Savings that featured Little L'Eggs Tights in seven colors for $1.67 a pair. If I bought six pair or more at a time, they'd cut the price further to just over a dollar a pair.

A week or so later I armed myself with The Oriental Trading Company catalog to plan Libby's birthday party. This catalog offers a wealth of inexpensive ideas for party favors and stocking stuffers—everything from dinosaur erasers to bangle bracelets for pennies. Because little girls love (and usually lose) jewelry, I was in search of some affordable jewels. I came across a 36-piece birthstone-ring assortment for only $10.80 and an assortment of rhinestone-encrusted bangle bracelets for $10.80 a dozen. Twelve little girls, bedecked in their new jewels, left that party very happy!

I'm like most parents I know—with so many of us working nowadays, no one wants to spend precious lunch hours or leisure time trekking from store to store. Even in major metropolitan areas, it's often impossible to find what you're looking for. If you do, you're often too pressed for time to do any comparison shopping. If you try to shop on the weekends, you may still come up empty-handed, particularly if your kids are along. After all, kids don't necessarily make the most cooperative shopping companions. Even the best behaved havé been known to run from aisle to aisle pleading for presents. Consequently it's not uncommon for parents to flee their local mall with nothing to show for their efforts.

Shopping by mail for your kids can change all that. You don't need a babysitter, you can browse to your heart's content, and in many instances you can realize substantial savings. Besides, the variety of goods available by mail is staggering—everything from clothing, bedding, and furniture to dinosaur cake pans, piñatas, and screenplays for your kids' favorite shows.

To make your life easier, I've culled here the best kids' catalogs and brochures out of the thousands vying for a share of the $85-million-dollar-a-year mail order market. Whenever possible, each entry includes not only the catalog's mailing address but its phone number and cost as well. I have also listed each catalog's number of pages, although by the time you order a company's catalog this number could change.

In most entries I've also tried to give you an idea of prices for specific purchases. Keep in mind that prices change frequently. All the same, I felt it was important to let you know whether you're dealing with a Neiman Marcus or a J. C. Penney.

Finally, I have included a few choice foreign catalogs available through the mail.

In cases where prices are not listed in U.S. dollars, you can easily find out the exchange rates for the French franc and English pound by calling a large bank and asking for the foreign-currency teller. You'll need an international money order (IMO) to buy foreign catalogs or to purchase goods from them, but these can be purchased at a bank or post office. Or you can use your credit card to make purchases and let the bank figure the exact exchange rate for you.

I should also point out that many catalogs, because of the variety of quality merchandise they offer, defied the categorizing system I adopted for this book. They almost forced me to emphasize one line of their products at the expense of other, equally fine, lines. That's where my cross referencing comes to the rescue; it lets me remind you that these other fine products are available, too. So don't think that the cross references suggest products of inferior quality; to do so will be doing yourself a disservice.

I have received and read every single catalog listed here and have made every attempt to provide you with accurate and up-to-date information. But the mail order business has a high turnover rate, so it's entirely likely that, by the time this book gets to you, a handful of the companies will already have gone out of business. Another handful will have disconnected their old 800 number in favor of a new one offered at a better rate by a competing telephone company. I apologize in advance for any inconvenience this may cause, but it is truly unavoidable.

The Kids' Catalog Collection is meant to be referred to again and again. I hope you'll keep it with your phone book or on your desk—wherever you'll be able to refer to it easily for those many occasions when you need to buy something fun or something useful for your kids.

Sincerely,

Jane Smolik

Jane Smolik

P.S. Please let me know if you discover a wonderful new catalog that isn't listed here. You can write me c/o The Globe Pequot Press, 138 West Main Street, Chester, CT 06412.

■ What to Do If You're Not Satisfied with Your Order

Mail order businesses are required by the Federal Trade Commission's Mail Order Rule of 1975 to ship goods within thirty days after receiving your order. If they cannot send the merchandise by then, they must notify you by sending you an option notice. This notice gives you a revised shipping date and offers you the option of waiting for the merchandise or canceling your order and receiving a refund.

If you have another complaint with your order, a letter (save a copy for your files) usually gets results. If not, contact The Direct Marketing Association. The oldest trade organization of mail order businesses, the Direct Marketing Association has maintained a free mediation service for twenty years that resolves problems between mail order customers and companies at no charge. Send a letter clearly explaining your problem and with copies of documentation to:

> Mail Order Action Line
> 6 East 43rd Street
> New York, NY 10017

If you have paid for your purchase with a major credit card, you have another option available to you. Suppose you have been billed for merchandise that you haven't received. Write your credit card company, and they will credit your account for the amount of the purchase. Then they'll contact the company to see what the hold-up is. When the merchandise is shipped, they will rebill you. This method works for any sort of dispute, including disputes over defective merchandise. You will not be required to pay for the disputed portion of your bill (nor will you be assessed a finance charge) until the dispute is resolved.

Arts and Crafts

■

■ The American Needlewoman

Box 6472, Fort Worth, TX 76115, (800) 433–2231
Minimum phone order is $19.95, but there is no minimum when ordering by mail.

Free 72-page color catalog

In business since 1976, The American Needlewoman has gathered some attractive and unusual items. Chicken or bunny Easter baskets with plastic canvas needlepoint kits cost as little as $9.49 (all supplies included). You can appliqué a furry animal on your child's sweatshirt either by hand or machine sewing for $11.95 per pet. Each kit includes fur, eyes, nose, fabric, drawings, and instructions.

This catalog offers mostly adult fare, but a nice sampling for children includes baby quilts, afghans, and accessories. They offer twenty-two different pillowcases for stamped cross stitch, many of which are designed for children.

A very merry treat are the fourteen Christmas stocking kits in felt appliqué or counted cross stitch at $13.95 each. Ten gaily decorated tree skirts in felt or latch hook are equally appealing.

■ Annie's Attic

Rt. 2, Box 212B, Big Sandy, TX 75755, (800) 527–8452; in Texas, (800) 456–2131; in Alaska, Hawaii, and Canada, (214) 636–4353

$1.95 for 24-page color catalog

Annie's Attic is chock-full of crochet patterns for children's items. You will find seven slipper patterns in mother and daughter sizes for $7.95 per kit. Several patterns in crochet fashion outfits for 11½-inch dolls are included. Among the more unusual patterns are whole roomfuls of doll furniture made with 7-mesh plastic canvas and worsted-weight yarn. Twenty-three doll family-room projects, eleven projects for a doll living room, and twenty-seven pieces that can be used to create a soda shop for 11½-inch dolls are priced right at $5.95 for each room of patterns.

Patterns for twelve crocheted animals that hold their grip with Velcro on the inside of their arms are only $5.95.

Clothing patterns to crochet for babies include boys' and girls' styles in newborn, 6-, and 12-month sizes. An adorable sailor outfit includes a matching hat. Instructions for five different outfits come in one full-color pattern set for only $5.95.

■ California Stitchery

Judaic Designs, 6015 Sunnyslope Avenue, Van Nuys, CA 91401, (800) 345–3332

Free 32-page color catalog

California Stitchery has hard-to-find Judaic needlework with many items to complete for children. Needlepoint kits for Bar Mitzvah or Bat Mitzvah include Paternayan persian wool and an alphabet and numerical graph that help you personalize your project with a name and date; these kits range from $29.95 to $52.95.

Tallit bags and tallis cases to make for girls and boys are offered in needlepoint designs for $32 and up. Table linen kits offer embroidered designs on tablecloths, napkins, and challa covers.

The catalog also offers how-to books and charts for Judaic needlework designs, including such projects as yarmulkes, mezuzah covers, and prayer shawls.

■ Carolyn Warrender

Stencil Designs Ltd., P.O. Box 358, London, SW11 4NR U.K., Phone: 01–622 8275

Write for current price of their 35-page color catalog

If you have been searching for charming stencils to decorate your little one's bedroom or play area, this catalog will provide some nice ideas. Sailboats, seashells, teddy bears, soldiers, puppy and dog houses, a happy cat, rocking horses, circus figures, trains, alphabets, and more will bring your child's room to life. You can personalize toy chests and furniture with these stencils and others, including miniature pigs, whales, gingham cats, and calico dogs.

The catalog provides instructions and helpful hints on stenciling successfully and also tempts you with wall paint in terrific colors.

Payment may be made by Barclaycard/MasterCard and American Express, but no cash or postal orders will be accepted. Prices are quoted in the British pound.

■ Chaselle, Inc.

A huge inventory of arts and crafts supplies, from paints and papers to looms and kilns. See page 87 under **Educational Materials.**

■ Cherry Tree Toys, Inc.

Belmont, OH 43718-9989, (614) 484–4363

$1.00 for 60-page color catalog

Cherry Tree Toys specializes in woodworking kits, parts, plans, tools, books, and supplies for all skill levels. They have several popular children's clock kits with themes taken from beloved nursery rhymes and fairy tales. Peter Rabbit, Hansel and Gretel, Jack Be Nimble, Three Men in a Tub, The Three Little Kittens, and more are all waiting to be assembled and painted by you. Plans alone are $2.95 each. Kits that include some parts are $9.95 each. Kits that contain all necessary parts but are uncut are $14.95, while complete, precut kits are $19.95. Finished clocks sell for $79.95.

The catalog also includes plans and kits for colorful, old-fashioned whirligigs, toys to ride on, children's furniture, wooden toys, miniature toys, boats, vehicles, dollhouses, and dollhouse furniture.

This catalog is a not-to-be-missed treat with many potential heirlooms.

■ Childcraft

Modeling wax, fabric pens, markers, easels, rubber stamps, art books, and craft kits. See page 217 under **Toys.**

■ Claudia Pesek Designs

P.O. Box 1184, Grants Pass, OR 97526

Free 9-page black-and-white illustrated catalog

If you would like to try your hand at sewing some of your baby's things, you might want to consider a soft baby carrier in the material of your choice. Claudia Pesek Designs sells full-size patterns with explicit instructions for their own Close 'N Comfy design. The carrier can be worn either on the front or back, has an adjustable infant seat, a handy pocket, and a padded headrest. The pattern is $4.95.

Modeled after the full-size pattern, a "Just Like Mama" doll carrier pattern is $4.00. Lastly, hard-to-find infant wear patterns are specially designed for the premature baby; choose from seven styles priced at $4.00 each.

■ Clotilde Inc.

1909 S.W. First Avenue, Ft. Lauderdale, FL 33315-2100, (305) 761–8655

Free 67-page color catalog

Clotilde (rhymes with Matilda) offers hundreds of sewing notions at 20 percent off retail.

The catalog includes a number of books of interest to parents. *Jami's Special Appliqué Patterns* features such classic children's designs as a snowman, helicopter, train, and sailboat. *Kid's Holiday Appliqué Patterns* has five patterns for each of the major holidays. *Easy Halloween Costumes For Children* contains patterns for sixty costumes for children aged three through twelve. Other titles of interest are *Sewing For Baby, Sew For Toddlers, French Hand Sewing by Machine, Heirloom Doll Clothes, Bearly*

Beginning Smocking, *Picture Smocking*, *English Smocking*, and *English Smocking On the Sewing Machine*. The books are also available at a discount; most titles are $8.00 to $12.00.

■ Constructive Playthings

Stenciling, beadwork, make-you-own bonnet kit, puppet factory kit.
See page 218 under **Toys**.

■ CR's Crafts

Box 867-3652, Leland, IA 50453, (515) 567–3652

$2.00 for an 80-page color catalog

If you enjoy making your children's toys, this catalog is well worth the price of admission. CR's Crafts has loads of craft supplies and dozens of original copyrighted patterns for bears, dolls, toys, and puppets. Complete kits for cuddly Butterscotch and Brandon Bear, which have jointed arms and stand 36 inches and 48 inches tall, are $26.75 and $30.25 respectively; you can buy the patterns alone for $6.00 for both bears.

■ The Crafters' Gallery

P.O. Box 4238, Huntington Station, NY 11750-0076, (800) 323–1800

Free 96-page color catalog

The Crafters' Gallery offers a large selection of needlecraft kits, many of which are exclusive designs. The holiday catalog has dozens of charming, unusual Christmas stockings to cross-stitch, candlewick, knit, needlepoint, or cut and paste with sequins, metallic thread, and felt.

Adorable sampler kits for newborns list name, weight, and birth date. For the dinosaur lover, a stamped or counted cross-stitch kit for $14.98 features seven of these huge reptiles with their species name embroidered beneath them.

You receive a free 3-piece needleworker's accessory kit with every order, a free needlecrafter's tote bag with orders over $30.00, and free shipping and handling with orders over $50.00. You can order, toll free, 24 hours a day.

■ Crate and Barrel

Easels. See page 94 under **Furniture and Bedding.**

■ Creative Crafts International

P.O. Box 819, (16 Plains Road), Essex, CT 06426, (800) 666–0767

Free 48-page color catalog

Creative Crafts International provides basic arts and crafts supplies as well as beautifully crafted kits in a variety of media. For the junior yachting enthusiast, the catalog offers unpainted wooden boat kits at $8.40 each. A small sailboat, brigantine, cruising sloop, pirate ship, sport fisherman's boat, tug boat, shrimp boat, or schooner will provide hours of assembling, painting, and sailing fun.

Kits are also available for children who prefer woodworking, leathercraft, basketry, ceramic tiling, and beadwork. Bulk packs are available for nursery schools and birthday parties.

In addition, Creative Crafts carries a large selection of quality art supplies. Papers, glues, paints, markers, pencils, and pens are available at good prices and quantity discounts. T-shirt decorating supplies are best-selling items and include glitter glues, "puff" paints, write-on fabric pens, and more.

■ Current

Stickers, ribbons, and papers; some stencils and rubber stamps.
See page 204 under **Stationery and Birth Announcements.**

■ Daisy Kingdom, Inc.

134 N.W. 8th Avenue, Portland, OR 97209, (800) 234–6688

Free 52-page color catalog

Create your own nursery decorations or clothing with the original fabrics, borders, and graphics available separately or as kits from this unique company.

This beautifully illustrated catalog sells balloon pant overalls, ready-made or in kits ($24.98 per kit) in sizes 1T through 6X. Or maybe you are looking for a quilted jacket with Beatrix Potter designs on the back, frilly party dresses, overalls, sweatshirts, coats, crib sheets, bumper pads, or bibs. Cut 'n Stitch Fabric Kits feature original designs on polyester/cotton fabrics printed with the shapes of the major pattern pieces; just cut along the lines and sew the pieces together.

Personalize sweatshirts, T-shirts, and more with iron-on transfers in a variety of designs. Noah's Ark, bunnies and ducks, ballerinas, rocking horses, balloons, lambs, and others are $4.98 each.

■ Demco

Box 74488, Madison, WI 53707-7488, (800) 356–1200

Free 50-page color catalog

Creative early learning supplies for child care professionals are made available to individuals in this colorful catalog that includes a wide selection of crayons, clay, markers, specialty paints and tools, how-to books, glitter, glue, foam shapes, sequins, spangles, and more.

You and your child are bound to be intrigued by the dozens of exciting ideas presented here. To aid your imagination, many pages of the catalog include a photograph of the crafts that can be made with the items sold on the page.

Bags of pom-poms, chenille stems, colored paper rolls, books, ethnic dolls, puppets, puzzles, blocks, anti-dust chalk, flannelboards, and felt cut-outs are just a few of the items filling the pages. Demco even sells bright, unusual furniture you might buy for your budding Picasso's studio; these sturdy pieces include some great storage systems in which to save your youngster's masterpieces.

■ Dollspart Supply Co., Inc.

46-50 54th Avenue, Maspeth, NY 11378 (800) 336–3655; in New York, (718) 361–1833

$3.00 for 32-page color catalog

"Anything and everything for dolls" is this catalog's motto. Here you will find a wide assortment of quality items that can be bought in quantity for a substantial discount. Choose from an array of doll stands, beautifully detailed doll kits, eyes, eyelashes, socks, underwear, shoes, antique-looking porcelain doll kits, hats, doll bodies, patterns, repair and craftsman's supplies, and books. For those who prefer their dolls ready-made, a nice selection of Madame Alexander dolls will fit the bill. The minimum order of $25.00 does not include shipping and handling.

■ Dover Publications, Inc.

Sticker books, cut-and-assemble dioramas, pre-cut stencils, coloring books, paper dolls, cut-and-assemble masks. See page 28 under **Books.**

■ Enterprise Art

2860 Roosevelt Boulevard, Clearwater, FL 34620-1998, (813) 536–1492

Free 80-page color catalog

One of the best ways to keep kids away from your jewelry is to let them make their own with a variety of inexpensive rhinestones, sequins, beads, clip or pierced earring backs, bracelets, pins, and barrettes.

These items and others that are similar are the main attraction at Enterprise Art, which also supplies some doll-making items and craft supplies such as styrofoam balls and discs and flocked animals.

Jewelry making may not be appropriate for the younger child, but it will provide hours of entertainment for your older kids. As with most craft catalogs, if you buy in bulk you can realize substantial savings. For instance, a package containing two 3-inch barrettes is $.75, a 72-piece package is $14.19, bringing the cost down to just under $.20 per barrette.

■ Florida Jewelry Crafts, Inc.

P.O. Box 2620, Sarasota, FL 34230, (813) 351–9404

$2.00 for a 23-page black-and-white illustrated catalog

Florida Jewelry Crafts offers a large selection of jewelry-making items, including many styles of pierced earwires and earposts in surgical steel, rhodium, gold-filled, or gold finishes.

Unadorned French-style barrettes can be ordered for $6.45 for 36. The company also sells foundations for stick pins, bar pins, clasps, key rings, necklaces, and bracelets. All items are offered in bulk packages only. The inventory specializes in jewelry foundations, but pearl beads are offered for decorative work. A small but complete selection of craft tools will help you complete many projects.

There is a $2.00 service charge for any order under $20.00

■ First Step, Ltd./Hand in hand

Stencil kits, paints, easel, moldable soap dough.
See page 140 under **Infant Products and Equipment.**

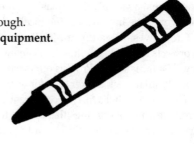

■ Gail Wilson Duggan Designs, Inc.

Box D Summer Street, Charlestown, NH 03603, (603) 826–5630

Free 8-page black-and-white illustrated catalog

Gail Wilson Duggan, a craftsperson and dollmaker, presents dozens of felt bears and their clothing, miniature accessories and furnishings, and toys, folk dolls, and pull toys. Small wooden-furniture kits (some available already finished) are carefully pre-cut from solid wood and are ready to assemble.

Kits come with detailed instructions, notions, and high quality materials like wool felt and cotton fabrics.

Choose from nine 7½-inch country folk doll kits, each with a tiny doll in its pinafore pocket ($12.75 per kit). Many of the kits have unique details, making this catalog a delight.

■ The Gifted Children's Catalog

Woodworking set, wooden loom, cut-and-assemble alphabet kit, mask-making kit, puppet projects, pour-and-paint plaster kits, flower press.
See page 222 under **Toys.**

■ Greiger's, Inc.

Jewelry-making foundations, gems, and tools. See page 131 under **Hobby Supplies.**

■ Grey Owl Indian Craft Co., Inc.

P.O. Box 507 (113-15 Springfield Boulevard), Queens Village, NY 11429, (718) 464–9300

$2.00 for 202-page black-and-white illustrated catalog

Need a Sioux war bonnet? Here is where you can get it. This catalog is an unbelievable resource for Indian clothes, craft kits, breastplates, accessories, beadwork, books, tomahawks, blankets, masks, rattles, and much, much more. You can even make your little Indian an authentically designed Sioux or Cheyenne tipi.

Grey Owl stocks authentic leathercraft and beadwork kits—great for social studies projects or scout activities. You can even buy ceramic elk teeth! A section called Low Cost Indian Craft Projects offers easy-to-make kits that come ten to a pack. A colorful Indian neck choker sells for $8.50 for a 10-kit pack.

This is Grey Owl's forty-second year of service, and it has put together an incredible array of offerings that are not to be missed. Returns must be made within thirty days and may be subject to a 15 percent re-stocking fee.

■ Hamleys

A whole section devoted to arts and crafts includes coloring and painting materials and plaster casts. See page 222 under **Toys.**

■ Hearthside Quilts

P.O. Box 429 (2048 Shelburne Road), Shelburne, VT 05482-0429, (800) 451–3533; in Vermont, (802) 985–8077

$2.00 for 49-page color catalog

If you want to stitch up a vibrant, beautifully designed quilt for your child's bed, crib or doll, but you are not feeling ambitious enough to do all the intricate cutting required, Hearthside Quilts is the catalog for you.

These quilt kits are 100 percent complete. Included are precision pre-cut pieces, thread, instructions, needle, batting, and backing. Pillow kits include pillow forms. Hearthside offers a few dozen pattern choices and rates each quilt as to skill level from 1 to 4. You may choose from easy designs like the Double Irish Cross or the more difficult Laurel Leaf and Primrose patterns.

Windmill, Trip Around the World, and Patchwork 22x30-inch doll quilts are $19.50 per kit. A popular design for·children features appliquéd hearts; the kit for a 34x50-inch crib quilt costs $39.50.

All kits are crafted in Vermont and are made from 100 percent cotton domestic fabrics.

■ HearthSong

Modeling beeswax, knitting kits, candle-making kit, basketry, doll-making, and more. See page 224 under **Toys.**

■ Hummingbird House

P.O. Box 4242, Palm Desert, CA 92261-4242, (619) 360–2275

$3.00 for 33-page color catalog

Hummingbird House offers lovely patterns and kits for English smocking, needle-point, and counted cross-stitch.

If you have the talent and/or the patience for smocking, you will be pleased with the beautiful items offered here, including darling Kathy Crisp patterns for babies, elegant christening outfits, and Chery Williams patterns for little girls' dresses and playsuits. Smocking patterns are $4.00 to $9.00; many include instructions for embroidery topstitching. Books that will help you complete smocking projects are also available.

The Hummingbird House staff has worked every sample in the catalog and their notes are included in each of these lovely kits.

■ Ideal School Supply

Arts and craft supplies and creative activities. See page 89 under **Educational Materials.**

■ Imaginative Inroads

Shirt-painting kits, mask-making kit, and more. See page 225 under **Toys.**

■ Just for Kids!

Easel, hat-decorating kit, face paints, balloon-painting kit, arts and crafts materials. See page 226 under **Toys.**

■ Keepsake Quilting

P.O. Box 1459 (Dover Street), Meredith, NH 03253-1459, (603) 279–3351

$2.00 for a 94-page black-and-white illustrated catalog

Pour yourself a cup of tea and curl up with this catalog from the largest quilt shop in New England. Offering one of the most extensive selections of cotton quilting fabric available anywhere, Keepsake stocks more than 600 cotton solids, prints, and designer fabrics. Also available here are delightful quilt kits for wall or crib, as well as pattern books featuring full-size appliqué patterns for kids and strip-pieced log cabin jackets and vests. One book offers a pattern for a little girl's dress and matching pattern for her doll; another allows you to design your own jumper.

Presto-chango! *The Big Book of Sweatshirt Designs* shows how to transform a plain sweatshirt or T-shirt into wearable art. This softcover book ($12.95) contains dozens of illustrations and more than sixty full-size appliqué patterns that will help you complete your design in one afternoon. *Patterns For Making Amish Dolls and Doll Clothes* (also $12.95) features authentic patterns in both jointed and Lizzie Lapp styles.

■ KidsArt

P.O. Box 274, Mt. Shasta, CA 96067, (916) 926–5076

Free 8-page black-and-white illustrated catalog

The KidsArt inventory includes creative activities and art supplies for home and school. The catalog features inexpensive rubber-stamp alphabets and non-toxic tempera paint in many colors, including sparkling silver and gold metallics.

Fun Mix Kits sell for $3.95 each and come with just enough materials to create a small but special project. Funtastic Finger Puppets, Magnet Pom-Pom Pets, or Creative Clothespin Characters will make great stocking stuffers or party favors.

Among the offerings are a few art activity books by the popular Ed Emberley and one that is the best-selling item in the whole catalog—Dan O'Neill's *Big Yellow Drawing Book*. At $5.95, the latter is a how-to drawing workbook that emphasizes the basic principles of drawing, expression, and perspective through cartooning.

Fashion-conscious kids will love the buddy bracelet kits for $9.95. This popular friendship jewelry is easy to make by knotting and braiding, and the kit includes lots of beads to add a bit of sparkle.

■ Kirchen Bros.

Box 1016, Skokie, IL 60076, (312) 676–2692

$1.50 for a 48-page catalog

Kirchen Bros. has been providing craft materials, do-it-yourself kits, and holiday decorations since 1919. You will find dolls as well as clothing patterns to crochet for them, together with dozens of softly colored painted wood scenes to hang on the walls of baby's nursery. Prices are incredibly reasonable. A 7½-inch doll with moving eyes, head, arms, and choice of four hair colors sells for $1.25. A colorful wooden alphabet scene is $4.77, and a door hanger that warns, "Shh, Baby Sleeping" is $3.43.

You can also assemble your own dolls from the parts list available here. The stock includes heavy-gauge, flexible vinyl doll heads with hand-painted features, hands, hats, shoes, eyes, and other quality parts. The same low prices apply for how-to books on an endless variety of projects, including dolls' clothes, Christmas ornaments, needlecraft designs, and macramé for beginners.

Kirchen Bros. also offers miniatures, flocked and plush animals, colorful beads, sock doll kits, and more.

■ Learn and Play for Kids

Picture frame and handprint kit, wooden dinosaur kits, and many other crafts. See page 227 under **Toys**.

■ Martha Hall

46 Main Street, Yarmouth, ME 04096, (207) 846–9746

Free 32-page color catalog

If you don't have the chance to visit this wonderful shop tucked into a historic sea captain's house on the Maine coast, you can still enjoy their delightful offerings in the prettiest catalog I've seen for knitters.

Martha Hall offers sweaters, kits, and books for the whole family, and many of the kits feature designs for children. The books also include lovely patterns for you to knit for children. Kits range in price from $20.00 for a rolled collar baby sweater and hat set in your choice of colors to $45.00 for a Peace Fleece cardigan.

You should have no trepidation about ordering through the mail because the yarns—all of them gorgeous—are photographed beautifully in color.

You can also order wonderful ceramic buttons and old-fashioned Christmas stocking kits that are knit on size 8 needles. That way you can finish them before it's too late to hang them by the fire!

Gift certificates are available.

■ Mary Maxim Inc.

P.O. Box 5019, 2001 Holland Avenue, Port Huron, MI 48061-5019, (313) 987–2000

Free 80-page color catalog

This needlework and crafts catalog for adults offers a nice selection of items to make for children. A needlepoint Easter basket and candy dishes with duckling, bunny, and lamb motifs are typical of the catalog's seasonal offerings. Thirteen-inch-doll kits and the clothes to crochet for them are available here, as are Beatrix Potter pictures and pillows to cross-stitch or needlepoint. Delicate animal designs on crib quilts or bibs can be worked in both counted and stamped cross-stitch.

For the knitter, the catalog presents machine-washable layette sets, back-zippered sweater sets, and children's bulky weight, jacket-style sweaters with designs (cat, stars, fire truck, puppy, polar bear, kitten, or dinosaur) on the back. Priced from $12.99 to $16.99, the patterns are available in sizes 2 through 12, and their matching zippers and liners can be ordered with them.

Mary Maxim's Christmas catalog features stocking kits and Christmas Teddy sweater vests in sizes 2 through adult. If you are at all handy with a needle, you are sure to find an appealing project at Mary Maxim.

■ Nasco Arts & Crafts   *sent for*

901 Janesville Avenue, P.O. Box 901, Fort Atkinson, WI 53538-0901, (800) 558–9595

Free 352-page black-and-white illustrated catalog

Directed to the educational market but available to parents as well, the huge Nasco catalog is packed with thousands of supplies at very reasonable prices.

Parents and children will find enjoyable craft projects that involve leatherwork, beads, basket weaving, calligraphy, collage, woodcrafts, stenciling, and origami. Sketchables—blank postcards waiting for your child's artwork—are a neat idea at $5.50 for a pack of fifty.

Look here also if you are in the market for audiovisual tapes and equipment, paint brushes, paints, storage ideas, pens, markers, paper, mask-making materials, drawing and drafting sets, clays, or ceramics.

■ North Island Designs

Main Street, North Haven, ME 04853, (800) 548–5648; in Maine, (207) 867–4788

Free 14-page color catalog

These people like kids, knitting, and Maine—and it shows. Their book entitled *Maine Island Kids: Sweaters and Stories from Offshore* offers twenty sweater patterns for sizes 2 through 12 that are knit on large needles (typically size 5, 6, 7, or 8) so you can finish the sweater before your child outgrows it! Trains, schoolbuses, and barnyard animals are some of the fun designs that scamper across cardigans and pullovers.

Striking in its simplicity is the Starry Night pullover kit in machine-washable, sport-weight wool for children (sizes 2 through 12) or worsted-weight wool for adults. You will find wonderful downeast sweater kits with wildflowers, apple trees, spruce trees, or fish. A very practical lightweight sweater jacket features pewter buttons and a farmyard motif. Prices start at $35.00.

■ Platypus

Box 396, Planetarium Station, New York, NY 10024

Free 30-page black-and-white illustrated catalog

Platypus sells dozens of patterns and instructions to help you make cloth dolls, toys, and quilts for your children. The catalog tells you how complicated each project is so you really have a good idea of what you are ordering.

Contemporary and historical dolls and costume designs can be found here, as well as instructions for making doll and cradle quilts, three lovely muslin angels, holiday decorations, a cloth train, a menagerie, a mermaid, a unicorn, and a dragon. Most patterns sell for $3.00 to $7.00. The catalog also provides an inventory of supplies you need to finish these projects.

Platypus's minimum order is $8.50. All patterns have been tested before being offered to the consumer, but if you run into problems, a letter to Platypus will bring help quickly.

■ PlayFair Toys

Sticker books and craft kits, rubber stamps, tabletop easel, weaving loom, flower press. See page 230 under **Toys.**

■ Pyramid School Products

Art supplies and craft projects. See page 92 under **Educational Materials.**

■ S & S Worldwide

Colchester, CT 06415, (800) 243–9232

$5.00 for 132-page color catalog
$25.00 minimum order. A $5.00 service charge will be added to all orders below this minimum.

Schools have ordered from the S & S catalog for the past eighty years. Now individuals, too, can order thousands of fun, inexpensive kits and supplies for kids, including such old favorites as Red Heel Sock Toys, felt bookmarks, octopus yarn dolls, sand art, mask-making kits, jewelry-making kits, paint-by-number sets, packs of construction paper, velour paper, doilies, tempera paints, and Lego building sets. The company also offers leather-making kits for purses, wallets, key cases, moccasins, and belts. What a bonanza!

A typical project kit for wearable beadcraft includes patterns, pinbacks, glass beads, wire, cement, and instructions for $9.85 per pack of twenty-four projects.

Supplies for basketry and candlemaking are also stocked, as is a large line of ceramic tiles, trivets, and trays. To simplify construction, many multi-project packs include pre-cut shapes. In most cases age-appropriateness guidelines for project kits are indicated in the catalog. Some projects can only be purchased in quantity.

■ San Francisco Museum of Modern Art

Paper crafts, watercolor paints, and pastel crayons, handbooks, and activity books. See page 152 under **Museum Shops.**

■ Shillcraft

8899 Kelso Drive, P.O. Box 7770, Baltimore, MD 21221-0770, (301) 682–3064

$2.00 for 48-page color catalog

In 1949 Shillcraft was the first catalog to introduce the craft of latch hooking and more than forty years later, they still offer interesting kits you can make for children.

The catalog presents ten latchhook kits for stuffed animals, including Fergie Frog, small and large teddy bears, and an adorable little monkey. Shillcraft's Baby Boutique section has five cute rug kits—one with marching ducks and the others with teddy bear motifs.

The selection of kits to make for children is limited to the offerings listed here; but if you like latch hooking, you just might be interested in this catalog.

■ Snowflake

N 1314 Nesoya, Norway

$5.00 for 8-page color catalog

Looking for beauty, warmth, comfort, and customer service par excellence? Look no more. Each of the nine snowflake pattern sweater and hat kits sold by this company is packed to order; so if there is a particular color you like that is not offered, send a swatch or crayoning, and they will do their best to match it for you. Each kit contains soft Norwegian wool, knitting needles, pewter buttons or clasps, and easy-to-follow patterns in English. The catalog is also printed in English and prices quoted are in U.S. dollars. (Snowflake is one of the few foreign companies I have come across that will accept personal checks drawn on U.S., Canadian, or United Kingdom banks.) Prices range from $24.00 for leggings and mittens to $48.50 for a white, navy, and red traditional Norwegian sweater.

■ Standard Doll Co.

P.O. Box 5128, Woolsey Station, Long Island City, NY 11105, (800) 543–6557, ext. 31

$3.00 for a 76-page color catalog, refundable with first order

Since 1922, Standard Doll has served as a complete supply house for the dollcrafter.

Besides selling parts and accessories separately, the company also offers a large selection of doll-making kits. These include china heads, arms, and legs plus patterns and instructions for making costumes and bodies. China doll kits range from $11.50 to $57.00; most offerings are in the $20.00 area.

Porcelain bisque parts and kits are among the choices offered, as are those made from vinyl and plastic. If you would rather concentrate on making the clothes and not the doll, all sizes and shapes of ready-made dolls are available at very reasonable prices.

Doll furniture kits from Realife Miniatures, books, and doll clothes pattern books are just a few more of the thousands of products sold here.

■ The Stitchery

120 North Meadows Road, Medfield, MA 02052-1593, (800) 225–4127; in Massachusetts, (800) 222–4136

Free 80-page color catalog

Since The Stitchery opened twenty-five years ago, the company has introduced many leading needle artists and their exciting designs. This catalog sells a large variety of stitchery kits, with several pages devoted to designs especially for children.

A musical carousel kit is a temptation to the needlepoint enthusiast and comes complete with canvas, floss, needle chart, music box, trims, and decorations for $34.95. Sure to flatter your child's teacher is a counted cross-stitch picture with a school design above the words, "My Favorite Teacher _____" (name to be filled in by you) for $10.95.

Gifts for the new baby include a colorful prequilted stamped cross-stitch alphabet quilt ($19.95), and a bunny-shaped bottle cozy you hand or machine sew ($12.95).

Several wall hangings offer appealing number and alphabet charts and a variety of children's maxims. Beatrix Potter is charmingly represented here with a birth sampler and small needlepoint sculptures of Hunca Munca and Peter Rabbit.

■ Suncoast Discount Arts & Crafts

P.O. Box 40963, St. Petersburg, FL 33743, (813) 577–6331

$2.00 for a 290-page black-and-white illustrated catalog

You will need an afternoon to thumb through this huge catalog of art supplies, but you will find tons of crafts ideas for you and the kids. With all that you will want to buy, you will be thrilled with the reasonable pricing.

Suncoast has a tremendous selection of art supplies, beads, blackboards, felt products, wooden boxes, chenille products, colored pencils, and construction paper. The catalog also lists craft sticks, crayons, crepe paper, drawing supplies, scissors, posterboard, and more. Kids' special craft sets include potholders, pottery sets, fun-to-color stickers, and classic wooden car kits.

For the dollmaker, the offerings include doll joints, hats, and stands. The catalog is also a good source of dollhouses and dollhouse wallpaper.

■ Timbers Woodworking

Timbers Building, Carnelian Bay, CA 95711-0850, (916) 581–4141

Free 24-page black-and-white illustrated catalog

If you are talented with a hammer, you can build your own heirlooms. Timbers has been in the woodworking and pattern supply business since 1972 and they have dozens of full-size patterns for cradles, furniture, and toys.

A variety of patterns for children's rockers include some traditional horses, but you might want to saddle up the kids for a ride on a rocking giraffe, elephant, donkey, or bull. Full-sized patterns for rockers sell from $4.49 to $9.98. Kid-sized tables and chairs, play kitchens, doll cradles and classic toy cars are also among the temptations. You can construct a full-size bedmobile, combination chalkboard and desk, trucks, trains, and wood banks. All the projects featured here can be made much less expensively at home than they can be purchased for in retail stores. Make a choice and start a family project!

■ Toys to Grow On

Stickers, rubber stamps, art supplies and craft projects.
See page 234 under **Toys.**

■ Vanguard Crafts, Inc.

P.O. Box 340170, Brooklyn, NY 11234, (718) 377–5188

$1.00 for 68-page color catalog

Just when you think you have enough crafts catalogs, you will open this offering and be hooked again. This catalog is loaded with kids' crafts and project ideas including hundreds of supplies for felt and fabric crafts, jewelry, paint-by-number, calligraphy, Indian crafts, macramé, metal tooling, shells, pom-poms, decoupage, leathercraft, and much more.

Small, unfinished pre-cut wood shapes are ready to paint, stencil, or decorate for ornaments, plaques, and key chains. A 72-piece package of shapes is $9.98. Disposable plastic aprons protect messy Picassos and are $17.98 for a pack of 100. No-bake suncatchers can be painted to look like stained glass and are available in several designs. Clowns, balloons, rainbows, kittens, and others are $.75 each. A 12-project pack of dinosaur designs sells for $11.98.

Books

■

■ Alaska Craft

Alaskan culture, geography and natural history in books and coloring books.
See page 101 under **Gifts.**

■ American Camping Association, Inc.

Bradford Woods, 5000 State Road (67 North), Martinsville, IN 46151-7902,
(800) 428–CAMP

Free 100-page catalog

The ACA catalog is aimed primarily at schools, and educators. The ACA, however,
also offers hundreds of interesting books from various publishers of interest to parents.

Many nature books and nature activity books are described in detail so you can
easily decide what is suitable for your child. Titles such as *The Unhuggables: The
Truth About Snakes, Slugs, Skunks, Spiders, and Other Animals That Are Hard To Love*
($14.95) by The National Wildlife Federation are real child pleasers. The many na-
ture identification books listed are perfect for kids and parents to use together.

You may also request the ACA flyer; many camping and nature videocassettes
are available through the ACA.

■ Anatomical Chart Co.

Inexpensive books on health-related issues.
See page177 under **Science and Nature.**

■ baby-go-to-sleep center

Fairy tales, folk stories, old and new favorites. See page 171 **Records, Tapes, and CDs.**

■ A Baby's Secret Garden

Parenting books and videocassettes. See page 103 under **Gifts.**

■ Barnes & Noble

126 Fifth Avenue, New York, NY 10011-5666, (201) 767–7079

Free 64-page black-and-white illustrated catalog

Famous for hefty discounts, Barnes and Noble offers a constantly changing array of books. Although none of the catalogs I have received have had a special children's section, the company offers lots of books of potential interest to teens, who might well find a good read under History Bargains, The World As It Was, Mythology, Games, Puzzles and Humor, Reference, or History.

■ Barron's Educational Series, Inc.

P.O. Box 8040, 250 Wireless Boulevard, Hauppauge, NY 11788, (800) 645–3476; in New York, (800) 257–5729

Free 55-page color catalog

Barron's, a large children's book publisher, offers books by mail on just about every topic of interest to children. The catalog shows color photographs of the book jackets and gives a brief synopsis of the story. All of the titles in the catalog are published by Barron's.

Lots of traditional board books for little ones are offered as well as brightly colored Woodbooks that are bound with leather thongs.
Many skills books for math and spelling are available as well as animal stories, a
"Famous People" series, adventures for young readers, children's encyclopedias, fairy tales, biographies, and classic adventures.

■ Bellerophon Books

36 Anacapa Street, Santa Barbara, CA 93101, (805) 965–7034

Free 15-page color catalog

Bellerophon Books offers gorgeous art books for children. Beautifully illustrated coloring books on topics as varied as cowgirls, Rome, clowns, U.S. presidents, and pirates are available for $3.50 each. Colorful paper dolls of the Royal Family, Civil War soldiers, great women, and Queen Elizabeth sell for similar prices. Extraordinary cut-outs of castles of Scotland, chariots, magnificent helmets and old cars have been gathered here, as have been wonderful posters to color of unicorns, China, Japan, dinosaurs, and ancient Egypt.

■ Better Beginnings Catalog

345 North Main Street, West Hartford, CT 06117, (800) 274–0068;
in Connecticut, (203) 236–7739

$1.00 for 15-page catalog

After reading hundreds of books to my own children, I can safely say you cannot go wrong with any of the selected books and tapes offered here for very young children. *Mr. Brown Can Moo, Can You?* is always a big hit with the over-12-months set, and *The Baby's Book of Babies* lets little ones look at photos of their favorite subjects—other babies! Margaret Wise Brown's *Goodnight Moon* is such an often-read classic that many parents can recite "In the great green room. . ." by heart. *Caps For Sale* has been a tremendous child pleaser since its publication in 1940.

Some fine holiday treasures include Chris Van Allsburg's *The Polar Express* and other choices for Chanukah and Christmas. Some of the cassette tapes appropriate for all ages are *Just in Time for Chanukah!*, Raffi's *Baby Beluga,* and *Lullaby Magic.*

■ Blacklion Books

9 East Oxford Avenue, Alexandria, VA 22301

Free 18-page catalog

Blacklion is a quality concern offering only the best children's classics for every age. The catalog lists a full range of titles from board books for babies to modern classics such as *Tuck Everlasting.* A smaller selection of cassette music tapes is also available for $8.95 each—at least 10 percent less than the usual retail price.

The catalog offers a synopsis of each book and suggests appropriate age levels, a feature parents and grandparents always appreciate.

■ Book Passage

51 Tamal Vista Boulevard, Corte Madera, CA 94925, (800) 321–9785;
in California, (415) 927–0960

Free 40-page black-and-white illustrated catalog

Book Passage has hundreds of guidebooks, maps, and arm-chair travel books. There is nothing here for the younger child, but teens will be interested in some of the language tapes and books in thirty-seven languages.

The catalog is a real treasure trove for those who love to travel, and several books are designed to help parents plan family vacations. *Learning Vacations* by Gerson Eisenberg describes hundreds of active vacations in the United States and more than sixty foreign countries. Parents will find vacation ideas that will intrigue the whole family, such as music festivals, safaris, archaeological digs, and whale watching.

Here and there you will also find a title such as *Kid's London*, which describes everything from toy museums and children's theatres to rowing clubs and riding schools.

■ Books of Wonder

132 Seventh Avenue, New York, NY 10011, (212) 989–3270

$3.00 for three illustrated catalogs: Adventures In Reading, The Oz Collector, and An Eric Carle Celebration. Also available is a catalog of old and rare collectible children's books for an additional $3.00.

From New York's largest children's bookstore come three catalogs of distinguished childhood classics and modern masterpieces.

For *Wizard of Oz* aficionados, a special 15-page catalog features books, movie memorabilia, toys, posters, and more.

Adventures in Reading contains 8 pages of favorite fairy tales and other titles especially popular with young listeners. Among these are *Froggie Went A-Courting; Wynken, Blynken and Nod; Eloise;* and *The Random House Book of Fairy Tales*. Most of these books are available with the illustrator's autograph.

A separate 6-page Eric Carle catalog features this innovative illustrator's well-loved picture books. Eight of the titles are available with the artist's autograph at no additional charge.

■ The Book Stork

Mail-order Children's Book Service, 44 Tee-Ar Place, Princeton, NJ 08540

Free 12-page color catalog

This firm has assembled a choice collection of books for children from toddlers to teens. The owner, Mary Jane Rossi, will personally make a selection for your child if you tell her his or her name, age, interests, and needs. She has had more than fifteen years of experience as a teacher, author, and reviewer.

But don't miss the fun of browsing through the catalog, which is chock-full of beautiful jacket illustrations. Age recommendations are included with each book's description.

■ Broadfoot's of Wendell

6624 Robertson Pond Road, Wendell, NC 27591-9506, (800) 444-6963;
in North Carolina, (919) 365-6963

Free 97-page black-and-white illustrated catalog

Broadfoot's is a fascinating catalog devoted exclusively to books and teaching aids
for the study and enjoyment of North Carolina. Hundreds of titles abound on the
history, geography, folklore, legends, traditions, famous Carolinians, plants, minerals, and sea life of the Cardinal State.

The works of authors who hail from North Carolina are featured, and you will be
delighted by the large selection of children's books by Betsy Byars, Gail Haley,
William Hooks, Carole Marsh, and, of course, Carl Sandburg.

A sizable section for young adults has been included as well as wonderfully
eerie books for all ages on witches, ghosts and goblins, and pirates.

■ Cahill & Company

A Division of Regnery Gateway, Inc., Federalsburg, MD 21632-0039,
(800) 333-6583, ext. 22

Free 56-page black-and-white illustrated catalog

Although this catalog offers mainly fine adult literature, it is worth including here
for its excellent children's selections. For *The Nutcracker* fan in your house there is a
ballet cut-out book with its own small theater of sturdy cardboard and a cast of more
than fifty beautifully costumed dancers (scissors and a ruler are needed). Lots of
children's classics are also offered here, including Madeleine L'Engle's *The Twenty-
Four Days Before Christmas, Anne of Green Gables, A Little Princess*, a seventy-fifth-
anniversary edition of *The Wind in the Willows, The Light Princess*, and more. You
can't go wrong ordering from this little treasure.

■ Carousel Books

P.O. Box 755, West Hartford, CT 06107, (800) 233-5573;
in Connecticut, (203) 561-4780

Free 16-page black-and-white illustrated catalog

Now in its third year, Carousel Books has the advantage of being run by a children's
librarian. You will find about a hundred well-chosen books here described in clear,
readable copy.

Parents may select baby board books, fairy tales, Chanukah and Christmas stories, poetry, picture books, and titles to please young dance enthusiasts. The catalog

carries fiction in categories for children five through eight, seven through twelve, and ten through fourteen. You will also find a good selection of non-fiction titles such as *The Littlest Dinosaurs*, *Monarch Butterfly*, and *The Book of Eagles*.

■ Carousel Press

Family Travel Guides, P.O. Box 6061, Albany, CA 94706, (415) 527–5849

**$1.00 or a long, stamped ($.45) self-addressed envelope for a 32-page
black-and-white illustrated catalog**

If you are planning a vacation or even just a long car trip to Grandma's, send for a copy of the Family Travel Guides catalog. Offerings include more than 200 family-oriented travel guides, game books, and related items, all reasonably priced. Among the catalog's most popular titles are the *Rock 'n Roll Oldies Car Songbook and Audio Cassette*, *Are We There Yet?*, and *Recommended Family Resorts*.

All areas of the United States are represented as are Europe and Asia. Where else will you find books like *A Children's Guide to London*, *Kids Love Israel/Israel Loves Kids: A Travel Guide*, and *The Candy Apple: New York For Kids*? This catalog makes terrific reading, even for the armchair traveler.

■ Chaselle, Inc.

Look in *Pre-School and Elementary School Materials* catalog for great selection of children's classics and teacher-tested favorites. See page 87 under **Educational Materials.**

■ Child Art Studios

Personalized books to commemorate baby's birth.
See page 116 under **Gifts.**

■ Children's Book and Music Center

2500 Santa Monica Boulevard, Santa Monica, CA 90404, (800) 443–1856;
in California, (213) 829–0215

Free 80-page black-and-white illustrated catalog

The Children's Book and Music Center carries an extensive line of books, recordings, and videos. You will find not only favorite classics and award-winners but also lots of the new and noteworthy choices on the market today. *I Was So Mad* and *Shake*

My Sillies Out are two wonderful books that help kids to cope with common childhood dilemmas.

You will also find an interesting selection of multicultural books and recordings, poetry, and holiday books and recordings. Record and cassette players and a large collection of musical instruments are also part of the huge inventory.

It is easy to find what you want in this catalog as the contents are grouped into chapters by age range.

■ The Children's Small Press Collection

719 North Fourth Avenue, Ann Arbor, MI 48104; in Michigan, (313) 668–8056; outside Michigan, (800) 221–8056

Free 44-page black-and-white illustrated catalog

A terrific resource for parents looking for a unique book, record, or game, this catalog presents the selections of more than 100 small publishers on the forefront of children's issues. Instead of the big-name publishing houses you see in all the bookstores, you will find original titles by the likes of Parenting Press, Windswept House, and Giggles to Gumdrops Publishing.

The table of contents is divided into such categories as self-esteem, fantasy, heroes and heroines, safety issues, and science and environment.

Some eye-catching titles are *Come and Get It: A Natural Foods Cookbook for Children*, *How Do You Draw Dinosaurs?*, *Making Your Own Traditions: Around the Year*, and *The Black Mother Goose*.

Under records, tapes, and CDs, you will find learning titles like *Months, Seasons, and Weather Songs; Instant Piano Fun;* and *Games for the Road*.

■ A Child's Collection

Response Service Center, 3200 South 76th Street, Box 33901, Philadelphia, PA 19142-0961, (215) 492–9628

Free 46-page color catalog

This beautiful catalog features a color photograph of every book jacket. The books offered include some classics but most are terrific new books by some of the finest authors and illustrators working today.

You will find a nice selection of board books (good for toddlers' inquiring fingers) as well as wonderfully whimsical pop-up books. The winter catalog features many Christmas and Chanukah choices.

■ Chinaberry Book Service

2830 Via Orange Way, Suite B, Spring Valley, CA 92078-1521, (800) 777–5205

Free 96-page catalog

Even if you never buy a book from this wonderful catalog, the advice it gives on reading to very young children is so good that you should order it for that reason alone. Helpful guidelines explain simply and clearly how to encourage children to enjoy books from infancy onward.

Chinaberry offers the tried-and-true classics such as *Goodnight Moon* and *Pat the Bunny* but also includes new books worth mentioning. *First Things First: A Baby's Companion* is a new title that provides information through pictures. Sitting, smelling, eating, the alphabet, and the days of the week are some of the early learning topics covered here for $12.95.

Organized by age level, the catalog gives a thorough description and critique of each book. Page counts and other specifics follow every entry.

■ Chronicle Books

275 Fifth Street, San Francisco, CA 94103, (800) 722–6657;
in California, (800) 445–7577

Free 41-page color catalog

Chronicle publishes mainly adult books, but its few children's titles are choice. Robert Louis Stevenson's *A Child's Garden of Verses*, for example, is colorfully illustrated in a soft, old-fashioned style. *Mrs. Mustard's baby faces*, a vibrantly colored folding board book with six smiling babies on one side and six cranky babies on the other, is perfect for babies eager to pursue one of their first pastimes—looking at other babies' faces. My daughter and I also liked two clever craft books, *Things I Can Make With Paper* and *Things I Can Make With Cloth*.

■ Claudia's Caravan

P.O. Box 1582, Alameda, CA 94501, (415) 521–7871

$1.00 (refunded on first order) for 12-page catalog

This fascinating catalog specializes in multicultural/multilingual books, records, and games that have been carefully evaluated for their accuracy and positive imagery.

The catalog's bookshelf features reference titles that represent Alaska, Hawaii, Black history, the Chinese, Europeans, and Japanese; many include "hands on" cultural activities. Bilingual books in German, Spanish, and French are stocked, as are illustrated vocabulary books entitled *The First 1000 Words In English (or French, German, Hebrew, Italian, Russian* and *Spanish*). Each of these dictionaries is $10.95.

The line concentrates on nonfiction titles; the current list includes books about Africa, American Indian groups, volcanoes, The United Nations, earthquakes, and many other subjects.

Unusual games as well as records and tapes make this catalog an excellent resource for teachers and parents looking for materials to complement the school curriculum. The game *Where in The World* helps children learn geography; *Robot* develops the concept that a wide variety of work opportunities exists for both men and women.

■ Clotilde Inc.

Books on sewing, smocking, knitting. See page 3 under **Arts and Crafts.**

■ Cobblestone Publishing, Inc.

30 Grove Street, Peterborough, NH 03458, (800) 341–1522

Free 12-page color catalog

Cobblestone offers three award-winning special interest magazines for children eight through fifteen. *Cobblestone,* a history magazine, focuses on a single theme in each issue: The Alamo, Albert Einstein, the Amish, baseball, and children who shaped history are some recent themes. *Calliope* offers stories and legends to enhance appreciation of English and American classical literature and includes a one-act play in every issue. *Faces* explores cultures in far-off lands and is published in cooperation with New York's American Museum of Natural History. Back issues are clearly listed by theme and are available for immediate delivery for $3.95 each, plus shipping and handling. The annual subscription rate for twelve issues of *Cobblestone* is $22.95; *Calliope* sends out five issues yearly for $17.95; *Faces* is $21.95 for nine issues a year.

■ Discount Books and Video, Inc.

930 North Main Road, P.O. Box 928, Vineland, NJ 08360-0928, (800) 448–2019

Free 72-page black-and-white illustrated catalog

Directed mainly at adults, Discount Books has some bargains for kids. The Children's Corner section offers *Aladdin and His Wonderful Lamp;* beautifully illustrated and originally published at $12.95, it is only $3.50 here. *The Three Sillies,* published at $9.95, is $4.00. Thirty picture books are offered, all at similar discounts.

A small section, Stories on LP, sells titles like *The Emperor's New Clothes* and *The Gift of The Magi and Other Stories* for $4.00 each.

Older children should find something of interest in one of the dozens of other sections such as Earth, Sea and Sky, Foreign Language, Hobby, Nature, Reference, Sports, Ships, Sailors and Oceans, Biography and Autobiography, or Mystery and Suspense.

■ The Disney Catalog

Popular titles from the Disney library, some with audiocassettes.
See page 105 under **Gifts.**

■ Diversions

One Hart Street, Dept. 198, P.O. Box 1834, Newark, NJ 07101-1834,
(800) 772–9200, Ext. 198

Free 48-page color catalog

Diversions offers some of the best titles in books, music, and video entertainment for the whole family.

One book sure to be welcomed is *Nintendo Strategies* ($5.99). After that edition has been mastered, your child can move on to *More Strategies For Nintendo Games,* also $5.99. *My First Baking Book, My First Camera Book,* and *The Garden Book and the Greenhouse* are fun selections.

The 56-volume set of Nancy Drew mysteries and the 58-volume set of The Hardy Boys are also part of the Diversions line.

Some family video titles are *The Legend of Sleepy Hollow, Bambi, Bedknobs and Broomsticks, Family Circus, The Yearling, Annie Oakley,* and *Pecos Bill.*

■ Dover Publications, Inc.

31 East 2nd Street, Mineola, NY 11501-3582, (516) 294–7000

Free 47-page illustrated catalog. Be sure to request the Children's Book Catalog as this company publishes catalogs on many different subjects.

Book lovers of all ages will enjoy the Dover Children's Book Catalog. In addition to its original line, Dover specializes in reprints offering facsimile editions of classic children's favorites.

More than 500 books, most between $1.00 and $3.95, include *Peter Rabbit Notepaper to Color, Original Shirley Temple Paper Dolls in Full Color, Cut and Make Cat Masks in Full Color, The Emerald City of Oz, Kate Greenaway Stickers and Seals, My Alice in Wonderland Notebook,* and Gelett Burgess's *Goops and How to Be Them.*

Dover sells wonderful little activity books for just $1.00, pre-cut stencil books, sticker books, stationery, bookmarks, cut-and-assemble productions, coloring books, and several full-color paper doll collections. Many items are perfect stocking stuffers and party favors. Several children's classics and fairy tale anthologies are wrapped as gift sets along with related paper dolls or activity books.

This is one of my all-time favorite catalogs, filled with unusual treats, and I am sure you will agree.

■ Down East Books

P.O. Box 679 HC, Camden, ME 04843, (207) 594–9544

Free 31-page illustrated (some color) catalog

Some of the most interesting selections of books come from the small regional publishers and it is thus with Down East. Specializing in titles about Maine or of interest to Mainers and those that love her, Down East presents titles that will interest parents, as well as a small but choice collection of children's picture books.

Head to Toe by Helene Rush is a collection of thirty original designs to knit. Patterns are for a special Christmas stocking, soft hats, socks, and slippers. *Maine Woods Woolies* provides patterns for thirty kids' sweaters decorated with puffins, penguins, whales, and the like. This latter book is Down East's best seller and I can see why. I could not resist the wonderful patterns and I have made three of the sweaters for my daughter. If your needles are raring to go, *Fox and Geese and Fences, More Maine Sweaters, Flying Geese & Partridge Feet,* and *The Mitten Book* will keep you busy in front of many a winter fire.

The carefully selected children's books include *Crystal: The Story of a Real Baby Whale,* Robert McCloskey's classics *Blueberries for Sal* and *One Morning in Maine,* and other tales of Maine lobstermen, lighthouses, and moose.

■ EDC Publishing

Div. of Educational Development Corp., P.O. Box 470663, Tulsa, OK 74147, (800) 331–4418; in Oklahoma, (918) 622–4522

$2.00 for a 26-page color catalog (with $2.00 rebate coupon for use with your first purchase)

A great source of how-to and reference books for children from toddler to teen, EDC Publishing is the largest U.S. distributor of Peter Usborne books. His First Experiences line, with titles such as *Going to the Doctor, The New Puppy,* and *Going On A Plane,* is helpful to preschoolers and children in the lower grades. Older children will enjoy *How To Draw Spacecraft* and *How To Draw Ghosts, Vampires, & Haunted Houses,* and *The Young Cartoonist*. All are designed with step-by-step instructions to guide the young artist.

Usborne also writes practical guides like *The Usborne Book of Ballet*, *The Usborne Guide to Make Your Own Jewelry*, and *The Usborne Guide to Soccer*.

Car Travel Games and *Air Travel Games* can keep youngsters busy on long trips as can brainteasers like *Picture Puzzles*, *Brain Puzzles*, and *Number Puzzles*.

More than 300 information and reference books for children, most with the Usborne imprint, offer children interesting choices on a wide variety of subjects.

■ Family Communications

Marketing Dept., 4802 Fifth Avenue, Pittsburgh, PA 15213, (412) 687–2990

Free 13-page color catalog

Producers of *Mister Rogers' Neighborhood*, this non-profit company has packed their catalog with Mr. Rogers' *First Experience Books*, records and cassettes, activity kits, T-shirts, posters, and tote bags.

Books for parents offer insights into how families grow or how they deal with divorce. The award-winning *First Experience* series for children includes *Going on an Airplane*, *Making Friends*, *Moving*, and *The New Baby*. Dozens more offer comforting or funny stories inspired by the perennially popular PBS series.

A good selection of videos makes kids feel like they really are Mister Rogers' neighbors as they are educated and entertained on subjects like wearing a cast, having an operation, music and feelings, and dealing with parents going away.

■ First Step, Ltd.

Interactive board books and more, especially for infants and toddlers.
See page 140 under **Infant Products and Equipment.**

■ Friendship House

Dozens of reference books on music and great composers; coloring books and bookmarks with a musical theme. See page 160 under **Music.**

■ Geode Educational Options

Resources For Whole Life Learning, P.O. Box 106, West Chester, PA 19381, (215) 692–0413

$1.00 for a 52-page black-and-white illustrated catalog (refundable with first purchase)

For titles to intrigue budding scientists and encourage attitudes that will help restore the Earth, take a look at this most interesting catalog. Packed with a collection of more than 500 items, the catalog focuses on non-fiction books for children from preschool through high school.

Math and logic puzzles such as *Aha! Gotcha: Paradoxes to Puzzle and Delight* stimulate older kids to think about questions like why do mirrors reverse left to right but not top to bottom? *What Color is Newton's Apple? Inquiry Science For Young Children* has thought-provoking activities and questions for use with children two through eight.

Geode also sells cooperative board games that encourage children to work with each other instead of competing against each other. *Save the World* is an environmental board game which educates players about ecological problems.

■ The Gifted Children's Catalog

Titles on earth sciences, dictionaries, mythology, and more.
See page 222 under **Toys.**

■ Gospel Light Publications

Order Dept., P.O. Box 6309, Oxnard, CA 93031, (805) 644–9721

Free 24-page color catalog

As its name suggests, Gospel Light sells books, videos, and games to meet your child's Christian education needs. Parents and group leaders of religious education classes may find the Gospel Light selections useful for children from infancy to teens.

The King Who Lives Forever and *Peter* are just two of the dramatic, illustrated books offered for $3.95 each.

Worshiping in God's Family is a kit with student pages, puppet skits, puppet patterns, songs, a music cassette, and a story cassette. It is recommended for use in grades one through six.

Bible Pictures for Children is a series of books with sixteen full-color illustrations of Bible stories. Choose from *The Beginnings, Jesus Our Savior, Jesus and His Followers,* and *Favorite Bible Stories* at $7.95 each.

Most families probably will skip the video of Franco Zeffirelli's *Jesus of Nazareth* for $129.95, but, at $14.95, *The Donut Hole—Jesus Shows His Love* is a video with a family message.

■ Green Tiger Press, Inc.

435 East Carmel Street, San Marcos, CA 92069-4362, (800) 424–2443; in California, (619) 744–7575

Free 21-page black-and-white illustrated (some color) catalog

Among my favorites in the small press category, Green Tiger Press sells new titles, classics, and unusual older picture books, each one beautifully illustrated. I loved many of the lesser known offerings with titles that tickle the imagination. Among them are *Now is the Moon's Eyebrow, Sky Jumps into Your Shoes, Grandma's Scrapbook, Woolman, Legend of the Flying Hot Dog, Hole in the Ocean,* and *Mama, Were You Ever Young?*

Each catalog listing has a photograph of the jacket illustration and a brief description of the story.

Green Tiger also sells premium quality note cards with illustrations taken from *The Teddy Bear's Picnic* (Alexandra Day), *The Tales of Peter Rabbit* (Beatrix Potter), and the works of Jasper Tomkins, Paul Cline, Cooper Eden, and others. Hand-lettered messages and fine papers define the line, which also offers blank cards suitable for birth announcements and other special celebrations. Ask for the separate stationery catalog.

■ Grey Owl Indian Craft Co., Inc.

Native American culture and crafts. See page 8 under **Arts and Crafts.**

■ Gryphon House Inc.

P.O. Box 275, Mt. Rainier, MD 20712, (800) 638–0928; in the Metro Washington, D.C., area, (301) 779–6200

Free 42-page black-and-white illustrated catalog

For nineteen years, Gryphon House has been providing a terrific assortment of Early Childhood books to teachers, parents, and librarians. They have also created an excellent catalog that aims to make easy the job of finding an appropriate book for your child. A terrific table of contents and a handy subject index point shoppers in the right direction, but you may find yourself stopping along the way just to browse. Photos of the book jackets spice up the layout, and each title listed is accompanied by a short description and suggested appropriate age ranges.

The contents are divided into sections such as Early Experiences, Friendship and Sharing, Multi-Cultural Stories, and Science and Nature. A wide variety of titles include *I'm Going To School, Are You My Friend Today?, Mufaro's Beautiful Daughter: An African Tale*, and *Where Fish Go In Winter*.

Take a look at the selection of titles for and about Special Needs children, and at the new collection of Spanish language books. Finally, Gryphon House presents a section of books about parenting.

■ Hatchards

Mail Order Dept., 187 Piccadilly, London W1V 9DA, England, Phone: 01-439 9921

Free 33-page catalog

Booksellers since 1797, Hatchards displays the warrant that signifies they are merchants to the Royal Family. Three pages are devoted exclusively to young children, and the appealing titles include *Oh! Get Off Our Train* and *A Bear-y Tale*. The catalog lists the title, a short description of the story, the number of pages, and the price in British pounds. The story descriptions hint at great fun for titles such as *Quentin Blake's ABC, The Pooh Gift Box, A Foxwood Counting Frieze, The Monster and The Teddy Bear, Easy Peasey People, Cupid, The Market Square Dog, Gruesome Games* and *Postman Pat's Zodiac Storybook*.

Ordering information for foreign catalogs is provided in the "Dear Reader" letter on page ix of this book.

■ Hazelden Educational Materials

Pleasant Valley Road, P.O. Box 176, Center City, MN 55012-0176, (800) 328–9000

Free 12-page black-and-white illustrated catalog

The Hazelden Clinic in Minnesota is well known for its treatment of people with various addictions. Their catalog lists dozens of books that address these addictions and offer coping strategies for sufferers and their families. All the materials are based on the Twelve Steps principle developed and used so effectively by Alcoholics Anonymous.

Families will find useful titles covering such areas as meditation and inspiration, chemical dependency, living with AIDS, chronic illness, depression, eating disorders, nicotine addiction, physical and sexual abuse, and children of alcoholics. Many of the titles have been written for teenagers.

■ HearthSong

Well-chosen collection of folktales, bedtime stories, craft books, and parenting books. See page 224 under **Toys.**

■ Highlights for Children

2300 West Fifth Avenue, P.O. Box 269, Columbus, OH 43272-4002

Free color brochures

Order this packet of brochures from *Highlights for Children* and you will receive proof positive that wonderful things do come in small packages. A highly regarded children's magazine, *Highlights* has been educating and entertaining kids for years. Now, they also offer thirty-three practice workbooks to develop and reinforce arithmetic, reading, handwriting, phonics, and spelling skills. Designed for children in preschool through grade six, they are very reasonable at $2.50 each (for every five you buy, you get an extra book free). They will also send you a color brochure of books on crafts, writing, brainteasers, first dictionaries, science and nature, and hidden pictures. A rubber stamp kit and a great set of twenty-four sturdy plastic stencil cards in their own storage box has nearly 200 designs to trace, color, and cut out. The set is $14.95 and includes numbers, letters, dinosaurs, zoo and farm animals, geometric shapes, and holiday decorations. This one proved to be a big hit under our Christmas tree and is still being enjoyed months later.

■ Hispanic Books Distributors, Inc.

1665 W. Grant Road, Tucson, AZ 85705, (800) 634–2124; in Arizona, (602) 882–9484

Free 65-page black-and-white illustrated catalog

If you are trying to reinforce bilingualism at home or supplement school materials, you will find hundreds of quality Spanish-language books for children and young adults listed here. Core literature, science, bilingual, and picture books are offered in age-appropriate groupings with titles in Spanish and book synopses in English.

Black-and-white jacket illustrations of the book give shoppers a feel for the book, and the descriptions below the title are very clear.

Six pages of resource books offer a good selection of bilingual dictionaries, encyclopedias, and atlases. Paperback collections of plays, children's cookbooks, and special activities make this catalog a valuable source of cultural materials.

■ inkwell

P.O. Box 178, Hanover, MA 02339, (617) 826–9793

Free 12-page catalog

This little catalog specializes in books that are especially suitable for reading aloud to children over the age of five. The proprietor suspects that many parents stop reading to children who have learned to read, risking the loss of a joyful habit that encourages children to explore new kinds of books. She feels that good books need to be "advertised" to kids and, to that end, has assembled a fine collection of titles to set your child's imagination soaring. Among the choices are *Custard the Dragon*, *Three Tales of My Father's Dragon*, *Just So Stories*, *Every Living Thing*, and *James and the Giant Peach*.

■ La Leche League International

P.O. Box 1209, Franklin Park, IL 60131-8209

Free 23-page black-and-white illustrated catalog

La Leche League is the recognized leader in providing information and support for breastfeeding.

Most of this catalog is devoted to books and pamphlets about breastfeeding, nutrition, childbirth, and parenting. About three pages offer special needs items such as breast pumps. Gifts, sweatshirts, and T-shirts are also offered.

A small selection of paperback and picture books for children includes titles like *My Body is Private*, *How You Were Born*, and *I Love My Baby Sister (Most of the Time)*.

■ LibertyTree

134 Ninety-Eighth Avenue, Oakland, CA 94603, (800) 872–4866

Free 32-page color catalog

LibertyTree is a semi-annual review and catalog of more than 800 books, audiotapes, videos, puzzles and games, and gifts on our heritage and practice of liberty. The catalog includes both popular and educational books in American and world history, economics, politics, ethics, literature, humor, and much more, including an extensive selection of books on education at home. History selections include the *Landmarks in America* series, *American Revolution* series, *If You Lived Then* series, Laura Ingalls Wilder's *Little House Books*, and the *Childhood of Famous Americans* series. Two excellent books on economics are *Whatever Happened to Penny Candy* and *Capitalism for Kids*.

Many book prices are discounted, and an additional 10 percent discount is available with a $25 annual membership/subscription to *LibertyTree*. Each issue focuses on a particular theme such as the Constitutional Bicentennial, the Civil War, or the American Revolution. Books on schools and educating children include *Home Schooling for Excellence* and *How to Tutor*.

Popular puzzles include *The Statue of Liberty, Declaration of Independence, Revolutionary War Battlefield Map, Weapons of the Revolution, Famous American Flags*, and *Presidents of the U.S.*

■ Linden Tree

Classic children's books. See page 174 under **Records, Tapes, and CDs.**

■ Manzanita Publications

1731 Hendrix Avenue, P.O. Box 1366, Thousand Oaks, CA 91360

Free 10-page black-and-white illustrated catalog

With a choice from this catalog, your child can have hours of fun cutting and assembling a three-dimensional Emerald City of Oz ($5.00) or completing a coloring book of dinosaurs ($1.50).

Sixteen coloring books include wonderful titles like *Let's Go Whale Watching, The Lewis & Clark Expedition, Peter Cottontail, American Indians, Cowgirls*, and *Soup to Nuts*. The latter features cartoons of nutritious food pals such as Comical Cucumber, Clean-Cut Peanut, and Bandana Banana.

The rest of the catalog is devoted to eleven paper doll and cut-out books: a romantic Princess Di and Prince Charles are $3.50; a Curious George paper doll kit recreates some of this famous mischief maker's wildest adventures.

■ The Metropolitan Museum of Art

Baby books, journals, and pop-up books; illustrated classics for children. See page 150 under **Museum Shops.**

■ National Geographic Society/Books

Christmas Gift Catalog, P.O. Box 2118, Washington, DC 20013-2118

Free 20-page color catalog

With National Geographic's reputation for quality, you can feel comfortable about ordering any of these gorgeous books.

Books like *The Incredible Human Machine* contains photomicrographs (pictures taken inside the body). *Into the Unknown* crosses the seven seas to tell the story of exploration.

The Just For Kids section contains several lively non-fiction books with easy-to-read texts. You might choose from *Let's Explore a River, How Animals Talk, Saving our Animal Friends, Explore a Spooky Swamp,* and *The Wild Ponies of Assateague Island.* While no age recommendations are provided, parents should have no problem determining the titles most appropriate for their child. The catalog includes selections of interest to all age groups.

■ The Norman Rockwell Museum at Stockbridge

A small selection of children's books. See page 151 under **Museum Shops.**

■ Orchard Books

10 Golden Square, London W1R 3AF, England, (phone) 01-734 8738

Free 32-page black-and-white illustrated catalog

A newcomer among small presses, Orchard Books began publishing in 1986 and has built a list that, while small, offers good quality fiction, picture books, poetry, novelty, and gift books for children. A photograph of each book's jacket appears with each listing as does a brief synopsis of the story.

You will be treated to some wonderful books with titles like *The Twins In France, The Twins in Greece, The Get Better Book, Mr. Loopy and Mrs. Snoopy, British Folk Tales,* and *The Apple Pie Alien.*

Orchard Books is a British company and its prices are listed in pounds, so be prepared to call the bank for the latest conversion rate when you actually order. You may also charge your order and let your credit card company do the conversion for you at current rates.

■ Picture Book Studio

P.O. Box 9139, 10 Central Street, Saxonville, MA 01701, (800) 462–1252

Free 31-page color catalog

This publisher is noted for presenting unusual, quality crafted picture books. Among the eighty-three beautifully designed books are *Aesop's Fables,* illustrated by Lisbeth Zwerger, and *The Baby Who Would Not Come Down* with illustrations by Deborah Santini. *Jeremy Quacks* and *Where is Mr. Mole?* are nice gifts for the toddler set. I am always struck by the gorgeous illustrations in the books. *The Greatest Treasure,* the story of adventures in a wonderful kingdom, is painted in fabulous watercolors by the award-winning Spanish artist Arcadio Lobato. The distinctive collages of Eric Carle's books are among the extras you will find.

Parents may also choose from a small selection of toys, gifts, calendars, and Christmas cards.

■ Plays, Inc.
120 Boylston Street, Boston, MA 02116

Free 12-page catalog

If the kids in your house love to put on a show as much as the kids I know, you will want to get your hands on this catalog. Plays, Inc. has assembled collections of one-act plays sure to be hits with your young thespians. *The Big Book of Comedies* offers twenty-five funny plays and skits, including adaptations from classic tales. *The Big Book of Christmas Plays* presents twenty-one traditional and modern choices. Also popular is *Plays From Favorite Folk Tales*, which offers children the roles of Little Red Riding Hood, Rapunzel, Rumpelstiltskin, Robin Hood, Aladdin, and many others.

Even the junior sleuth will find an outlet for his or her talents with *Mystery Plays For Young People*. Also available are workbooks on mime and plays for puppets.

Prices range for $6.95 to $16.95.

■ Pleasant Company
Book series about American girls from pioneer, Victorian, and WW II eras.
See page 239 under **Toys.**

■ Piragis' Northwoods Company/Boundary Waters Catalog
Campfire stories and other books with outdoor themes.
See page 80 under **Clothing.**

■ Practical Parenting
Dept. 5M-90, 18326 Minnetonka Boulevard, Deephaven, MN 55391, (800) 255–3379

Free 4-page black-and-white illustrated brochure

Divorce, toilet training, sibling rivalry, ear tube surgery, and birthday parties are just some of the topics discussed in this collection of books by Vicki Lansky. Ms. Lansky writes the Practical Parenting column in *Sesame Street* magazine's Parent Guide section as well as the HELP column in *Family Circle* magazine.

One of her most popular books, with more than a million copies sold, is *Feed Me I'm Yours*, a baby food and toddler cookbook with 200 child-tested recipes plus feeding advice for new parents.

■ Rand McNally & Company

Publishing-Direct Mail, P.O. Box 1697, Skokie, IL 60076-9871, (800) 234-0679

Free 48-page color catalog

These people have a lot more to offer besides maps and atlases, and it is hard to go wrong with any of their quality, educational offerings for kids and adults. After all, they have been in business for more than 130 years.

Among the items of interest to children are write on/wipe off world maps and a variety of globes from $9.95 to $745.00. Dozens of travel and animal videos include titles from National Geographic, National Parks Videos, and Readers Digest. A great addition to a child's home library is a three-book set that consists of the Rand Mc-Nally's Children's Atlas of the United States, Children's World Atlas, and Children's Atlas of World History. The set is $35.00.

■ Reference Book Center, Inc.

175 Fifth Avenue, New York, NY 10010, (212) 677-2160

Free 16-page catalog

Reference Book Center has gathered an extensive list of reference books from a wide variety of publishers on a broad spectrum of subject areas. This collection is aimed primarily at older children and will be most valuable to teenagers.

The inventory includes dozens of encyclopedias, dictionaries, thesauruses, atlases, gazettes, and companions to American history and literature. Also offered are manuals of style and usage, as well as anthologies of Shakespeare and children's literature.

Books are listed alphabetically by title within subject categories, and include price but no descriptions.

■ Sailors Bookshelf, Inc.

623 Ramsey Avenue, Box No. 643, Hillside, NJ 07205, (201) 964-4620

Free 16-page black-and-white illustrated catalog

The nautically minded will find lots of treasures here with books on racing, cruising, survival, basic and advanced seamanship, and navigation. Nautical charts and videos complete the list.

The highly regarded *Annapolis Book of Seamanship series* is among the choices and is also available on video.

The selection is terrific and provides lots of good, informative reading for teens and adults.

■ Salad Days

P.O. Box 996, Harpers Ferry, WV 25425, (800) 248–3274

Free 27-page black-and-white illustrated catalog

Parents will find a carefully selected library of children's literature, picture books, and non-fiction for all ages and tastes. Key categories are Board Books, Alphabet and Counting Books, Bedtime Books, Picture and Story Books, Poetry and Verse, and more. The Favorite Authors and Illustrators section steers readers to the beloved works of A. A. Milne, Maurice Sendak, Tomie de Paola, Dr. Seuss, and Arnold Lobel.

Parenting books are among the extras. There is also a small selection of music on audio and video cassette.

■ San Francisco Museum of Modern Art

Illustrated classics, activity books, art handbooks.
See page 152 under **Museum Shops.**

■ Savanna Books

72 Chestnut Street, Cambridge, MA 02139, (617) 876–7665

Free book list

Savanna Books was started by a mother initially frustrated in her efforts to find literature that would give black youngsters positive role models.

Her perseverance resulted in an assemblage of nearly 300 books for toddlers through teens. Categorized according to age-appropriateness, the book list gives the titles, author, and price of each book.

Synopses are not provided, but many titles are sufficiently descriptive. Intriguing titles include *Africa Dream, Afro-Bets: ABC, Black Achievers—Great Women,* and *Why Are People Different?*

■ Schoolmasters

Books with science and nature themes. See page 183 under **Science and Nature.**

■ Script City

1770 N. Highland Avenue, #608, Hollywood, CA 90028, (213) 871–0707

$2.00 for 33-page catalog

Movie and television scripts, film and media books, and photos and posters are the order of the day in this fascinating catalog.

Script City offers the actual scripts of hundreds of movies and television shows. For $19.95 each, you can choose Academy Award winners like *The Adventures of Robin Hood* (1938), *Back to the Future* (1985), *Ben Hur* (1959), *Doctor Doolittle* (1967), *The Wizard of Oz* (1939), and *Splash* (1984).

If television is more your taste, for $16.95 each you can buy a script of *The Addams Family*, *Alf*, *Born Free*, *Dennis the Menace*, *Faerie Tale Theatre*, *M*A*S*H*, and others.

Script City also offers dozens of books on film direction and production as well as the history of the big screen and television.

■ Sensational Beginnings

Good selection of infant board books, picturebooks, songbooks, poetry, and parenting titles. See page 232 under **Toys.**

■ The Sesame Street Catalog

Preschool titles featuring favorite characters from Sesame Street.
See page 233 under **Toys.**

■ Skippack

Box 326, Kulpsville, PA 19443, (215) 362–8868

Free 24-page black-and-white illustrated catalog

Mary Martha Whitworth, the president of Skippack, has used her twenty-year experience as an educator and child care specialist to select books that reflect excellence in children's literature and that bring the most enjoyment to her students.

A happy variety of infant and toddler cloth and board books feature touch-and-feel and peek-a-boo books, Mother Goose rhymes, and a few titles that positively reinforce toilet training skills.

Social issues and special situations are addressed in books on divorce, death, feelings, friends, and safety. Also among the array are activity books, adventures, poetry, fairy tales, songbooks, and finger plays for all ages.

Books are divided into sections according to age appropriateness. Titles that have won the prestigious Caldecott or Newbery Medals are specially marked.

■ Tiger Lily Books

Kathy Epling, P.O. Box 111, Piercy, CA 95467

Free 40-page catalog

From her cabin in the fir and madrone forests of northern California, proprietress Kathy Epling shares her wisdom about good children's books. Three children and twelve years of employment in a bookstore have shaped her philosophy on the joys of reading.

With a great deal of warmth, she recommends some new and unusual preschool books to take the place of standard board (she calls them "bored") books. Nonetheless she often stands by some wonderful classics, encouraging readers to try titles by Robert McCloskey and Maurice Sendak, to name just two.

This catalog is really a charmer, and Ms. Epling writes such clear and complete copy about each book that you will know exactly which one suits your child.

■ Travel Books

113 Corporation Road, Hyannis, MA 02601-2204, (800) 869–3535

Free 34-page catalog

The armchair traveler will be in seventh heaven while browsing through this descriptive catalog. Titles such as these will appeal to parents and kids: *Walt Disney World* (the "official" guide by Steve Birnbaum), *Kids London, The Norse Myths, Family Vacations USA, In and Out of Boston with (or without) Children,* and *The Candy Apple: New York for Kids.*

A special section devoted to books about student opportunities includes *Work, Study, Travel Abroad; The Teenager's Guide to Study, Travel and Adventure Abroad;* and *Learning Vacations,* to name just three.

■ World Almanac Education

1278 West Ninth Street, Cleveland, OH 44113, (800) 521–6600

Free 47-page color catalog

A wide selection of books for toddlers through teenagers awaits you here. The classics are represented with the likes of *The Velveteen Rabbit, Charlotte's Web,* and *The Very Hungry Caterpillar,* as well as *Dr. Seuss* sets, the tales of *Babar,* and the *Little House on the Prairie* books. Interspersed with the award winners by well-known authors are hundreds of other good choices for elementary, middle, and high school readers. Many are available at slightly discounted prices. For example, Laura Ingalls Wilder titles that list for $13.95 are offered here for $12.82.

Jacket illustrations of each title appear with a brief description of the story, so your selection is made pleasant and easy.

■ World Around Songs, Inc.

Pocket-sized songbooks for church, camp, and school; folksongs, carols, trail songs. See page 160 under **Music.**

■ World of Science/Merrell Scientific

Identification guides, reference texts, and many earth science titles. See page 184 under **Science and Nature.**

■ Yellow Moon Press

P.O. Box 1316, Cambridge, MA 02238, (617) 628–7894

Free 47-page catalog

Yellow Moon Press concentrates on books, audiocassettes, and videos related to the oral tradition. Many of their materials explore the history of storytelling and breathe new life into that age-old art.

Yellow Moon has made a wonderful selection of quality items. For instance, Judith Black's audiocassette *Glad to Be Who I Am* is the winner of the 1988 Parent's Choice Gold Award. It contains a contemporary version of *The Three Billy Goats Gruff* and stories about kid-related issues such as having a new baby around the house (60 minutes for $8.95). *Medley of Tellers & Tales* is an audiocassette collection of seven stories by different storytellers; for ages 8 and up, it sells for $8.95.

The titles are divided into toddler, young children, and young adult categories. Many of the books are unusual and hard to come by elsewhere.

Some nicely varied folktale and fairy tale books are *Arab Folktales, African Folktales, Elijah's Violin and Other Jewish Fairytales, The Bread Sister of Sinking Creek, Magic Orange Tree,* and *Seven Arrows.*

A very small section of videos features imaginative and interesting educational stories.

RECORDED BOOKS

■ Alcazar Records

Narrations of children's classic and folktales.
See page 171 under **Records, Tapes and CDs.**

■ Children's Book and Music Center

Narrations of children's classics, holiday stories, and more.
See page 24 under **Books.**

■ Children's Recordings

Classics and Poetry read aloud by celebrities and authors.
See page 171 under **Records, Tapes and CDs.**

■ Discount Books and Video, Inc.

Classics on LP. See page 27 under **Books.**

■ The Disney Catalog

Recordings of Disney versions of fairy tales and children's classics.
See page 105 under **Gifts.**

■ Dove Books on Tape

12711 Ventura Boulevard, Suite 250, Studio City, CA 91604, (800) 345–9945;
in California, (818) 762–6662; in Vermont, (800) 533–0024

Free 35-page color catalog

In an era when many children have more electronic equipment than their parents, it is no surprise that books on tape are so popular among the young crowd. In fact, the whole family will enjoy the recordings of Dove Books on Tape, which uses the finest quality audiotape for every cassette.

Small children will enjoy cassettes of Walt Disney's *Bambi, The Little Mermaid, Oliver & Company, The Jungle Book, Winnie the Pooh,* and *The Fox and the Hound.* Other titles are *The Summer Friend, The Little Grey Men,* and *Peter Pan.*

Older children can choose from *Batman, Indiana Jones, The Princess Bride,* and the works of Charles Dickens. The tapes are priced at $9.95 or $14.95 each.

If parents feel the need for some enlightenment, they can listen to Dr. Sirgay Sanger's *You and Your Baby's First Years* for $14.95.

■ Durkin Hayes Publishing Ltd.

One Columbia Drive, Niagara Falls, NY 14305, (800) 962–5200

Free 23-page color catalog

Would you and your child like to hear Katharine Hepburn read *Beauty and The Beast, Jack and the Beanstalk, The Nightingale,* and *The Musicians of Bremen*? Durkin Hayes sells these audiotapes and others of plays, novels, and short stories for the whole family. All are recorded on high quality, music grade tape, with Dolby noise reduction. Most of the tapes are about two hours long and include such favorites as *Ring of Bright Water, Through the Looking Glass, The Secret Garden, The Snow Goose, The Wind in the Willows, Tom Brown's School Days, The Jungle Book, Little Women, Peter Pan, Black Beauty,* and more.

Older children will enjoy *Born Free, The Lost World, A Christmas Carol, The Canterbury Tales,* and *The Red Badge of Courage.*

Most of the titles sell for $14.95 each.

■ A Gentle Wind

Contemporary and traditional tales on audiocassette.
See page 173 under **Records, Tapes and CDs.**

■ LibertyTree

Audiotapes on our heritage and practice of liberty.
See page 35 under **Books.**

■ The Mind's Eye

Box 6727, San Francisco, CA 94191, (800) 227–2020;
in California, Hawaii, Arkansas, (415) 883–7701

Free 40-page color catalog

You can build your listening library from the terrific list offered in this catalog of cassettes for children of all ages. A comprehensive selection of children's classics, folktales, and contemporary favorites is sure to please most shoppers.

A set of four Roald Dahl classics are $29.95, as is a set of four tapes recounting the glorious tales of King Arthur and his Knights of the Round Table.

A set of seven cassettes of *The Chronicles of Narnia* are read by Claire Bloom, Michael York, Anthony Quale, and Ian Richardson. Young listeners are sure to enjoy *Winnie-the-Pooh, Alice in Wonderland, Aladdin, Cinderella, Amelia Bedelia, Hawthorne's Great Short Stories, Treasure Island, The Pied Piper of Hamelin,* and *Sarah, Plain and Tall.* The line also includes audio biographies of inventors, explorers, and history shapers like Susan B. Anthony, Benjamin Franklin, Eleanor Roosevelt, and many others.

The catalog also offers foreign language instruction tapes for children and adults.

■ Recorded Books, Inc.

270 Skipjack Road, Prince Frederick, MD 20678, (800) 638–1304

Free 29-page catalog

Recorded Books offers an interesting option that will help you keep some of your money in your pocket: You can rent (for 30 days) any of the cassettes they offer for the whole family. All titles are also available for purchase.

Complete and unabridged narrations, the cassettes are a lifesaver on long car rides. The kids are sure to enjoy *Black Beauty, The Wind in the Willows, The Secret Garden,* and Kipling's *Just So Stories,* and *The Jungle Book.*

Older children will enjoy *Ann Frank: The Diary of a Young Girl, The Red Badge of Courage, Pocahontas, The Oregon Trail,* and *The Call of the Wild.* To give you an idea of the prices, Mark Twain's *The Adventures of Tom Sawyer* runs for seven hours and sells for $34.95. You can rent it for 30 days for $11.50. *The Adventures of Huckleberry Finn* runs for nine and a half hours and sells for $39.95. It can be rented for 30 days for $13.50.

Next time your kids are on a plane, in the car, or at the beach, slip one of these cassettes in the tape player and let their imaginations soar with some truly enduring literature.

■ Spoken Arts

P.O. Box 289, New Rochelle, NY 10802, (800) 537–3617

Free 64-page black-and-white illustrated catalog

Let Julie Harris read Nathaniel Hawthorne's *Tanglewood Tales* to your kids at naptime, hear Francis Sternhagen bring Beatrix Potter's *Treasury of Animal Stories* to vibrant life, or perhaps have Ossie Davis explain *How the Snake Got Its Rattles*.

Established in 1956, Spoken Arts has been bringing some of the best in children's literature to families and schools. Hundreds of cassettes include several with companion videos or filmstrips of classic tales and new releases.

■ Yellow Moon Press

Storytelling favorites on tape. See page 43 under **Books**.

Clothing

■

GENERAL MERCHANDISE

■ Aerie Design

P.O. Box 36, Asheville, NC 28802, (800) 233–0229; in North Carolina, (704) 645–3285

Free color brochure

Aerie Design, a small company located in the Blue Ridge mountains of North Carolina, creates colorfully silkscreened wildlife designs on T-shirts for men, women, and children.

All printed by hand, the nine designs feature flora and fauna beautifully and whimsically represented. "Last One In" shows baby turtles rushing across the sand to the surf. On "Close Encounter" a panda reaches up from a bamboo forest to touch a butterfly.

Children's designs are on the front of 50/50 poly-cotton T-shirts. Sizes are: small (6-8), medium (10-12), and large (14-16). T-shirts are $4.50 each.

■ After the Stork

1501 12th Street NW, Albuquerque, NM 87104, (505) 243–9100

Free 66-page color catalog

This is a great place to stock up on sensible, everyday clothes in natural fibers. After the Stork offers versatile cotton sweats and turtlenecks in twelve colors, including very pretty ones in coral, emerald, and marigold. Crew socks in matching colors are 97 percent cotton. Winter jackets and hats are offered in the Fall/Winter catalog, bathing suits and shorts are staples in the Summer issue. Long- and short-sleeved T-shirts are so sturdy, classic and inexpensive that you will want to order in bulk for every kid in the house.

Several styles of sweatpants, slacks, shorts, and skirts are offered in matching colors and fabrics. (Colorful playcord pants for the bargain price of $6.75 were so well made and fit so great that I ordered them in all six colors for my four-year-old.) Terrific long underwear sets are like a second skin to most kids; buy these and you may never buy pajamas again.

The popular Soupçon label provides mix-and-match sets for infants. After the Stork also carries Zoo Shoe sneakers and canvas shoes in a variety of colors and styles.

You can fill up the order form with more basics like cotton sweaters, knee socks, overalls, jumpers, raincoats, boots, shoes, slippers, hats, and more. Clothes sizes start at 0-6 months and continue to size 16.

■ Athletic Supply

NBA and NFL jackets, sweats, jerseys, T-shirts.
See page 189 under **Sports Equipment.**

■ Baby Clothes Wholesale

70 Ethel Road West, Piscataway, NJ 08854, (201) 842–2900

$2.65 for 44-page color catalog, refundable with first order

Don't hesitate to send for this one. It is loaded with unbelievably priced bargains on kids' clothes from newborn to size 7 with a very few items up to size 14.

Mail orders under $50.00 will have a $5.00 handling charge, but you will save at least that much on every outfit.

For babies, 100 percent acrylic sets for $5.99 include shirt, pants, and matching booties in soft colors and designs. A permanent press, cotton blend appliquéd romper and hat set are $4.99; boys' cotton shirt and matching diaper shorts are $3.99 a set; girls' 100 percent cotton corduroy overalls with matching blouse are $6.99 a set.

Coats, jerseys, dresses, and sleepers are all stocked at similar fantastic savings.

Gift certificates are available; all merchandise is accepted for return or exchange if it is in original "unused and unwashed" condition.

■ bear-in-mind

Teddy bear motifs on T-shirts and sweatshirts.
See page 249 under **Toys.**

■ Biobottoms

Fresh Air Wear, P.O. Box 6009, Petaluma, CA 94953-6009, (707) 778–7945

Free 44-page color catalog

First known for its breathable wool diaper covers, Biobottoms now sells cotton clothing in colorful, practical, and fashionable styles for boys and girls, newborn to size 14.

Their specialty is cotton prefold diapers and comfortable, absorbent, pin-free wool or cotton diaper covers. These covers are expensive ($16.00 for smaller sizes and $16.50 for babies 18 lbs. and up), but they are incredibly durable and allow you to use cotton diapers without the fuss (and pain) of pins. Since 18 billion plastic diapers are buried in landfills every year at great cost to the consumer and the environment, a switch to cloth diapers and covers will be a favor to your baby *and* the Earth.

Biobottoms has done a great job with gorgeous, natural-fiber clothes for kids by Well-Made Widebody, Padders, Sara's Prints, Wibbies, Widgeon, and Flapdoodles. The line includes rompers, dresses, T-shirts, underwear, sweaters, jackets, hats, pants, and tops.

You will also find a nice selection of footwear. Choose from booties, moccasins, slippers, sneakers, and boots.

■ Boston Proper Mail Order

One Boston Plaza, P.O. Box 7070, Mt. Vernon, NY 10551-7070, (800) 243–4300

Free 56-page color catalog

Boston Proper devotes six pages of its women's catalog to kids' clothes and (a few) toys. Unusual outfits by Eagles Eye, Hartstrings, Mother-Maid, Kitestrings, and Lyka Bear offer something for almost every taste.

Cute cotton rompers or shortsets by Pattycakes that depict a turtle playing frisbee are $34.00 for the romper, $41.00 for the shortset.

A lunchbox from Metrokane comes with an adjustable strap, thermos jug, a built-in quartz clock, and batteries for $25.00.

Let the kids express themselves by stenciling dinosaurs, airplanes, or alphabets on their T-shirts. Paint-on kits ($19.95 each) come with stencils and seven shiny textile paints. Extra sets of five paints sell for $12.50.

■ Brights Creek

Bay Point Place, Hampton, VA 23653-3116, (800) 622–9202

Free 80-page color catalog

Brights Creek offers reasonably priced mix-and-match clothes, shoes, and costumes for newborn to size 16. Bold prints and cute appliqués are trademarks of the inventory, which includes cotton blend and acrylic knits, corduroys, and fleecewear. Shirts, pants, skirts, shorts, bathing suits, pajamas, and layette items are easily coordinated with colorful socks and a fabulous assortment of nylon tights. Many of the pajamas can do double duty as costumes, especially the Superhero and skeleton styles.

The shoe line includes dress-up Mary Janes, cotton sneakers in several styles and many colors, ballet slippers, rain boots, deck shoes, and cowgirl and cowboy boots.

Jackets, sweaters, turtlenecks, and more make this a good place for back to school shopping. You can order toll-free 24 hours a day.

■ Brooks Brothers

350 Campus Plaza, P.O. Box 4016, Edison, NJ 08818-4016, (800) 274–1815

Free 62-page color catalog

It is never too early to introduce future gentlemen lawyers and bankers to Brooks Brothers. The ultimate symbol of the Boston Brahmin and preppydom, Brooks Brothers catalog caters to men and boys.

Along with classic and beautifully constructed quality clothing, you will get extraordinary service. I ordered by phone some of their justifiably famous shirts one afternoon during the Christmas rush season. They were delivered to my door late the next morning!

The exclusive Brooks 3-button navy wool blazer for boys is $85.00 for sizes 8 to 12 regular. Sizes 13 to 20 prep are $110. Cotton broadcloth, button-down, bold stripe shirts are $35.00 each in sizes small, medium, large, or extra large. Cotton boxer undershorts are $8.00 in sizes 22 to 30. Pajamas, flannel robes, corduroy trousers, suede moccasin slippers, and other shirts are also available.

■ The Children's Shop

Box 625, Chatham, MA 02633, (800) 426–8716

Free 20-page color catalog; three seasonal mailings per year

If you never have the chance to go to Cape Cod and visit this delightful shop located in an old fishing village, you will still find plenty to charm you in their catalog.

They carry quality, traditionally styled clothing for boys and girls in sizes newborn to 14. I was especially impressed with the good-looking clothes for boys—for years designers seemed to think we wanted only Batman or The Incredible Hulk splashed across our sons' clothes. Smart-looking jumpshorts and walk shorts in Tartan plaid are $24.00 and $17.50, respectively. They look great paired with a piped, Peter Pan collar shirt ($11.50 to $13.50).

Navy blue sailor suits are available as dresses or as shortalls for boys. The stock includes lots of pretty dresses, coats, vests, turtlenecks, jumpers, blouses, overalls, raingear, fleecewear, and sleepwear. Most items are 100 percent cotton and nearly all are machine washable.

■ Children's Wear Digest

2515 East 43rd Street, P.O. Box 22728, Chattanooga, TN 37422-2728, (800) 433–1895

Free 32-page color catalog

Children's Wear Digest features well-made clothes in attractive colors and styles for boys and girls. If discounted OshKosh overalls don't draw your attention, you might be tempted by the other familiar manufacturers here, including Carters, Izod, Eagle's Eye, Sweet Potato, and Florence Eiseman.

The fall catalog offers cold-weather gear and nice things for school with lots of practical slacks, sweaters, and rugby-style jerseys, as well as some adorable dresses that would be fine for church but are not too fussy for school days. The holiday catalog features more winter wear, including coats, jackets, snowsuits, and sleepwear. The spring catalog lightens up for warm weather with cotton playwear, bathing suits, rain gear, cotton tights, and more.

Clothes are available in sizes 12 months to 14.

■ Chock Catalog Corp.

74 Orchard Street, New York, NY 10002-4594, (800) 222–0020;
in New York State, (212) 473–1929

$1.00 for a 61-page black-and-white illustrated catalog

In business since the 1920s, the Chock family continues to bring you nationally advertised name-brand underwear and sleepwear for the whole family at approximately 25 percent off the manufacturer's suggested list price.

Hanes T-shirts for boys that list at three for $5.99 are sold by Chock for $4.50. Briefs listed at three for $4.99 sell here for $3.75. Dozens of styles of Carter's training pants, crib sheets, receiving blankets, infant gowns, and terry jamakins as well as blanket sleepers and underwear are available. Tic Tac Toe sells boys' and girls' socks with slip-proof rubber on the soles; they list for $5.00 each and are offered here at three for $11.25. Similar discounts are taken on Trimfit tube socks and anklets.

■ Classics For Kids

Dept. KC, 10501 Metropolitan Avenue, Kensington, MD 20895, (301) 949–3128

Free 34-page black-and-white illustrated catalog

Classics For Kids specializes in children's natural-fiber clothes up to size 10, wooden toys, and a small selection of OK waistband maternity clothes.

Traditional and functional kids' clothing from snow hats and hoods to six styles of cotton tights is the hallmark here. Colorful rain jackets, pants, and capes are machine washable and priced from $9.50 to $18.95. Soft cotton sweat dresses, jumpers, and flightsuits all by Jeanie Mac make for easy and comfortable dressing. A lamb's wool sweater handknit by Peruvian women is done in a variegated pattern and sells for $39.00.

With more and more parents switching to environment-friendly cotton diapers, Nikky cotton or wool diaper covers are a popular item. The waterproof, washable, vinyl-lined cotton covers are their biggest seller. A single pair sells for $9.95; for six or more, the price drops to $8.95 each.

They also carry WrapUp diaper covers at $5.50 each or six for $29.50. All of these diaper covers have Velcro closures that make diapering easy and painless.

■ Cohen's

64 Cranbrook Road, Yorktowne Plaza, Cockeysville, MD 21030, (800) 736–1667

Free 12-page color catalog

Cohen's claims to be "Always In Good Taste" in providing fine classic clothing for boys and men since 1904. Cohen's carries clothes from size 6/7 to husky size 20 in regular, short, or long lengths. Cohen's has traditionally catered to the young man who needs a private-school wardrobe, so you will find very preppy cotton pants, Gant corduroy slacks, navy blazers, washable grey flannel pants, cotton oxford dress shirts, knit ties, polo shirts, and more. All are the finest quality available at reasonable prices.

■ Cot'n Kidz

P.O. Box 620159, Newton, MA, (617) 964–2686

Free 10-page black-and-white illustrated catalog

Formerly called Cot'n Tot Fashions, Cot'n Kidz still features 100 percent cotton clothing that is both comfortable and stylish. The selection is small, but the merchandise is very attractive and often unique. Best of all, the clothes are machine washable, machine dryable, colorfast, and preshrunk. A seashell print Hawaiian shirt and bloomer shorts set is $20.00 and is available in sizes 0-6 months and 18-24 months. If you want to protect your child from the sun, $8.00 will buy a flap hat like the legionnaires wore in the desert.

Beautiful sleep or play outfits made in Japan by Fusen Usagi have delightful prints and are available as shirt and pants or coveralls. They sell for $24.00 each and are durable enough to be passed on to the next child.

Cot'n Kidz also offers stylish bathing suits, extenderalls that add a couple of inches to the length of overalls, jackets, hats, and more.

■ Cove Knitters

Mary Brown, R.F.D. #2, Lincolnville, ME 04849, (207) 338–3419

Free information sheet with sample yarn

You will receive only a flyer from this concern, but yarn samples are enclosed and the information is clear and concise. Cove Knitters makes the most adorable "rollup" hats I have ever seen. You will find them in many children's catalogs, but this is the direct source. Designed in four styles (all clearly illustrated on the flyer), they are made of machine washable 100 percent cotton. This hat is the *only* hat my daughter will keep on—it doesn't itch, and it doesn't lose its stretchiness either. You choose the color(s) for the solid or striped styles from a nice assortment of beautiful, clear hues that will easily match any jacket or snowsuit available. Prices range from $9.50 for x-sm (0-6 mos) to $14.50 for kids (5 years and up). Postage is included in these prices. You just cannot go wrong.

■ Daisy Kingdom, Inc.

Children's clothing and nursery materials ready-made or in kits.
See page 5 under **Arts and Crafts.**

■ The Disney Catalog

Disney clothing for the whole family. See page 105 under **Gifts.**

■ Eddie Bauer

Sweaters, turtlenecks. See page 78 under **Clothing.**

■ Eisner Bros.

76 Orchard Street, New York, NY 10002, (800) 426–7700;
in New York State, (800) 426–7900

Free 30-page black-and-white illustrated catalog

Eisner Bros. is one of the largest wholesalers of T-shirts and other printables with
sizes from 6 months through 4XL. They sell Hanes, Monsanto by Pannill, Jerzees by
Russell, Screen Stars, Fruit of the Loom, and Auburn—and they are cheaper by the
dozen. You *must* order at least a half dozen of an item, but the savings are so good
here that it is still a deal.

Sweatshirts and sweatpants are stocked in a variety of colors. Made from a 50
percent cotton/50 percent acrylan acrylic blend, they are sized for youths, juveniles,
toddlers, and infants. A dozen sweatsuits in sizes 12 months to 6X-7 are $48.00 a
dozen. Where else can you buy a quality Pannill sweatsuit for $4.00? Get together
with a few other parents with children the same size as yours and you can realize
some very substantial savings. They also sell infant T-shirts by Screen Stars for
$15.00 per dozen in sizes 6 to 24 months.

Choose carefully because all sales are final.

■ Flap Happy

2322 Walnut Avenue, Venice, CA 90291, (800) 234–3527;
in southern California, (213) 391–1316

Free 6-page black-and-white illustrated catalog

The Flap Happy Flap Hat for kids was first produced by a mother who needed a hat
that would protect her fair-skinned baby from the sun. That original design has
evolved into eight different styles that protect kids of all ages from the elements. A
100 percent cotton or cotton flannel version has a visor and a flap around the back
that looks like a legionnaire's desert garb. You may be tempted to giggle at first, but
remember that these hats are well-made and practical solutions to the problem of
harmful sun exposure.

Sailor hats, baseball caps, Surf Visors, and adorable Flapper Caps or Bands (with
a sassy bow in the front) are also available in a wide range of solids and assorted
prints. A Polar Fleece hat with a special Velcro-like closure under the neck is itch-
free and comes in black, red, frost blue, or electric pink for $10.95 each.

■ F. Rubbrecht

Grand-Place 23, B-1000 Brussels-Belgium

Write to request current cost of 14-page color catalog

Their own front cover best describes the quality of real Belgian lace that F. Rubbrecht offers. "The best is something which costs more, requires more individual effort, and is often created with a passionate disregard for the practical outcome."

Turn past the doilies, traycloths, and tablerunners offered here, and you will find one page with two of the most exquisite christening gowns you can imagine. One is thirty inches long and sells for $230.00; the other is 32 inches long and is $323.00.

Rubbrecht also has two styles of delicate babycaps. One is lined with silk and sells for $36.00; the other is $26.00. Silk-lined booties are $38.00, and bibs far too lovely to spill on are $18.00 or $35.00.

■ Garnet Hill

The Original Natural Fibers Catalog, 262 Main Street, Franconia, NH 03580, (800) 622–6216

Free 50-page color catalog

Bedding, bath needs, and clothes—all in natural fibers—are Garnet Hill specialties.

Classic madras pull-on shorts or sundresses in sizes 2 through 12 are $15.00 and $26.00, respectively. Handcrafted "Bear Feet" sandals, are naturally shaped and feature rubber soles to allow lots of freedom of movement.

Garnet Hill features hard-to-find breathable cotton swimsuits, cotton pants by Jeannie Mac, and terrific striped Absorba coveralls and rompers for infants. You will find brushed cotton jumpsuits and simply styled cotton knit dresses that can be worn for party and play. Cotton shorts with coordinating T-shirts (both by Absorba) are a high-quality essential in children's summer wardrobes. Look here in the fall for cotton tights, jackets, sweaters, and coats.

A few choice maternity options include a floral batiste nursing gown, a cotton nursing bra, and two rather cleverly designed nursing shirts by Gale River for $44.00 each.

Any baby should have sweet dreams on the all-cotton flannel crib sheets. Pillowcases and a crib comforter cover are also offered.

■ Gymboree Catalog

577 Airport Boulevard, Suite 400, Burlingame, CA 94010, (800) 222–7758

Free 16-page color catalog

The Gymboree Play Centers have a catalog of sportswear and equipment for children from three months to four years.

Fleece sweatsuits in five colors are priced at $15.00 for the top and $15.00 for the pants. There are poly/cotton jumpsuits for infants, GymSox leggings, and shoes by Toddler University.

You can also purchase some of the items that Gymboree uses in their classes. A Play Parachute that is 10 feet in diameter (adult supervision recommended) sells for $30.00; an inflatable Gym Baby Bolster sells for $12.00; SoftShapes Beanbags are $10.00 each; and some fun music and exercise cassettes are $12.00 each.

■ half pint

23010 Lake Forest Drive, Suite 187, Laguna Hills, CA 92653, (800) 477–4704

$2.00 for an 8-page color catalog

These hand-painted cotton playclothes make wonderfully unique gifts. Jazzy designs on girls' and boys' clothes are reasonably priced and fun to wear.

Little girls will like the vibrant fuchsia or teal cotton interlock tops with matching leggings and hand-painted black stars in sizes 12M, 2, 4, and 6 ($25.00). Geometric shapes painted on poly/cotton fleece sweats will keep active boys and girls looking their best; they are $23.50 for sizes 2, 4, and 6.

A string of hearts run down a float style dress for $30.00. Mom can order an oversized matching T-shirt for $22.00.

■ hanna Andersson

1010 N. W. Flanders Street, Portland, OR 97209-9902, (800) 222–0544

Free 52-page color catalog

When I ask people which catalogs they shop from for their children's clothes, they invariably name hanna Andersson. You will understand why when you see the 100 percent cotton, Swedish clothes offered for infants and children up to size 8-10. The colors and patterns are irresistible, and the styling is snappy and fresh yet very practical.

Twelve shades of 100 percent cotton sweatpants are great for mixing and matching with bold striped socks ($14.00 for three pair) and striped double-neck turtlenecks ($17 or $19 each). Several color combinations of soft Swedish sailor's neck pullovers are $24 or $27 each, depending on size.

Infant clothes include lots of comfy, stylish cotton cover-ups, dozens of snappy caps, snowsuits ($48.00), mittens, shoes, bibs, and bright plaid jackets. A few terrifically comfortable outfits are also provided for mothers; among this collection of casualwear are maternity basics in pretty cotton solids and soft stripes.

The quality fabric and construction are so good that you will use these clothes for your next child—and probably the next. Or, if you can send items back to hanna in gently used condition, they will donate the clothes to a local charity and give you a 20 percent credit off their purchase price, which you can apply to the purchase of any current catalog item.

■ Heir Affair

Christening gown. See page 107 under **Gifts.**

■ Hog Wild!

Pig motifs on T-shirts and sweatshirts, booties and hats. See page 120 under **Gifts.**

■ Initials

Personalized hooded sweaters and T-shirts. See page 117 under **Gifts.**

■ Jim Morris

Environmental T-Shirts, P.O. Box 831, Boulder, CO 80306, (303) 444–6430

Free 32-page color catalog

With these beautifully silkscreened T-shirts and sweatshirts you can express your concern for the environment while contributing to the cause financially. The company will donate ten percent of its profits to environmental groups, whose names are listed on the order sheet for your review.

Dozens of images and environmental messages draw attention to global problems such as the destruction of the rain forest and water pollution. In addition to messages about endangered environments, attention is given to endangered species like the tiger, whale, and bald eagle, among many others.

T-shirts are $9.95 and come in children's sizes small (6-8), medium (10-12), and large (12-16). All of the designs are also available in adult sizes.

■ Kids At Large, Inc.

Building 32, Endicott Street, Norwood, MA 02062, (617) 769–8575

Free 11-page color catalog

Finally—a spot to buy fun and fashionable clothes for large kids (boys and girls from 55 pounds to 230 pounds). The company was founded about five years ago by two women who had been overweight as children and had hated the limited choices they found when shopping. Their efforts will make heavy children feel and look great. This is a collection with a lot of pizzazz.

An easy-to-read sizing chart at the beginning of the catalog lets you accurately choose your child's size by weight and height.

Boys' brightly colored swimsuits with a 100 percent nylon shell are $22.00 to $26.00, depending upon size. Girls' floral swimsuits are classic one-piece tanks made of nylon/lycra; they sell for $32.00 to $36.00.

One hundred percent cotton canvas pants by Zeppelin in up-to-the-minute styling are $32.00 to $36.00.

They offer acid-washed denims, dress clothes, school outfits, bathing suits, and great acrylic blend tights. Most outfits have elasticized waists.

■ Lands' End, Inc.

One Lands' End Lane, Dodgeville, WI 53595-0001, (800) 356–4444

Free 123-page color catalog

It would be difficult to say enough good things about Lands' End. I buy about a third of our children's summer and winter clothes here and have never been disappointed.

About ten pages are devoted to kids' sizes 12 months to size 14-16. Do not hesitate to order elastic waistband shorts, slacks, T-shirts, and turtlenecks in a terrific variety of mix-and-match solids and stripes. I have ordered many of these and they are all so well made that they are able to be passed down to the next child.

Shortalls, tank dresses, T-dresses, and dozens of other items for boys and girls are all fairly priced and guaranteed. Take it from me—you can count on Lands' End quality *every* time.

Teens and parents will find hundreds of items in the rest of the catalog that will take care of their needs for T-shirts, pants, shorts, casual dresses, jackets, turtlenecks, sweats, swimsuits, and much more.

■ Laura Ashley by Post

P.O. Box 891, Mahwah, NJ 07430-9990, (800) 367–2000

$3.00 a year for three "Mother and Child" 16-page color catalogs that come with a 48-page garment catalog for women

Gorgeous Laura Ashley fabrics and fine detailing are trademarks with this well-known firm.

If you are looking for mother-daughter or big sister-little sister outfits, the most lovely of all are offered here. Though expensive, the clothes have a classic, somewhat old-fashioned look with a timeless appeal. A navy blue sailor dress with red trim for mother is $140.00 while the same dress in size 3/4 or 5/6 is $70.00. In sizes 7/8, 9/10, and 11/12, the dress is $78.00. Baby sister's dress in size 12-18 months is $54.00; sizes 18-24 months and 2/3 is $62.00.

The line includes softly draped velvet and pinwale corduroy dresses, wool coats, sweaters, and delicate floral patterned dresses with touches of lace.

The fine fabrics and construction are worth the price, if your budget can allow, and the loose-fitting women's dresses can do double duty as maternity clothes for at least most of your pregnancy.

■ Les Petits

Response Service Center, 3200 South 76th Street, Box 33901, Philadelphia, PA 19142-0961, (800) 333–2002

Free 52-page color catalog

This lovely collection of beautifully made clothes for boys and girls in sizes newborn through 14 features dresswear and playwear designed and manufactured in France. Some prices are a bit high, but the quality is excellent.

The selection for girls includes 100 percent cotton and cotton blend blouses and skirts, plaid and corduroy slacks, denim skirts, cotton piqué polo shirts with long or short sleeves, turtlenecks, polo sweaters, hats, gloves, knee socks, and tights. The girls' dresses are particularly elegant, and are made from top quality fabrics with embroidery and smocking exquisitely done. A cotton flannel dress with dainty cotton piqué collar is $34.00; another with smocked front and covered buttons is $49.00.

Les Petits also has traditional styles for boys. You will find shirts in 100 percent cotton, pants in plaid, corduroy, denim, twill, and gabardine, Bermuda shorts in dress flannel or summer-weight cotton, sweaters, stone washed denims, belts, suspenders, and socks. Beautiful wool blend coats made in Brittany in sizes 4 to 12 are $99.75.

Look for fleecewear, cotton infantwear, nylon raingear, snowsuits, terrycloth bathrobes, and boots, shoes, sneakers, and slippers.

■ maggie moore, inc.

P.O. Box 1564, New York, NY 10023, (212) 543–3434

Free 48-page color catalog

maggie moore delivers stylish, good quality kid's clothes in sizes newborn to 14 with a smattering of wooden toys, little girls' jewelry, and fantasy costumes.

They carry sweaters and sweater sets in 100 percent cotton. Beautiful patchwork jackets made from antique quilts are custom-made works of art for $170.00 each. One hundred percent cotton jumpsuits range from $46.00 to $90.00. Shirts and matching leggings constructed from 100 percent cotton knit come in colors suitable for boys and girls. Have fun mixing and matching—shirts are $12.00 and leggings are $10.00.

One of the best (and most reasonable at about $25) ideas I have seen for fast-growing babies are the "Baby Bloomer" outfits. These are adorable one-piece bloomer suits that you roll up at the arms and legs at first, then roll down as the baby grows. Mostly cotton or cotton interlock, they are available in eight solid or plaid colors. Match them with 100 percent cotton jackets for a complete "look."

■ The Mast General Store

Striped overalls by Liberty and OshKosh.
See page 264 under **General Merchandise Catalogs.**

■ Patagonia for Kids

Tees, polos, shorts, sweats. See page 80 under **Clothing.**

■ Performance

Jackets, pants, jerseys, vests, shorts, and more.
See page 191 under **Sports Equipment.**

■ Pleasant Company

Girls' clothing in size 6X to 16 in styles to match The American Girls doll collection.
See page 239 under **Toys.**

■ The R. Duck Company

650 Ward Drive, Suite H, Santa Barbara, CA 93111, (800) 422–3825;
in California (805) 964–4343

Free 15-page color catalog

R. Duck specializes in diapering accessories. Rubber Duckies pull-on diaper covers
come in blue, red, yellow, purple, green, turquoise, pink, and white for $4.00 each or
three for $11.00. Pinless Wrap-Up diaper covers with Velcro closures are also offered.
These waterproof covers come in the same colors as the Rubber Duckies and are
$5.50 each or three for $16.00. For beach or warm-weather playtime, you can buy
both styles in bright jungle prints or wild duck motifs.

■ The Red Flannel Factory

P.O. Box 370, Cedar Springs, MI 49319, (800) 533–9276; in Michigan, (616) 696–9240

Free 7-page color catalog

The Red Flannel Factory has been offering good, old-fashioned quality since 1936.
You can keep all your children warm with 100 percent fire-retardant, interlock or
brushed flannel fabrics in sizes for infants to teens. Cozy red granny gowns, nightshirts, princess sleep gowns with matching booties, nightcaps, and dustcaps are well
made and appealing. A variety of cotton and cotton interlock shirts are stocked in
seasonal and year-round styles.

The catalog also carries Baby Rompers in sizes from 6/9 months to 4T for $15.00
and $17.00.

Christmas stockings and gift certificates are also available.

■ Richard Hanten For Children

4209 Craftsman Court, P.O. Box 9665, Scottsdale, AZ 85252, (602) 994–4383

Free color photographs, descriptions, and price list

Richard Hanten sells a limited selection of exceptionally attractive clothes best
known for their whimsical appliqués. Almost all are designed in brother/sister
styles: You can order a gingerbread house motif on a red jumper for girls and the
same design on a pair of shortalls for boys. Outfits are carefully coordinated with
matching barrettes, hairbows, fancy underpants, shirts, and blouses.

Most of the clothes are made from washable poly-cotton blends. The fabric and
construction are of the finest quality, and the outfits are very eye-catching and detailed. That stated, I must add that prices are high. A pair of boys' appliquéd shortalls size 2T-4T are $67.50; a girls' jumper in the same size is $68.50.

■ Richman Cotton Company

529 Fifth Street, Santa Rosa, CA 95401. In California: (800) 851–2556;
Outside California: (800) 992–8924

Free 30-page black-and-white illustrated catalog sent out twice a year

Richman offers 100 percent cotton clothing for kids and adults in practical, basic
styles. They dye many of the garments themselves, so a large selection is available in
white (undyed), as well as in beautiful dyed colors. Take your choice of long johns
and turtlenecks in sea green jade, bubble gum pink, lemon chiffon, or any of the
twenty-one colors offered.

Prices are reasonable: a girls' peasant blouse sells for $10.00; mom can own a
matching blouse for only $12.00.

Also look for leotards, tank dresses, sunsuits, jumpers, shorts, tank tops, slacks,
sweats, socks, hats and gloves, as well as underwear in infant-to-adult sizes.

About ten pages have been devoted to some original and charming toys, books,
and cassette tapes. Imaginations will be helped along with sidewalk chalk, face
paint, an old-fashioned knitting Suzi, bags of beads, and a half dozen kids' crafts
books.

■ Rubens & Marble, Inc.

P.O. Box 14900, Chicago, IL 60614-0900, (312) 348–6200

Free black-and-white illustrated brochure

In business since 1890, Rubens sells infant garments at remarkably low prices
because the items are all seconds. Soft and durable, these seconds have small knitting flaws that do not affect wear. Sold for many years to hospitals all over the country, these garments may have been the first clothes your baby wore.

Among the inventory are white, all-cotton babyshirts available in sizes from
preemie through 32 pounds. Heavier cotton pullover shirts are two for $1.99.
Babyshirts with mitten cuffs are $1.99 the pair. Crib sheets are two for $8.99 and will
fit a 30 x 54-inch crib mattress. Baby gowns, training pants, and bassinet sheets are
also sold here.

■ Sears, Roebuck & Co.

Clothing for the whole family. See page 266 under **General Merchandise Catalogs.**

■ The Sesame Street Catalog

T-shirts and sweatshirts with Sesame Street motifs.
See page 233 under **Toys**.

■ Showcase of Savings

P.O. Box 1010, Rural Hall, NC 27098-1010, (919) 744–1170

Free 52-page color catalog

Save up to fifty percent on L'eggs and Hanes slightly imperfect hosiery and under
wear. Mostly devoted to pantyhose, Showcase of Savings has two pages of items for
kids. Hanes ShowToons underwear for boys in sizes 3, 4, 6, and 8 are $5.00 for three
pair. ShowToons briefs of 100 percent cotton are three for $3.59. A three-pack of
Hanes boys' T-shirts is $4.19; buy six and they are $7.18.

Little L'eggs Tights come in seven colors and are $1.67 if you buy one or two pair.
If you buy six or more pairs, you will save fifty percent off retail at $1.19 a pair. (I
like these tights.)

First-quality Hanes sweats come in sizes 2 through 16 and are available in six colors. Regularly $10.00 for each piece, the sweatpants and tops are offered at $8.99
each.

You will also find L'eggs Sheer Energy maternity pantyhose and maternity
stretch briefs at savings of up to forty percent.

■ Socks Galore and More

P.O. Box 1515, Franklin, TN 37065, (800) 626–SOCK; in Tennessee, (615) 790–SOCK

Free 14-page color catalog

Need socks? More than 600 sock styles for the whole family are offered here at great
prices. All are made in American mills, and all are 100 percent guaranteed.

A good selection of children's socks starts with Humpty Dumpty for infants, at
two pair for $2.49. They also have Giggles, with 100 percent stretch cotton feet and
cotton/nylon tops.

The styles are great, the colors terrific, and the prices right. These folks know
their socks.

■ Sweats and Surf, Inc.

9145 Deering Avenue, Chatsworth, CA 91311, (800) 822–2104

Free 40-page color catalog

California hip is a look that seems here to stay, judging by the success of the thirty Sweats and Surf stores located throughout the Golden State. Now they offer their activewear goods nationwide in this colorful catalog.

Bassett-Walker sweats are offered in sizes for men and women, and in youth and toddler sizes for children. You will find shorts and T-shirts with lots of pizzazz in 100 percent cotton and poly/cotton blends.

This catalog is a bonanza for the style-conscious teenager who wants the California look at the beach.

■ Taffy's-By-Mail

Dance and exercise wear; sweats.
See page 192 under **Sports Equipment.**

■ Talbots Kids

175 Beal Street, Hingham, MA 02043-1586, (800) 543–7123

Free 36-page color catalog

For years the bastion of classic women's clothing, The Talbots now offers their traditional look to the younger set.

Some of the best-looking sweater/hat sets I have seen anywhere are here, and they are mostly in ramie/cotton so the kids won't yank them off complaining that they itch.

Beautiful holiday outfits feature details such as hand-smocking, pin tuck pleats, and full linings.

Dresses run $40.00 to $90.00, so this is definitely not discount shopping, but the quality and styling are unbeatable. If the price stalls you, remember that these things can be passed on to another lucky child.

Many of the items wear the Talbots label, but other lines are sprinkled throughout the pages. Among them are Eagle's Eye, L'Amor, Miss Ashley, J.G. Hook, Cottontails, Marisa Christina, Sara Kent, and L.C. Tailor Wear.

Boys' and girls' clothing is offered in sizes 4 through 14.

■ Tortellini

23 East 17th Street, New York, NY 10003, (800) 527–8725; in New York, (212) 645–4266

Free 7-page color catalog

This is a small but charming catalog with excellent quality clothes for boys and girls. Tortellini makes most of their clothing in the United States, but their buyers also look to Europe for special items not found in this country. The Tortellini line and their contributors' lines are 100 percent cotton, except for socks, tights, leggings, and an occasional wool sweater.

A machine washable 100 percent wool sailor sweater comes in navy/red or navy/cream and sells for $53.00; a matching sailor cap is $15.00.

A great denim jumper features a raised waist, two patch pockets, and red buttons on the shoulder for $32.00. It coordinates with traditional striped Breton sailor shirts, imported from France for $38.00 each.

Pretty dresses in paisley, plaid, or tiny prints are offered for $24.00 to $74.00. From dress-up clothes to playwear, traditional styling and fine quality are the order of the day from this company.

■ The White House

51 New Bond Street, London, W 1 E 8XQ, England, Phone: 01-629 3521

Write for current price of a 25-page color catalog

Since it was established in 1906, the "House" has earned a reputation for quality and service. They are known for fine household linens, women's fashions, and classic children's clothes for daytime and formal occasions. This firm lists all their prices in pounds, so you will have to get the latest exchange rate to figure out the costs. That accomplished, you will be in for a treat with these elegant, traditional clothes. This is the place to find a girl's navy and white sailor dress and a matching suit with shorts for her brother. You can even buy the navy leather button bar pram shoes and high white cotton socks to complete the outfits.

You will also see delicate, hand-embroidered newborn nightgowns, baby dresses, matinée jackets, booties and other items for the layette. A few baby linens round out the collection.

■ The Wooden Soldier

North Hampshire Common, North Conway, NH 03860-0800, (603) 356–7041

Free 48-page color catalog

Fine detail and elegant styling make these clothes for girls and boys some of the most eye-catching you will find. This is not the place to look for everyday play-clothes at bargain prices. You will pay high prices for the quality clothes in this catalog, but if you need a special outfit, the most beautiful temptations are here.

The dressy clothes lean toward Victorian styles with lots of lace collars and velvet. You can buy bright Mousefeathers dresses and Lanz sleepwear, Vermont-made Scandinavian design wool jackets, Nanook wool coats, knitwear, and rain gear. Sizes range from 12 months to 14, and they include sister outfits, mother-daughter dresses, and brother-sister ensembles.

An assortment of cotton/polyester costumes are offered for children and adults. Designs include a pumpkin, ladybug, witch, bumblebee, dragon, fairy, and others.

The Wooden Soldier also sells an exceptional collection of toys and gifts, many of them handcrafted or imported. Kids' tableware, doll furniture, snow globes, night-lights, Christmas ornaments, music boxes, and more are among the treasures. And if you happen to win the lottery, for $3,850.00 you can buy a six-foot, three-story doll's house superbly crafted of varnished pine.

■ World Wildlife Fund Catalog

Animal print T-shirts. See page 122 under **Gifts.**

COSTUMES

■ Algy Costumes and Uniforms

440 Northeast First Avenue, P.O. Box 090490, Hallandale, FL 33008, (305) 457–8100

$3.00 for 63-page color catalog

Algy has been providing costumes and uniforms for cheerleaders, bands, dancers, skaters, drill corps, and others since 1937. The originators of the All-Over stretch sequin leotard, they offer every cut, color, and design you can imagine.

Dozens of accessories are also available such as reversible capes, nylon trunk pants, tights, lamé gloves, and sequined belts, ankle warmers, cuffs, and bow ties.

A variety of colored pom-poms are shown as well as several styles of batons, tiaras, shoes, and boots.

■ Allstar Costume

Catalog Dept. 1, 125 Lincoln Boulevard, Middlesex, NJ 08846, (201) 805–0200

Free 17-page color catalog

Buy quality Allstar Costumes direct from their workshop, and with the money you save, you can buy extra treats for your goblins and ghouls!

You will find mysterious Ninjas, adorable rabbits in hats, and glamorous harem girls, priced from $29.99 to $49.99. A small Dracula, skeleton, glow ghost, or twelve-legged spider are costumes sure to scare up a full bag of Halloween treats.

Perhaps you are handy with a sheet, needle, and thread; all you may need to buy in that case is an angel's glitter wand for $3.99. If you want something fancier, a fairy princess ($29.99), bride ($29.99), or old-fashioned girl ($39.95) costume will make any young lady feel all dressed up and ready to go. Boys will love Eddy the Nightmare ($29.99), Bat People ($29.99), and Pirate Man ($24.99). Infants and toddlers can join in the festivities in a bunny suit ($19.99) or a pumpkin outfit ($19.99).

Allstar Costumes only shows a fraction of the 27,000 costumes, masks, and accessories they have available by mail. If you do not see what you want, call and they will most likely have it.

■ Brights Creek

Sleepwear sets that double as spider, skeleton, pumpkin, and superhero costumes. See page 52 under **Clothing.**

■ Chaselle, Inc.

Costumes and dress-up clothes. See page 87 under **Educational Materials.**

■ Childcraft

A variety of costumes for Halloween fun. See page 217 under **Toys.**

■ F.A.O. Schwarz

Fantasy playwear for dress-up and Halloween. See page 220 under **Toys.**

■ Grey Owl Indian Craft Co.

Native American clothes, masks, rattles, jewelry, and more. See page 8 under **Arts and Crafts.**

■ Just for Kids!

Gladiators, astronauts, Santas, wigs, boas, and more. See page 226 under **Toys.**

■ maggie moore, inc.

Fantasy costumes for boys and girls. See page 62 under **Clothing.**

■ Morris Costumes

3108 Monroe Road, Charlotte, NC 28205, (704) 333–0004

$2.00 for a 74-page color catalog of masks
$3.00 for a 144-page color catalog of costumes
$10.00 for a 423-page complete costume and mask catalog

Morris Costumes claims to be the largest costume store in the world. After rifling through this 423-page tome, I have no reason to doubt them. Nine pages of ready-made children's costumes and hundreds of pages of noses, wigs, accessories, masks, shoes, hats, crowns, headpieces, make-up, beards, mustaches, and prosthetics will tempt you to send out invitations to a masquerade.

You can get a top-quality adult's Easter Bunny suit for $225.00, the economy suit for $170.00, or just the plastic bunny head for $67.50.

A deluxe velveteen Santa suit will cost $205.00, but I am sure you can be just as merry in the economy suit for $48.00. The options continue: They offer a child's Santa suit, a Mrs. Santa, and many beards, belts, and hats sold separately for jolly old St. Nick.

You can also scramble the inventory to make your own mix-and-match extravaganza.

■ The Smithsonian Institution

Astronaut and baseball uniforms. See page 152 under **Museum Shops.**

■ Taffy's-By-Mail

Costumes for dance, gymnastics, and cheerleading, plus special costumes catalog. See page 192 under **Sports Equipment.**

■ Toys To Grow On

Costumes and girls' dress-up clothes. See page 234 under **Toys.**

■ **The Wooden Soldier**

Costumes for children and adults: ladybugs, dragons, witches, and more.
See page 68 under **Clothing.**

FOOTWEAR

■ **After the Stork**

Snowboots, rainboots, Zoo shoes, canvas sneakers, and slippers.
See page 49 under **Clothing.**

■ **Arctic Trading Company**

Handcrafted Inuit boots and slippers. See page 102 under **Gifts.**

■ **Biobottoms**

Booties, moccasins, slippers, sneakers, and boots. See page 51 under **Clothing.**

■ **Brights Creek**

Cotton sneakers, ballet slippers, boots, and more. See page 52 under **Clothing.**

■ **Brooks Brothers**

Suede slippers. See page 52 under **Clothing.**

■ **CAMPMOR**

Hiking boots, snow boots, slippers. See page 78 under **Clothing.**

■ **Eddie Bauer**

Snowboots, rainboots. See page 78 under **Clothing.**

■ Gymboree Catalog

Toddler University shoes. See page 58 under **Clothing.**

■ J & R Creations

23 Devereux Street, Utica, NY 13501, (315) 724–1492

Free 16-page color catalog

J & R Creations sells fine quality Minnetonka moccasins for the whole family. They are cut from only the best glove tanned leathers and fashioned into popular styles. You can also expect fast shipment from their large in-stock department.

To begin, they design seven styles of infant's moccasins, all attractive and beautifully crafted. A suede or deerskin fringed bootie is offered in five different colors for $10.95. A genuine sheepskin infant moccasin costs $18.95. A dozen styles for older children feature softsoles and cushioned insoles.

Whether you choose beadwork, fringe, or plain styling, you will definitely receive a quality moc to suit your taste.

■ Les Petits

European-made leather shoes, boots, terry slippers, sneakers. See page 61 under **Clothing.**

■ Livonia

Personalized baby shoes. See page 117 under **Gifts.**

■ Price Is Rite Women's & Children's Shoes

1840 Centre Street, West Roxbury, MA 02132, (617) 325–1250

Free 11-page black-and-white illustrated catalog

Specializing in shoes for extra wide feet, Price Is Rite carries infants' and children's shoes in E, EE, and EEE widths.

Traditional and stylish offerings include saddle shoes ($30.00), white glove leather tie shoes for babies ($29.00), boys' black wing tips ($30.00), and a girls' white leather dress shoe with swivel strap. Black or white patent leather styles for girls feature bows or floral perforated teardrop designs. Sneakers are available with Velcro or tie closures. Popular high-top sneakers are also featured here.

■ REI

Boots and slippers. See page 81 under **Clothing.**

■ Sears, Roebuck & Co.

Shoes, boots, slippers, and sneakers for the whole family.
See page 266 under **General Merchandise Catalogs.**

■ Starr Enterprises

Hiking boots, boot liners, slipper socks. See page 81 under **Clothing.**

■ Tener's

4320 West Reno, Oklahoma City, OK 73107, (800) 654–6715

Free 24-page color catalog

Tener's has offered Western-style boots, hats, and clothing since 1930. The only item
made especially for children is the Junior Ropers leather boot. It is of excellent quality and sells through the catalog for $49.95 (suggested retail price is $56.00). It is
available in tan, cameo, red, navy, black, and grey. Sizes range from Children's 8½ -
13½ to Youth's 1-6.

■ The White House

Booties, leather pram shoes. See page 67 under **Clothing.**

■ Zoo Shoes, Inc.

12000 Woodruff Avenue, Unit C, Downey, CA 90241, (800) 343–7463;
in California, (213) 803–9711

Free color brochure and price list

It will be hard to find a kid who can pass up this fun idea—zoo jogging shoes have
leather uppers and a front closure that is a cute animal face. The lightweight rubber
sole features the pawprint of that animal on the treads. Your child can slip into a
green or pink dinosaur, "Duke" the dog, or a sweet yellow duck. If your child is a
climber, he or she might prefer the monkey or koala bear. The Zoo Shoes menagerie
includes a frog, raccoon, killer whale, penguin, panda, moose, tiger, squirrel, fox,
bunny, unicorn, and a Kool Kat with sun glasses. Many of these styles come in infant

sizes 1-4, and almost all come in child sizes 5-12 and youth sizes 12½ - 2. The shoes range from $21.95 to $23.95 and really are cute.

If your youngster is past the age of liking animal faces on his or her shoes, Zoo Shoes also sells skateboard shoes and swirl print canvas sneakers for $21.95 and $20.95, respectively.

MATERNITY AND NURSING WEAR

■ Beegotten Creations, Inc.

P.O. Box 1800, Spring Valley, NY 10977, (800) 722–3390

Free 4-page color brochure

T-shirts, hats, sweatsuits, nursing nighties, and underwear are sold here for the "Family-To-Bee." A bee design on each garment cheerfully announces such phrases as "Sister to bee" and "Brother to bee." For the pregnant mother with a sense of humor, a maternity T-shirt reads, "It won't bee over til the fat lady thins."

A small selection of novelties continues the theme. May-"bee" you will enjoy the mugs, keychains, or bumper stickers.

■ Bosom Buddies

P.O. Box 6138, Kingston, NY 12401, (914) 338–2038

Free 8-page illustrated catalog

Started six years ago by a mother who had trouble finding good nursing bras, Bosom Buddies now offers both fashions and accessories for mother and baby.

Three styles of 100 percent cotton nightgowns with a concealed nursing opening in the center pleats are $29.00 for a short nightshirt style and $35.00 for a mid-length nightshirt.

Nursing bras are the main product offered, though, and Bosom Buddies sells nineteen styles. Made from 100 percent cotton as well as many blends, the bras sell from $15.00 to $29.00. All bra designs are available in white; some also come in champagne.

■ Designer Series

Mary Jane, 3015 Glendale Boulevard, Los Angeles, CA 90039, (213) 664–2177

Free color brochure

Mary Jane offers a dozen styles of nursing bras, including a comfortable cotton sleep bra.

Bras are made in sizes 32A to 46G and are made in the United States. All bras are available in white; some styles can be ordered in champagne. Prices start at $7.00.

Mary Jane also sells the Singlet tummy sling back supporter for pregnant women. Designed to ease back strain and provide tummy support, it sells for $30.00.

■ 5th Avenue Maternity

P.O. Box 21826, Seattle, WA 98111-3826, (800) 426–3569

Free 19-page illustrated catalog with fabric swatches

Feel-good dressing and easy styling are the watchwords here. All the illustrations have a fabric swatch attached, so you can see and feel the colors and textures as you browse.

All sweaters, pants, jackets, and swimsuits are designed for a thirty-pound weight gain. Many designs can be adapted for wear even when you are no longer pregnant.

Classic jumpers in soft jersey with a lined bodice come in royal or black for $86.00. Suits and skirts in fabulous colors and comfortable fabrics help keep you stylish right through your ninth month. Sweats and comfy non-bagging leggings help to complete your casual wardrobe.

■ Garnet Hill

Cotton nursing clothes and bras. See page 57 under **Clothing.**

■ hanna Andersson

Cotton clothes for maternity wear. See page 58 under **Clothing.**

■ The Mother Nurture Project

Box 111 A, 103 Woodland Drive, Pittsburgh, PA 15228, (412) 344–5940

$2.00 for 16-page catalog

This catalog is devoted entirely to everything that you need for breastfeeding. It should be noted that these clothes are designed for nursing and can be worn only in very early pregnancy. They are *not* maternity wear. Most items feature hidden breast access for convenient nursing, and all are machine washable and dryable. Blouses, tops, skirts, slacks, dresses, and nightgowns are sold at reasonable prices. If you have time to sew, you can buy the patterns for many of the designs. You can also buy nursing bras, breast pumps, nursing pads, and books on breastfeeding.

■ Mothers Work

1309 Noble Street, 5th Floor, Philadelphia, PA 19123, (215) 625–9259

$3.00 for a 32-page color catalog and swatches

I have purchased my own maternity clothes from Mothers Work, and they are more attractively styled and of better quality than most you will find for this time in your life.

As the name suggests, you will find heavy emphasis on an at-the-office wardrobe with many beautiful jumpers, dresses, blouses, and their exclusive three-piece suit. This particular suit has a specially designed jacket that you can wear in your ninth month *and* after you return to work. The companion adjuster skirt also works during and after pregnancy; its patented concealed button adjustment expands with your waistline and then adjusts back after you regain your figure.

Dresses in several styles and fabrics are pretty yet classic enough to be appropriate for the professional woman. And you can round out your weekend wear with jumpsuits, shorts, and casual tops. Elastic waist pants have versatile belt loops and can be worn after pregnancy. I particularly like their soft, comfortable ramie/cotton sweaters.

■ Page Boy Maternity

8918 Governors Row, Dallas, TX 75247, (800) 225–3103

$2.50 for 20-page color catalog

The maternity clothes carried here are more elegant than most regular clothing you see. Be prepared for high prices. Oversized, ramie-cotton, hand-knitted sweaters with bold prints inspired by Matisse are $109.00. An evening pantsuit with embroidered lamé tunic and faille pants sells for $229.00. A gorgeous hand-beaded imported tunic is $429.00, and a black velvet skirt to coordinate with it is $69.00. A bright red rayon twill tunic and skirt is $159.00.

Along with the formal designs are cotton T-shirts and pants and other clothes for daily wear. I have the fall/holiday catalog, but I feel confident that no matter which edition you receive, it will have maternity clothes you will love.

■ ReCreations

Box 091038, Columbus, OH 43209, (800) 621–2547; in Ohio, (614) 236–1109

$3.00 for a 16-page color catalog

You will finally believe the people who tell you how beautiful you look pregnant! Pants and skirts are specially designed to fit well throughout your pregnancy. Versatile dresses for casual, office, or evening wear are available in lovely fabrics, including 100 percent cotton, linen, and rayon. Also available are stylish jumpsuits, slacks, shorts, and tops in lively prints and elegant solids.

■ Sears, Roebuck & Co.

Maternity clothes, sleepwear, underwear.
See page 266 under **General Merchandise Catalogs.**

■ Showcase of Savings

Maternity pantyhose and briefs. See page 65 under **Clothing.**

OUTDOOR GEAR

■ American Widgeon

376 Brannan Street, San Francisco, CA 94107, (415) 974–6803

Free 8-page black-and-white illustrated catalog

Now you can buy the well-known Widgeon brand direct. If you are not familiar with the name, you will discover beautifully designed, durable outerwear for infants through size 12.

The catalog shows a selection of some of their perennial favorites like The Widgeon Jacket made of 16-ounce Polarfleece. Available in red, rose, royal blue, and charcoal gray for sizes 2 through 12, it is machine washable and sells for $37.50 or $43.50, depending on the size. Snowsuits for babies and toddlers made of Polarfleece are hooded and have fold-over ankle and wrist covers to protect hands and feet from the cold. They sell for $44.00 to $91.00.

Toddlers and older children will keep cozy in waterproof jackets, bib overalls, ponchos, and rain gear.

■ Bart's Water Ski Center, Inc.

Kid-sized life vests and wet suits. See page 201under **Sports Equipment.**

■ CAMPMOR

Box 997-R, Paramus, NJ 07653-0997, (800) 525–4784

Free 119-page catalog

CAMPMOR offers thousands of products for camping and outdoor needs. Warm, practical boots and clothes are offered in children's sizes, although most of the collection is for adults.

Hi-Tec Sierra Lite Hikers, designed for lightweight trail hiking, are available in sizes 10-13 and 1-6 ($29.99).

The Columbia Bugaboo System is three water-repellent jackets in one. Each jacket has an outer shell with a zip-out liner so either the shell or the liner can be worn alone. It comes in fifteen color choices.

Bugabibs water-repellent bib overalls match the Bugaboo jacket and sell for $43.50. The Whirlibird Parka is designed with the same interchange system, allowing shell and liner to be worn together or separately.

Check here for rainsuits, boots, ski hats, ski and hiking socks, long underwear, and slippers.

CAMPMOR outdoor equipment keeps kids in mind with sleeping bags in children's sizes, frame backpack infant and toddler carriers, soft infant carriers such as Snugli, and the Baby Bag snowsuit. Kids will love the compasses, canteen, campfire games, and other goodies for overnight trips.

■ The Company Store

Infant down snowsuit and down booties; stroller throw and carseat throw in Merino wool. See page 94 under **Furniture and Bedding.**

■ Eddie Bauer

Fifth and Union, P.O. Box 3700, Seattle, WA 98130-0006, (800) 426–8020

Free 124-page color catalog

Eddie Bauer is famous for their practical, yet goodlooking outdoor wear for the whole family. This year they are offering children's cotton Shaker sweaters, bivouac sweaters, turtlenecks, fatigue shirts, windfoils, parkas, and more in kids' unisex sizes 4 through 14.

Rugged, well-made snowboots, rubber rain boots, and ⟨...⟩ also available.

Cotton fatigue shirts in your choice of seven bright colors are grea⟨...⟩ and casual trousers; they sell for $16.00 each. Navy or red wool-lined parkas in a cover-the-hip length are $65.00.

A small collection of seasonal items children will enjoy are offered in each catalog.

■ Gorsuch Ltd., Vail

263 E. Gore Creek Drive, Vail, CO 81657, (800) 525–9808; in Colorado, (303) 949–4005

Free 36-page color catalog

Maximum mountain style! The Gorsuch family has traveled the world and assembled sensational ski wear for the whole family. Children's gear starts at size 4, and the colors are sizzling, the styles, fantastic. Be forewarned, though, these dazzling styles are not inexpensive. A child's Austrian-style skisuit sells for $222.00; a brilliant lavender one-piece suit is $275.00, and a parka by Joplin is priced at $165.00.

■ High Peaks Cyclery

Snowboots, snowsuits, shellpants, hats, gloves.
See page 199 under **Sports Equipment.**

■ Laura Ashley by Post

Wool coats for dressy occasions. See page 61 under **Clothing.**

■ L. L. Bean, Inc.

Infant Babybag snowsuit, Polarplus bunting, life vests, kid-sized sleeping bags.
See page 196 under **Sports Equipment.**

■ Les Petits

Dress wool coats, parkas, boots, hats, and scarves. See page 61 under **Clothing.**

■ Patagonia for Kids

Mail Order, Inc., 1609 W. Babcock Street, P.O. Box 8900, Bozeman, MT 59715-2046, (800) 638–6464

Free 24-page color catalog

I was delighted to find that Patagonia, designers of outdoor wear for adults, now has a terrific catalog for kids. Functional and durable, their clothes are designed to be layered and still permit unrestricted movement.

Patagonia does all this and still comes up with stylish clothing in terrific color combinations. Synchilla-lined jackets, shells, pull-on pants, and vests in mix-and-match colors come in sizes 3T to 14. For the littlest snowbird, soft synchilla baby buntings come in color combinations of surf/fuchsia, yellow/periwinkle, or periwinkle/red.

Alpine gloves, hats, shelled mittens, rainsets, and long underwear all help to keep the kids warm and dry.

Cotton-polyester sweatshirts have stylish stand-up polo collars; they can be matched with color-coordinated sweatpants. Sweatshirts and sweatpants are sold separately for $24.00 to $26.00. Seasonal catalogs offer tees, polos, and shorts.

Most of the items offered by this fine company are machine washable; nearly all come in mix-and-match colors. This is a must-have catalog of kid-sized staples.

■ Performance

Gore-Tex outerwear, Thermax long underwear, windbreakers, vests, hats.
See page 191 under **Sports Equipment.**

■ Piragis' Northwoods Company

The Boundry Waters Catalog, 105 North Central Avenue, Ely, MN 55731, (218) 365–6745

Free 40-page color catalog

Piragis is *the* source for northern wilderness enthusiasts and other outdoor buffs, and as you browse through these pages you can imagine your canoe gliding serenely down a glass-like river at dawn. The catalog is designed like a newspaper and two full pages are devoted to kids' items, although you will find other products, such as a child's canoe paddle, scattered throughout the pages.

Unbreakable sunglasses for children with 100 percent UV protection have impact-resistant lenses and are $12.00. An infant or child's collar life vest, designed to keep a child's face out of the water, is $23.00. You will also find sweatshirts and sleeping bags.

Three volumes of *The Family Camping Video Series* are designed for the involvement of the whole family and are $19.95 each. *Campfire Stories: Things That Go Bump in the Night* is a book sure to keep the kids close to their tents after dark. Other children's titles and coloring books with outdoor themes are on the bookshelf.

■ REI

P.O. Box 88125, Seattle, WA 98138-0125, (800) 426–4840

Free 84-page color catalog

Order by phone seven days a week from these purveyors of quality outdoor gear and clothing for the whole family since 1938. Down and polyfill styles of waterproof, breathable kids' parkas, bibs, and snowpants in bright colors are sold along with mix-and-match hats and gloves for sizes 4 through 18.

Thinsulate insulated snowsuits for tots in sizes 1-4 come in combinations of fuchsia, bright blue, and red for $55.00. Coordinating mittens ($12.00) with Velcro closures keep little hands warm and dry with nylon shells. Leather palms assure a good grip, and knit cuffs keep in the warmth.

Insulated winter boots, shearling slippers, long Thermax underwear, dinosaur flannel sheet sets, along with a few toys and a couple of sleds make this a worthwhile browse.

■ Sears, Roebuck & Co.

Outerwear and outdoor gear for the whole family.
See page 266 under **General Merchandise Catalogs.**

■ Starr Enterprises

P.O. Box 82, Long Creek, SC 29658, (803) 638–3180
Free 12-page color catalog

Started by hiking and canoeing aficionados who wanted to bring their little one with them, Starr serves as a clearing house for all types of outdoor products for children.

Child carriers, chemically activated bottle warmers, a child's fishing vest, and lightweight rainwear certainly will make a trip in the wilderness a little easier.

If you have ever struggled with the chore of putting mittens on your child, you will appreciate the Carapacho Zippen Mittens ($9.50 a pair) that zip from the wrist to the thumb for easy entry. Available in red, periwinkle, cobalt, and grey, they are made from 16-ounce fleece.

Hiking boots and slipper socks are durable and reasonably priced, as are the jackets, water-repellent gaiter boots, boot liners, long underwear, American Widgeon Pom hats with earflaps, infants' bunting bags, and overalls.

■ Stowe Woolens

R.R. #1, Box 1420, Stowe, VT 05672, (802) 253–7171

Free color catalog

Stowe Woolens sells gorgeous ski sweaters and hats for women, men, and children. If you fall in love with these beauties, get ready to pay dearly—the children's sweaters in sizes 4 to 12 start at $76.00.

Hats are designed to match or coordinate with the sweaters, and some are irresistible. One of the most winning styles offered is a red crewneck sweater with three gnomes on the front ($80.00) and a red and white earflap hat ($22.50) with the same gnomes circling the crown.

■ Wyoming Woolens

P.O. Box 3127, Jackson, WY 83001, (307) 733–2889

Free 8-page color catalog

From Jackson Hole, Wyoming, come colorful jackets, pants, vests, and knickers for men, women, and children.

Cozy polyester PolarPlus jackets make a great lightweight outer shell for layering and come in six bright colors for kids size 2 to 14. The jackets are machine washable and sell for $38.00.

Other caps, vests, jackets are color coordinated, and most items are machine washable.

Computers and Computer Software

■

■ Accolade

550 South Winchester Boulevard, San Jose, CA 95128, (800) 245–7744

Free 20-page color catalog

Accolade specializes in entertainment software. If you have a child from ten to twenty with a high regard for computer games, you are sure to find something in this catalog to suit him or her.

A variety of sports software lets players construct their own baseball "dream team" and deal with offensive and defensive strategies, base-running options, different ballparks, and several views of the playing field. Games of golf, basketball, boxing, tennis, and pool are also available.

Kids can test their skills with simulations of car racing, Blue Angels formation flights, and more. A handy chart in the back of the catalog lists the compatibility of each piece of software with seven top-selling brands of computers.

■ Best Products Co., Inc.

Nintendo games. See page 263 under **General Merchandise Catalogs.**

■ Chaselle, Inc.

Educational software. Ask for separate Educational Software catalog.
See page 87 under **Educational Materials.**

■ Computer Direct, Inc.

22292 North Pepper Road, Barrington, IL 60010, (800) 289–9473

Free 60-page black-and-white illustrated catalog
Request the catalog that is compatible with your brand of computer.

If you are in the market for computer hardware, software, or accessories, Computer Direct is an excellent source for you. Thousands of items are kept in stock, including a number of IBM-compatible computers, hard drives, laptops, monitors, modems, letter-quality and dot matrix printers, ribbons, paper, daisy wheels, envelopes and labels, two sizes of disks, and FAX machines.

If you need a computer desk or table, a copy machine, or disk storage system, you will find many choices here.

The large section of software, much of it educational, includes *Sesame Street First Writer*, which provides fun and easy learning games with letters, words, and simple sentences ($10.95). Kids can design stationery, bookmarks, banners, and signs with *Muppets Print Kit* software ($10.95). Other software deals with biology, grammar, reading, phonics, science, U.S. geography, U.S. government, and world geography.

■ D.C. Heath and Company

2700 North Richardt Avenue, P.O. Box 19309, Indianapolis, IN 46219, (800) 428–8071; in Alaska and Hawaii, (317) 359–5585

Free 23-page color catalog

This catalog of terrific software is usually directed to educators, but orders from individuals are welcome as well.

With programs for kids in kindergarten through grade 12, you will find the best software of the year here, including *Explore-A-Story, Explore-A-Science*, and *Read, Write, and Publish*.

Products are first listed under their subject category, and then they are broken down by suggested appropriate age. Headings include science, social studies, arithmetic, algebra, other mathematics, Spanish, and French.

A *Picture Dictionary* for kids in kindergarten through grade 2 is $51.00. *Climates of the World* is recommended for children in middle and junior high school and sells for $66.00. Heath mathematics software programs for addition, subtraction, multiplication, and division are sold separately for $51.00 each.

■ Electronics Boutique

Consumer Products Division, 1345 Enterprise Drive, West Chester, PA 19380, (215) 430–8100

Free 35-page color catalog

Electronics Boutique offers great entertainment software and the incredibly popular Nintendo games. If you can get the kids past all of that, a section in the back is devoted to educational software. You might choose *Math Blaster Mystery* ($36.99), *Reader Rabbit* ($29.99 for Apple, $36.99 for IBM), *Children's Writing and Publishing Center* ($47.99 for Apple, $49.99 for IBM), or *The Oregon Trail* ($29.99).

A budget section includes software that is $9.99 to $12.99. *Win, Lose or Draw Jr.; Muppet Adventure; Candy Land;* and *Concentration II* are some of the titles found here.

■ Freeware Unlimited

P.O. Box 685, Cardiff, CA 92007, (619) 436–2618

Free 56-page catalog

Freeware Unlimited sells a vast selection of public domain software for IBM and IBM-compatible computers. Public domain software is not copyrighted and thus may be freely copied. These programs are usually sold for little more than the cost of a disk.

Freeware has very helpfully rated all the programs they sell. According to their system, five stars indicate a product "as good as the best commercial program available." One star indicates a program that "can be found helpful or amusing." Each software listing gives the name of the program, its rating, a short description, and its price.

The catalog includes an index organized by program name and a table of contents with headings for games, education, music, astronomy, sports, religion, and more.

■ Manhattan Software

P.O. Box 148, Peterborough, NH 03458, (800) 432–5656

Free brochure

Manhattan Software specializes in a small selection of entertainment and games. Craps, Blackjack, Hold'em, Stud, Cribbage Master II, and Gin Rummy 4.0 are a few of the choices offered. All programs are for IBM PCs or IBM compatibles. They cost $35.00 each or two for $60.00.

■ National Educational Music Co. Ltd.

Passport MIDI Software for recording your own music. See page 156 under **Music.**

■ PC Enterprises

The jr Products Group, Box 292, Belmar, NJ 07719, (800) 922–7257; in New Jersey, (201) 280–0025

Free catalog

Dozens of PC jr add-on products are the hallmark of PC Enterprises. Look for memory sidecars, disk drives, ROM's, joysticks, optical mice, and lightpens. Basic manuals and other related books are offered, as well as game cartridges and other PC jr software.

■ Triton Products Company

Order Center, P.O. Box 8123, San Francisco, CA 94128-9986, (800) 227–6900

Free 16-page black-and-white illustrated catalog

Triton sells computer software for IBM and compatibles, Macintosh, Apple II, and Commodore 64/128 computers.

The hottest new games from favorite publishers are offered along with established bestsellers in this eclectic inventory. Some programs, including classics like *The Last Ninja*, are sold through a special offer: you buy four and get one free. In addition to the games, you will find software dealing with finance, productivity, and creativity.

The back page features a few dozen specials that are offered at savings of up to 75 percent below retail.

■ William K. Bradford Publishing Company

594 Marrett Road, Lexington, MA 02173, (800) 421–2009; in Massachusetts, (617) 862–2570

Free 9-page catalog

The creative software in this catalog provides fun and educational activities for all computer users in the family. You may choose a program that reviews basic skills or a program that takes you through the solar system on a simulated space mission. Some packages deal with algebra and arithmetic, others help develop science, French, and Spanish skills. Kids in kindergarten through grade two will have fun with home versions of *Rosie the Counting Rabbit*, *Just Around the Block*, and *The Bald-Headed Chicken*.

Age recommendations are provided for each product, and the listings indicate any specific types of hardware that are required with particular software. Each program includes one disk and a detailed user's manual with student activity sheets.

Educational Materials

■

■ American Foundation for the Blind

Educational games for the blind. See page 123
under **Health and Safety Products.**

■ Anatomical Chart Company

Nutrition posters, anatomy charts, exercise programs, skeletons, books.
See page 177 under **Science and Nature.**

■ Audio-Forum

Foreign language instruction and sign language instruction. Audiotapes for typing,
reading music, and vocabulary building. See page 175 under **Records, Tapes and
CDs.**

■ Berlitz Publications

Foreign language instruction and sign language instruction. Audiotapes for typing,
reading music, and vocabulary building. See page 176 under **Records, Tapes and
CDs.**

■ Chaselle, Inc.

P.O. Box 2097, 9645 Gerwig Lane, Columbia, MD 21046, (800) CHASELLE;
in Maryland, (800) 492–7840

**Free color catalogs (Specify Pre-School or Elementary School Materials, Arts and
Crafts Materials, Educational Software, General School Supply, or Lifeskills
Materials. The first two are best bets for parents.)**

Chaselle is a major supplier to preschools, daycare centers, and elementary schools,
and they will gladly sell to the individual as long as there is a $25.00 minimum
order.

Send for the 176-page Preschool and Elementary School materials catalog for a
vast array of educational games, wooden puzzles, waffle blocks, Lego systems,

building logs, beads, Duplos, toddler manipulatives, hand puppets, multiethnic dolls, dress-up clothes, cooking utensils, play food, water and sand play toys, plastic animal figures, musical instruments, doll furniture, clocks, carpentry tools, science kits, and much more. Many items are geared to sensory exploration and developing motor skills for infants and toddlers, and sorting, sequencing, measuring, counting, and other learning skills of the early grades. A nice selection of books, audiocassettes, and board games are also here.

A great selection of furniture includes storage units, tables and chairs, bean bag chairs, rocking chairs, easels, a woodworking bench, and wonderful roleplaying structures such as a "farmer's market" stand, a telephone booth, a puppet theater, and kitchen equipment.

Wagons, bicycles, whirl-arounds and gym sets are designed for active outdoor play, as are portable basketball hoops, tons of balls, a bulldozer chair, and play tunnels.

The arts and crafts selection is fantastic, both in this catalog and in the 400-page Arts and Crafts catalog. Buy paints, markers, crayons, beads, aprons, rubber stamps, glues, scissors, papers, clay, chalkboards, brushes, collage materials, and stickers. The large catalog also offers leathercrafts, basketry, jewelry-making materials, and macramé, looms, mosaics, calligraphy, pottery tools, silk-screening supplies, stained glass supplies, and much more.

■ Cuisenair Co. of America, Inc.

Math and science materials, workbooks, calculators, nature labs.
See page 178 under **Science and Nature.**

■ Davidsons Music

Self-instructional audiocassettes and books for piano, guitar, organ, dulcimer, ocarina, and harmonica. See page 158 under **Music.**

■ D. C. Heath and Company

Educational software for grades K-12. Many subject categories.
See page 84 under **Computers and Computer Software.**

■ Didax Educational Resources

One Centennial Drive, Peabody, MA 01960, (800) 458–0024;
in Massachusetts, (508) 532–9060

Free 108-page color catalog

Didax is aimed primarily at the school market, and though they welcome orders
from individuals, a minimum order of $25.00 is required. They have a large and in-
teresting supply of creative and educational games, books, and puzzles for
preschoolers and children in kindergarten through grade six.

The items are displayed under helpful chapter headings such as Readiness,
Games, Floor Puzzles, Playmats, Reading-games, Mathematics, and more.

A good part of the inventory is designed for teachers to use in the classroom, but
parents may appreciate the opportunity to buy updated materials that complement
the school curriculum. Lots of imaginative items will make it easier for parents to reinforce lessons in telling time, learning fractions, taking measurements, and counting money.

■ EDC Publishing

Educational books by Peter Usborne. Information and reference titles.
See page 29 under **Books.**

■ Edmund Scientific

Science kits, star maps, dissection instruments, more.
See page 179 under **Science and Nature.**

■ Ideal School Supply Company

11000 S. Lavergne Avenue, Oak Lawn, IL 60453, (800) 323–5131;
in Illinois, (800) 543–3449

Free 38-page color catalog

I have found some of the best quality, educational toys, arts and crafts, games and
books in the catalogs that are aimed especially at schools and daycare centers. A
minimum order of $15.00 is required, but the merchandise is reasonably priced.

Chalkboards, pegboards, blocks, flash cards, dinosaur and nature study kits,
magnets, and more are featured here.

Check out the science kits, experiments, and creative activities, all sold with age
recommendations for each product. A weather kit has nine experiments to help kids
understand temperature, humidity, air pressure, and precipitation. Dinosaurs and

Prehistoric Animals Flash Cards feature the animals in full color on one side, and a pronunciation guide, the creature's size, habitat, mode of movement, diet, and more on the flip side ($7.95).

If your child needs help learning cursive or manuscript letters, they sell those familiar classroom-size banners that show the upper- and lower-case form of each letter and numerals from 1 to 10. Each banner is $8.95.

■ Johnson and Johnson Child Development Toys

Learning toys for infants. See page 226 under **Toys**.

■ Judy/Instructo

4325 Hiawatha Avenue S., Minneapolis, MN 55406, (800) 526–9907

Free 62-page color catalog

Judy/Instructo sells an extensive line of educational materials aimed at educators but available to the individual.

You will find wooden inlay puzzles, craft books, calendars, stickers, flannelboards, alphabet wall charts, hand-held puppet masks, and stand-up figures of people, pets, and dinosaurs.

Science kits to help kids understand weather, sound, insects, light, seeds and plants, magnets, and more are designed to be educational as well as fun. Flash cards for opposites, rhyming, color identification, telling time, and vowels all help reinforce important childhood learning skills.

Walt Disney Skill Books are great for helping to teach upper- and lower-case letters, phonics, math skills, and hand-writing. A few dozen additional children's books, reasonably priced at between $3.50 and $5.95, round out this catalog nicely.

■ Kapable Kids/The Able Child

Developmental materials for special needs children.
See page 124 under **Health and Safety Products**.

■ Kimbo Educational

Records and cassettes on health, nutrition, safety, and science topics.
See page 173 under **Records, Tapes, and CDs**.

■ The Learning Factory

P.O. Box 297, Clearwater, KS 67026, (800) 426–3768; in Kansas, (316) 773–1280

Free 14-page black-and-white illustrated catalog

If you share the philosophy that learning should be fun, you will love this catalog. Each "Folder Factory" contains approximately twenty activities designed to help teach young children various skills in a variety of subject areas. For instance, The Early Years Math Folder Factory includes twenty project sheets that use the numbers 1 to 9 in counting, adding, and subtracting. Other Folder Factories concentrate on ABC's, holidays, consonants, vowels, and Social Studies. Each kit is sold for $9.95.

You will also find rubber stamps and stickers by the yard. A minimum order of twelve stickers is required and they cost $1.00 per dozen. Sticker collectors will love the sixty different designs. Look for alligators, balloons, cats, dinosaurs, dogs, frogs, penguins, bunnies, apples, fish, geese, bats, ghosts, jack-o'-lanterns, Christmas trees, bears. . . . Need I go on?

■ LibertyTree

Materials on our heritage and practice of liberty. See page 35 under **Books.**

■ Opportunities For Learning, Inc.

Selected Material For Reading, Literature and Language, 20417 Nordhoff Street, Dept. RD, Chatsworth, CA 91311, (818) 341–2535

Free 72-page black-and-white illustrated catalog

Teachers have enjoyed the products of this concern since 1973, but now parents are welcome to explore the bounty as well. Opportunities For Learning offers a variety of instructional materials for students ages five and up. This catalog overflows with terrific selections of videos, reproducibles, books, workbooks, filmstrips, cassettes, and microcomputer software.

The table of contents will steer you to such areas as Motivational Materials for Reluctant Readers, Beginning Reading Skills, Microcomputer Learning, Listening and Following Directions. Writing and Spelling, Thinking, Study and Reference Skills, and more.

Most, but not all, of the books have to be bought in sets, making the price and quantity a little too high for many individuals. Still, a careful look will reveal some good items available as a single purchase.

Opportunities For Learning also will send nine other catalogs upon request: *Selected Materials for Special Students, Expanding Horizons Materials for the Gifted (grades K-8), The Right Selections for the Gifted (grades 5-12, Discover Science, Selected Microcom-*

puter Software, The Computer Approach to English, Remedial Materials for Mathematics,
and *Selected Materials for Social Studies.*

■ Pyramid School Products

6510 N. 54th Street, Tampa, FL 33610, (800) 792–2644; in Florida, (813) 621–6446

Free 176-page color catalog
Be sure to request The Pre-School and Elementary Catalog

This huge school supply company sells everything from arts and crafts projects to
world maps. I have found that, in addition to their tremendous selection, these catalogs offer very durable products at more reasonable prices than many of the retail
catalogs directed at the individual consumer.

Look for storage and play furniture, musical instruments, carpentry tools, cooking toys, puzzles, math and science items, and games. Several types and sizes of
non-toxic paints, double easels, sand and water toys, stickers, building blocks, and
small toys useful for stocking stuffers or party favors are some of the thousands of
products offered here.

■ Rand McNally & Company

Maps, globes, atlases, videotapes. See page 39 under **Books.**

■ Schoolmasters

Earth science kits, charts, lab equipment, books.
See page 183 under **Science and Nature.**

■ William K. Bradford Publishing Company

Educational software for the whole family. See page 86
under **Computers and Computer Software.**

■ World of Science/Merrell Scientific

Earth science kits, books, chemistry sets, labware, more.
See page 184 under **Science and Nature.**

Furniture and Bedding

■

■ The Baby's Gallerie

Oak and maple bedroom and play furniture.
See page 138 under **Infant Products and Equipment.**

■ Boston & Winthrop

2 East 93rd Street, New York, NY 10128, (212) 410–6388

Free large 5-page color catalog and price sheets

If money is not an object, look here for hand-painted children's furniture that you
can custom-order in designs, patterns, and colors to suit your child's room. You
choose from a large variety of furniture and accessories that can be painted with
flowers, bunnies, sailboats, or anything else you request. The artists will also paint
coordinated pieces to match your walls and wallpaper—or even your child's quilt.

The simple, country-style furniture is made from selected hardwood and pine. It
is hand-painted in non-toxic Benjamin Moore paints and protected with two coats of
clear polyurethane.

You have a wide selection of fine pieces to choose from, including two- and
three-drawer armoires, bureaus, chests, wardrobes, desks, beds, bookcases, and tables and chairs. You can complete the look with accessories such as a rocking horse,
toy boxes, mirrors, footstools, peg racks, doll cradles, and more. Prices range from
$75.00 for a mirror to $695.00 for a chest of drawers. A 3-drawer armoire will set you
back $895.00.

■ Chaselle, Inc.

Storage units, rockers, tables, chairs, desks, cribs, mirrors, bookcases, clothes racks,
cots, easels, role-playing structures. See page 87 under **Educational Materials.**

■ Cherry Tree Toys, Inc.

Heirloom-quality kits for children's furniture, ride-on toys, clocks, and more.
See page 2 under **Arts and Crafts.**

■ Childcraft

Fold-out kid's couch, tables and chairs, easels. See page 217 under **Toys.**

■ The Company Store

500 Company Store Road, La Crosse, WI 54601-9957, (800) 356–9367

Free 92-page color catalog

The Company Store specializes in down comforters, bed linens, and duvet covers, with a few pages of their catalog devoted to special treats for the younger set. Down comforters start at $45; matching pillowcases, dust ruffles, and bumper pads are available as well.

Basic but luxurious accessories for infants and children are made from soft, washable 100 percent Merino wool. Among them are bicycle seat covers in three sizes from $10.00 each, a stroller throw for $22.00, and a car seat cover for $27.00. A Merino wool crib mattress cover is $39.99, and a playpen throw is $59.00.

To keep your child cozy in the winter, you might consider down baby booties and plain or ruffled down bonnets. A down baby sac comes in four colors and is $50.00. A snowsuit for size 6-18 months is $49.00. Children's down parkas, coats, vests, and mittens are cozy and comfortable for winter weather.

■ Constructive Playthings

Table and chair sets, puppet theatre, market stand, storage systems. See page 218 under **Toys.**

■ Crate and Barrel

P.O. Box 3057, Northbrook, IL 60065-3057, (800) 323–5461

Free 52-page color catalog

Innovative furniture, tableware, decorations, and home accessories chosen for their thoughtful design are standard fare in this catalog, and many of the products are suitable for or specially designed for children. The stock is displayed in seasonal catalogs, not all of which will have items for kids—but just wait. You can expect to find kid-sized furniture, summer playthings, beach toys, easels, puzzles, wagons, and more.

My latest edition includes a set of three durable cardboard suitcases in red, yellow, and blue. Made in Sweden, they offer kids their very own storage space and sell for $34.95 for the set of three. A Finnish-designed red apple dinnerplate, covered apple bowl, and mug look like they would make mealtime more fun for $13.95. A mini-town made of high density foam consists of five buildings, several road sections, and a park with grass, benches, and trees.

A special selection of kids' furniture in the winter edition included a child's oak rocker, a rocking horse, a set of table and chairs, a maple toddler sled, a puppet theater, and a maple toy bench. Simple, handcrafted Vermont spindle beds with headboards and footboards are available in natural ash or white lacquered maple in twin sizes.

■ Demco

Storage systems and furniture designed for arts and crafts purposes.
See page 6 under **Arts and Crafts.**

■ Domestications

Hanover, PA 17222-0040, (800) 782–7722

Free 56-page color catalog

If your child eats, drinks, and sleeps Batman, this is the place to buy the bed linens for the Bat Bedroom. Full-color polyester-cotton ensembles feature the Caped Crusader and the Joker on the sheet sets, and comforters, drapes, and even a Bat Slumber Bag. All are made in the United States by Bibb.

And that's not all: Domestications devotes six pages of its current catalog to bed linens for kids. You can buy glow-in-the-dark Ghostbusters sheets and comforters by J.P. Stevens, and Teenage Mutant Ninja Turtle and Nintendo Games sets.

Other kids' motifs are ABC Sesame Street, Playskool, Patch the Dog, Mickey and Minnie Mouse, Chip and Dale, Snoopy, and the wonderful Babar the elephant. For beachcombers, King Babar and Queen Celeste are also available on sunbathing-size towels ($19.99 each).

For the sports enthusiast, check out the football, baseball, basketball, or soccer sheet sets.

You can also buy a kid-sized bean bag chair ($19.99) and many other kid-friendly bed linens in floral, striped, and solid styles.

■ The Enchanted Forest

Wooden rocking horse, combination puppet theatre and chalkboard, table and chair sets. See page 220 under **Toys.**

■ First Step, Ltd.

Beechwood table and chair set, picnic table kit, collapsible chair.
See page 140 under **Infant Products and Equipment.**

■ Fun Furniture

8451 Beverly Boulevard, Los Angeles, CA 90048, (213) 655–2711

$1.00 for large color mailers and price lists

As the name implies, Fun Furniture sells creative, jazzy, whimsical beds, desks, chairs, dressers, and other pieces that address fantasy as well as function.

These pieces are a bit pricey, but they are wonderfully imaginative. A "bookhouse" is a bookcase built like a five-story building. It has windows and a peaked roof and sells for $350.00. Or, your child's fancy might run to a headboard castle, or a toy box taxi, or maybe a hamper house.

Fun Furniture is architect-designed and made from durable plastic laminates with an eye toward easy cleanups and space conservation. All the pieces are available in a wide choice of colors. Some pieces are available in several designs.

■ Hancock Toy Shop

Rock maple chairs, tables, toy chest, play kitchen equipment.
See page 223 under **Toys.**

■ Hearthside Quilts

Pre-cut quilts for crib and twin sizes. See page 9 under **Arts and Crafts.**

■ Just For Kids!

Stools, an easel, flip-top table and chair set, dinosaur-shaped chair that converts to sleep area. See page 226 under **Toys.**

■ Keepsake Quilting

Fabric and kits for wall, crib, or twin-sized quilts.
See page 10 under **Arts and Crafts.**

■ Laura D's Folk Art Furniture, Inc.

106 Gleneida Avenue, Carmel, NY 10512, (914) 228–1440

$2.00 for a 4-page color catalog and price list

Would you cavort on an ordinary horse if you could play on a brightly colored rocking frog? These folkart pieces will convince you to put your pony back in the closet. Artist Laura Dabrauski makes and then hand-paints detailed, whimsical children's furniture. All items are made from clear birch plywood, decorated in dazzling hues of non-toxic paint and given three coats of protective polyurethane. Functional as well as fanciful, each piece can be customized to the customer's wishes.

Cheshire cat chairs, bunny and "Ogden Dog" toy chests, cat wall murals, cowboy tables, and rocking mice will put a smile on your child's face and liven up any bedroom or playroom. Finely crafted designs carry a high price tag, though. Be prepared to pay $375.00 for a Velveteen Rabbit chair, $700.00 for a rocking pig.

■ Naturally British Ltd.

Hardwood rocking horses. See page 229 under **Toys.**

■ Periwinkles

546 Boston Avenue, Medford, MA 02155, (617) 623–1980

$2.00 for black-and-white illustrated info sheets

I was delighted to discover that Periwinkles has just started to publish a catalog of the most lovely handpainted children's furniture I have seen anywhere.

This charming artwork is more than just nicely stenciled. Each piece is an artistic delight. First sprayed white or antique white, the furniture is handpainted in designs of your choice, then decorated with a trim stripe in your color choice. Lastly, each piece receives a clear coating for protection.

Prices vary with different patterns or custom work, but you can expect to pay about $695.00 for a crib, $965.00 for a 36-inch three-drawer bureau, $295.00 for a changing table, and $450.00 for a straight-leg night table.

■ The Products Company

P.O. Box 8, Baldwinville, MA 01436, (508) 632–1269

Free 15-page black-and-white illustrated catalog

TPC is a supplier of replacement parts for baby cribs. They also have wheels for many brands of imported strollers and metal disk-type wheels for your old wooden red wagon.

If you need parts for old or new juvenile furniture, give these folks a call.

■ Pyramid School Products

School-quality storage and play furniture.
See page 92 under **Educational Materials.**

■ Sears, Roebuck & Co.

Wooden, plastic, and metal furniture for the whole family.
See page 266 under **General Merchandise Catalogs.**

■ Shaker Shops West

Child-sized New Lebanon rocking chair. See page 233 under **Toys.**

■ Shaker Workshops

P.O. Box 1028, Concord, MA 01742-1028, (617) 646–8985

Free 52-page color catalog

All of the furniture, kits, and accessories shown in this lovely catalog are produced by Shaker Workshops's own skilled craftspeople.

Beds with pine headboards have frames of rock maple and are available in kit form or partially assembled and finished; twin-size kits start at $327.50. Four styles of children's chairs are all lovingly made of rock maple; a handsome rocker is available in kit form for $86.25 or assembled and finished for $172.50.

"A Peaceable Kingdom" is a beautiful and imaginative toy that includes a wooden elephant whose back lifts up to reveal twelve small African animals and three trees. Dolls in complete Shaker costume are available finished or in kits. A miniature Shaker barn with animals is $15.00, and a beautifully illustrated book, *Angel Baskets*, tells what it was like to be a Shaker child; it sells for $9.85.

Detailed, very colorful Victorian soft toys of a dancing goose, tabby cat, bunny, Velveteen Rabbit, or a Cheshire Cat are all available finished or in kit form.

■ Squiggles and Dots

P.O. Box 870, Seminole, OK 74868, (405) 382–0588

Free color postcards and price list

These pieces are the sort you see in children's rooms in *House Beautiful*. Made of birch veneer fibercore and white pine, these bright, wonderfully imaginative pieces are painted by hand.

"Zac's Cool Cats" are blue, pink, and seafoam with blue tails; sunny yellow seats are attached to form a rocker or stool. Companion pieces in the same motif include bulletin boards, bookends, picture frames, and lamps. You can also buy cheerful black and white Holstein chairs that match a table with pink udders.

As with most handcrafted items, the prices are high. A dinosaur stool is $125.00; a palm tree hat and coat rack is $220.00. Colorful fossil fish bookends are $60.00; a matching picture frame sells for $40.00. Still, even one piece of this fanciful collection will make a real splash in a child's room.

■ Timbers Woodworking

Full-size patterns for cradles, rockers, table-and-chair sets, rocking toys, play kitchens and more. See page 17 under **Arts and Crafts**.

■ Think Big!

Giant crayons, oversized wooden-block toy chests, hanging desk, other decorative biggies. See page 115 under **Gifts**.

■ This End Up Furniture Co.

Attn: Marketing Department, 1309 Exchange Alley, Richmond, VA 23219, (800) 638–2234

Free 19-page color catalog

For a simple but sturdy look, this crate-style furniture satisfies function first, with attractive styling as a bonus.

A classic pine storage chest is also handy as an extra seat ($140.00). A trestle-style table and two armchairs are ideal for tea parties, art projects, and games ($95.00).

Two southern yellow pine toy boxes serve as storage, steps, and seats. Paired as a set, the smaller one nests inside the larger one ($155.00).

A solid-end bunk and trundle bed of southern yellow pine will sleep three; the trundle bed stows away under the bottom bunk. The bunk bed is $328.00; the trundle bed option is available at an additional $160.00. They also sell daybed and bunk drawer units and a wonderful solid-end bunkhouse that features two bunk beds, a five-drawer bureau, two shelf units, and an extra bed for guests. A whole roomful of furniture in one unit, it sells for $968.00.

■ Tully Toys, Inc.
Menagerie of wooden rockers. See page 234 under **Toys.**

■ Yield House
Route 16, North Conway, NH 03860-6000, (800) 258–0376

$3.00 for 56-page color catalog

This enticing catalog features reproduction 18th- and 19th-century American furniture and accessories at affordable prices. All photographed in beautiful, country-style rooms, the Yield House designs are carefully crafted from solid pine. Oak pieces from another manufacturer are also available. Many of the pieces can be purchased in kits for you to assemble and finish as you wish.

Parents might be interested in the desks, computer stations, pegboard coat hooks, bookcases, storage chests, rockers, stepstools, and bedroom furnishings.

■ You Name It!
Personalized clothes hangers, stools, bulletin boards, and wall hangings.
See page 118 under **Gifts.**

Gifts

■

■ Abbey Press

285 Hill Drive, St. Meinrad, IN 47577-1001, (812) 357–8251

Free 48-page color catalog

Hundreds of inexpensive items for the whole family are offered in this publication that is dubbed "The Christian Family Catalog."

Decorative plates and plaques, holiday gifts and decorations, toys, stickers, books, and more are all included in the selection. A musical ABC Block plays the calming tune "Jesus Loves Me" and is $19.95. Pillowcases with "Love You Grandma" or "Love You Grandpa" silkscreened on poly/cotton are $9.95 each. *My First Religious Books* are twelve storybooks about the life of Jesus ($8.25).

A neat kid's calendar entitled *365 New Words for Kids* is a junior version of the popular adult model; definitions, sample sentences, and a pronunciation key are given for each word. Recommended for kids seven and up, they sell for $8.95 each.

■ Alaska Craft

C 3 Box 11 -1102, Anchorage, AK 99511-1102, (907) 273–5498

$1.00 for 48-page black and white illustrated catalog

The cooperative marketing effort of more than sixty homebased Alaskan crafters is represented in this collection of handmade items for children. All the products are Alaskan in design or theme.

You can buy a child's sweatsuit with handpainted bear tracks moseying from its shoulder to its ankle, or you may prefer three puffins dressed in scarves and hats on the front of a sweatshirt. The crafter offers six other designs as well. Silk-screened T-shirts have wolves, puffins, caribou, or bears.

If you are handy with a needle and thread, you can buy patterns to make Eskimo dolls and clothes, and beautiful Alaskan parkas. The cooperative also sells customized wooden puzzles, rubber stamps, cookie cutters, and dolls. Children interested in Alaskan culture, geography, and natural history will enjoy a selection of books, videotapes, and coloring books.

■ The Arctic Trading Company

P.O. Box 910, Churchill, Manitoba, Canada ROB OEO, (204) 675–2164;
in Canada (800) 665–0431

Free 20-page color catalog

This is the tenth anniversary collection from Canada's last traditional trading post. Traditional and modern native Canadian arts and crafts are sold here. Slip-on Mukluks ($65.00) are hand-beaded boots lined with a half-inch borg throughout; they are fully Scotchguarded, and treated with Tundra Thread, a coating on the soles for firm footing on slick surfaces. Moosecream rabbit-trimmed slippers are $35.00.

Little dolls that the Inuit carve from caribou antlers and sinew come in size small ($5.00), medium ($6.00), and large ($8.00).

Children may be interested in some of the books available here. *A Guide to Watching Whales in Canada*, and *Building An Igloo* seem educational and fun, and *A Promise is a Promise* is a tale written by an Inuit storyteller for children and adults.

■ Armchair Shopper

P.O. Box 306, Grandview, MO 64030, (800) 624–5038

Free 40-page color catalog

The Armchair Shopper features treats for the whole family, specializing in children's gifts, home decorations, and novelty items. About nine pages are devoted to products for children. Look for dollclothes, safety gadgets, miniatures, kid-sized furniture, and much more.

Parents will like The Nanny Electronic Babysitter ($13.90, with batteries included), which alerts you if your child wanders more than fifty feet from you; it also features an automatic water safety alarm and an emergency call button.

Toys include a wooden puzzle ($9.90) that requires your child's use of special prongs to remove the "patient's" organs. Make a mistake and the patient wiggles; kids will enjoy this funny way to develop hand-eye coordination. A musical baby doll tucked snugly into a wicker basket plays Brahm's "Lullaby" when you tug at her string ($39.90). A plastic fold-out vanity with lighted mirror holds a working hair dryer, brush, comb, curlers, barrettes, a ring, and a perfume bottle.

Their Christmas catalog contains more than twenty pages of decorations and other holiday items—many suitable for kids to enjoy. A rolling cookie cutter with eighteen shapes makes fast work of creating a plateful of angels, stars, bells, and more.

■ A Baby's Secret Garden

P.O. Box 20508, Rochester, NY 14602-0508, (716) 272–7836

Free 24-page color catalog

You are sure to find the perfect baby present in this collection of lovely gifts. If you are the parent-to-be, you will find elegant birth announcements, some of which coordinate with decorative posters, stuffed animals, and crib quilts.

The traditional baby cup and spoon set is available in pewter for $34.95. A cuddly Peter Rabbit chimeball measures 8 inches in diameter and tinkles softly when baby rolls it. Hand-painted with Beatrix Potter illustrations, it sells for $16.95.

Colorful posters of ABC's, teddy bears, or rocking horses are available framed or unframed. You can also choose from elegant paper dolls, switchplate covers, and baby record books.

■ Barrons

22790 Heslip Drive, Novi, MI 48050, (800) 538–6340

Free 36-page color catalog

For such special occasions as christenings or Bar Mitzvahs, a special gift from Barrons will help commemorate the day. Purveyors of china, silverware and giftware, Barrons often offers items at discounted prices.

The inventory includes a 5 x 7-inch silverplated picture frame ($19.95), a 3-piece Royal Doulton Bunnykins china set with child's bowl, mug, and plate ($34.95), and a 3-piece silverplated baby cup, spoon, and fork for $29.95.

Instead of the proverbial spoon, your baby can be born with a sterling silver toothbrush in his or her mouth ($29.95). And to foster good saving habits, choose a Reed & Barton Bunny Bank ($24.95).

■ B.N. Genius

22121 Crystal Creek Boulevard SE, P.O. Box 3008, Bothell, WA 98041-3008, (800) 468–4410

64-page color catalog

Brought to you by the people that publish the Sporting Edge catalog, this is a collection of rather pricey, high-tech items for the whole family.

If you cannot be concerned with keeping score for yourself, an electronic dart game will automatically do it for you for $399.95. You can play four different dart games: 301, 301 double in/double out, 501, and count-up.

Instead of a plain old princess phone for your teen's room, why not order a handcrafted Quacky IV Mallard duck phone? Instead of ringing, this phone quacks, moves its beak, and lights up its eyes ($69.95). Radio-controlled hydroplanes will skip across the water at speeds of up to twenty miles an hour; the Thunderhawk model is $69.95.

Conspicuous consumers will like the graphite pool cue, a Word Finder electronic dictionary and thesaurus, a remote-control duck or dinosaur, and more.

■ Charms R Us

31 Brompton Circle, Williamsville, NY 14221, (716) 633–2485

$5.00 for a 64-page black-and-white illustrated catalog refundable with first purchase

Design the charm bracelet of your child's dreams through this amazing collection. More than 6,000 charm designs are photographed here in actual size, and they are all available in sterling silver, 22-karat gold over sterling silver, 10-karat gold or 14-karat gold. All designs can be ordered as tie tacks or pins.

An index divided by category lists such diverse interests as animals and pets, music and the arts, professions, sports, religion, zodiacs, graduation, boating, Christmas, and gambling.

They have charms with maps of countries, continents, and Caribbean islands. They have facsimiles of the queen's throne or the queen's coach. They have every kind of animal I can think of, and every kind of fish. Name your charm—planes, buses, ballet slippers, hockey sticks, ice skates, G clefs, teddy bears, hearts—they have it.

You can also purchase the bracelets here. Several designs are offered, and all are available in sterling silver or gold and gold overlay.

■ Country Store

5925 Country Lane, P.O. Box 612, Milwaukee, WI 53201, (800) 558–1013

$1.50 for a 68-page color catalog

This catalog celebrates all that is reminiscent of life on the farm. Parents may be interested in the home decorations, country clothing, and collectibles; youngsters should flip to the last several pages devoted especially to items that will appeal to children.

Young farm hands will enjoy dozens of durable and authentic $1/16$-scale roto-balers, John Deere equipment, deluxe farm sets, a toy barn with sliding doors, a belted elevator, and even vintage replicas of tractors. Speaking of vintage, when your child decides to escape the farm and get a little flashier, there are vintage vehicles like a Ford '57 "T"Bird, a Chevy '69 Camaro, and a Pontiac '68 GTO. Those and other models are $6.98 each.

After a night on the town, they can settle back down to business with a scaled-down milking parlor for the junior dairy farmer at $18.98. A good variety of animals about two inches tall (even a feed pen with calves) will help turn any backyard into a farmyard.

■ The Disney Catalog

CN 2100, 475 Oberlin Avenue South, Lakewood, NJ 08701-1050, (800) 237–5751

Free 28-page color catalog

Mickey and Minnie, Jiminy, Pinocchio, Winnie the Pooh, Goofy, Donald, and the rest of the gang cavort across sweatshirts and T-shirts, lunchboxes, pillows, storage jars, armchairs, stationery, stamp kits, watches, socks, and beach towels. You can even buy a Rocking Mouse—your child will ride on Mickey's back instead of in a horse's saddle.

The official Mousketeer's ears on a black felt hat come in one size and are $3.50. A pair of slippers with non-skid soles and Minnie, Donald, or Mickey heads on the tops will keep little feet warm for $9.00.

A wonderful sleeping bag has Mickey Mouse's face on the pillow and arms that hug your child. When naptime is over, the bag folds up and tucks into Mickey's body to create a 38-inch playmate. The bag is sized for children two through six.

If you have an adult Disney fan in the house, take a look at the men's and women's watches, T-shirts, sweatclothes, earrings, suspenders, and polyplush golf club covers that feature the heads of Goofy, Minnie, Mickey, Donald, and Pluto. A set of five covers is $45.00. A large collection of Disney books, videos, and cassettes are also sold in these pages.

■ The Dragon's Nest

31 Market Square, Newburyport, MA 01950, (508) 462–8802

Free 24-page color catalog

From pogo sticks and a 44-inch giant panda to Educational Insights I.Q. Games, this catalog offers a little bit of everything. One useful set of toddler books is called *My First Tools;* each book is shaped like a saw, wrench, hammer, pliers, drill, or screwdriver, and inside each "tool" is a related story. Real working binoculars are reasonably priced at $11.00.

Detailed miniatures of castles or cowboys and Indians snap together easily so children can arrange them in many ways. Brio wooden trains and tracks, Gotz dolls, doll clothes, a star machine planetarium, fossil and rock collections, science kits, and much more will please nearly every taste.

■ Exposures

475 Oberlin Avenue South, Lakewood, NJ 08701, (800) 222–4947; in New Jersey, (201) 370–8110

Free 48-page color catalog

An unparalleled selection of picture frames, albums, and accessories will show off your little ones in the best light. The holiday catalog offers several photo Christmas cards and a colorful, hand-painted tree ornament that holds your child's picture. You can buy a set of ornaments in Santa, angel, and horn designs for $11.50.

A grandparent might enjoy a personalized calendar. Seasonally coordinated designs surround each month with windows above the days for your own pictures.

Also see the Grandmother's Book, découpage frames, for children, and Fido 'n Fifi découpage frames for the pet lover who thought he had everything.

■ Family Communications

Books and videos from the producers of "Mr. Rogers' Neighborhood." See page 30 under **Books.**

■ Hamakor Judaica, Inc.

P.O. Box 59453, Chicago, IL 60659-9923, (800) 621–8272

Free 64-page color catalog

This large selection of gifts will help you celebrate the special life-cycle events unique to Judaism.

Fourteen Chanukah songs are performed as Hebrew, Yiddish, and English sing-alongs and are available on audiocassette ($11.95) or on compact disc ($16.95).

A nice gift from grandchild to grandmother is a "We Love Bubbe" apron that can include up to five grandchildren's names. It can also be ordered with "We Love Zayde" across the front.

For ages three through eight, an "Eight Gifts for Kids" bag includes a "walking" dreidel, a jigsaw puzzle, a Chanukah play-along piano book, a Jewish symbols puzzle cube, a brass menorah, and a Chanukah coloring and cut-out book.

You will also find a custom-made Bat Mitzvah doll, cuddly Bear Bitzvahs, The Young Reader's Encyclopedia of Jewish History, Hebrew Scrabble, kosher snacks and candy, Jewish symbols cookie cutters, a paint-a-kit Shalom T-shirt, and much more.

▪ Heir Affair

625 Russell Drive, Meridian, MS 39301, (800) 332–4347;
in Mississippi, (601) 484–4323

Free 40-page color catalog

Many of the carefully chosen items in this catalog are distinctive enough to become treasured heirlooms. If you are looking for luxury, an elegant handmade Swiss batiste christening gown with yards of handsewn French lace and a matching French lace bonnet sells for $375.00. A sterling silver Kiddush cup is $110.00.

On a more affordable level, a sterling silver bent-handled spoon is a lovely gift for $30.00. A sterling toothbrush, also for $30.00, will encourage good habits with a flair. A sweet hand-painted music box plays "It's a Small World" and opens to reveal a hand-painted giraffe, bear, doll, clown, and the like for $15.00. You will also find an infant's bracelet, a cross pendant, a ring, and a chai necklace, all in fourteen-karat gold. Sterling comb and brush sets and picture frames are included in the selection.

The inventory also includes toys, science and craft kits, doll furniture, safety products, and more.

▪ James Kaplan Jewelers

40 Freeway Drive, Cranston, RI 02920-9835, (800) 343–0712;
in Rhode Island, (401) 467–9112

Free 24-page color catalog

This jeweler offers a catalog of fine giftware at a discount, including beautiful luxuries for children. A sterling, curved-handle spoon can be personalized with a birth date and time by your local engraver. The spoon's bowl is engraved with a clock design, and you need only to have the hands engraved on the face to denote the time of your child's birth. The suggested retail price is $37.50, but Kaplan sells it for $29.95. A baby boy's sterling comb and brush set by Gorham is $33.95; a more intricate girl's version is $35.95. A Peter Rabbit plate, cereal bowl, and mug by Wedgwood with a suggested retail price of $39.00 is $22.95 here.

Also available at discounts are a Towle's sterling silver baby cup, a silverplated bottle, a silverplated Tooth Fairy box, a K.C. Backpacker preschool sleeping bag by Kids' club, and a children's smoke detector disguised as one of three colorful balloons being carried by Snoopy.

■ John and Jo Withers H.S.

Eaton House, 14 Station Road, Madeley, Telford, Shropshire, England TF7 5AY,
Phone: 0952 585131

Include a self-addressed, stamped envelope for a 6-page color brochure

If you would like a keepsake that is sure to become a treasured heirloom, you must
send for photos of the beautiful work of these enamelers and silversmiths. They will
paint a miniature portrait of your child, working from a photograph that you send
to them.

The Withers brochure shows seven full-color examples of their artistry. If you
choose to have the portrait painted on the cover of an enameled box, a personal
inscription of not more than twenty words can be painted inside the lid before the
last firing.

Prices are $350.00 for a miniature painting (watercolor or oils), $372.00 for a portrait on an enameled box lid, and $442.00 for a miniature painting on enamel that is
fired onto copper.

■ Lillian Vernon

510 South Fulton Avenue, Mount Vernon, NY 10550-5067, (914) 633–6300

Free 96-page color catalog

It is hard to imagine that there could be a family left in America that is not familiar
with Lillian Vernon's catalog. It is filled with organizers, home decorations, holiday
decorations, and thousands of inexpensive gifts and gadgets for the whole family.

Throughout the catalog you will find colorful toys, games, books, and accessories for children. A bright red lunch box shaped like a car with wheels comes with
a thermos for $8.98; four plastic apples that you pre-freeze to keep lunchbox food
cool and fresh are $6.98; a collection of 110 Giant Assorted Stickers in a matching
box are $5.98; and a huge 100 percent cotton beach towel that says "SUPER KID" in
bright colors sells for $14.98.

A great source for birthday party and baby shower gifts, seasonal editions have
a changing inventory that usually includes puzzles, bath toys, dinnerware, arts and
crafts supplies, rattles, umbrellas, nightlights, music boxes, and a score of personalized items like towels, pencils, baseball caps, terry robes, duffel bags, and more.

Look here at Christmas, Easter, Halloween, and Thanksgiving for inexpensive
decorations that are sure to be kid pleasers.

■ The Metropolitan Museum of Art

Books, games, crafts, and more. See page 150 under **Museum Shops.**

■ Miles Kimball Company

41 West Eighth Avenue, OshKosh, WI 54906-0002, (414) 231–3800

Free 66-page color catalog

Miles Kimball has been in the business of selling inexpensive but useful gadgets, toys, decorations, and novelties for the whole family for more than fifty years.

Authentic miniature replicas of old-fashioned Coca-Cola delivery trucks are made in England and sell for $7.98 each. A pack of ten balloons in assorted colors can be personalized with "Happy Birthday _____(your child's name)" for $3.49 a pack. A toothbrushing timer for $2.98 is a smiley-faced hourglass that keeps kids brushing for two minutes.

These are just a few of the hundreds of gadgets, gags, and gifts stocked here. You can fill a dozen party loot bags with the choices offered, from sponges-on-rope and wind-up toys to personalized placemats and name stickers, note pads, and crayon mugs.

■ Museum of Fine Arts, Boston

Unusual gifts, books, and games. See page 150 under **Museum Shops**.

■ My Favorite Pastimes

Box 4179, (411 Harrison), Oak Park, IL 60303, (800) 445–9575; in Illinois, Hawaii, and Alaska, (312) 524–9170

Free 16-page color catalog

Luxurious gifts for special occasions are the mainstay of this inventory. A stenciled pinafore of cream polyester/cotton is $36.95; a 14-inch imported porcelain doll named Deborah is $75.00; and a music box that plays "Für Elise" while a bird dances in and out of its house is $39.95.

If you enjoy embroidery, you can create an heirloom with a 17-inch, jointed teddy bear. "Mr. Beresford" is made of 18-mesh Zweigert brown canvas hand-painted with many patterns and designs. The kit is $120.00. A midget train with 4-inch railway cars is painted with its cargo names: COAL, CHOCOLATE PUDDING, FULL OF ICE CREAM, and LEMONADE; it sells for $32.95.

■ The National Trust Enterprises Ltd.

P.O. Box 101, Melksham, Wiltshire SN 12 8EA, England, Phone: 02-72 217000

Write for current cost of 24-page color catalog

The National Trust is a registered charity and your catalog purchases contribute to The Trust's work of conserving historic buildings.

A limited but interesting number of items for children include a Jacob wool cap and striped wool scarf made from the distinctive natural fleece of the Jacob sheep. Handmade wooden bookends of resting frogs or pecking woodpeckers will make nice gifts as will paper dolls based on the costume collection at Killerton House in Devon, England. A witty little circular jigsaw puzzle illustrates pond life above and below the water. Handmade wooden toys that resemble ducks or puffins have leather feet that make a flapping sound as they are pushed along; they are a big hit with the younger kids.

Prices are quoted in British pounds, so you will need to know the latest exchange rate. Of course, the simplest way to order is to charge your purchase to your Access/MasterCard, Visa, Diners Club, or American Express account.

■ National Wildlife Federation

1400 Sixteenth Street, NW, Washington, DC 20036-2266

Free 56-page color catalog

Nature lovers will enjoy this collection of cards and gifts, and the profits from each purchase will help the federation continue its work on behalf of clean water and air and the preservation of wildlife habitats.

Thrill a dinosaur lover with a 55-inch vinyl tyrannosaurus ($14.95) or an activities book about the giant reptiles ($6.00). A sky science kit includes project booklets, compass, test tube, thermometer, and more.

Silkscreened sweatshirts and T-shirts, bird feeders, and stuffed animals are offered along with dozens of Christmas cards, gift bags, calendars, and canvas totes decorated with Earth-friendly motifs.

■ The Oriental Trading Company, Inc.

P.O. Box 3407, Omaha, NE 68103-0407, (800) 228–2269

Free 66-page color catalog

The Oriental Trading Company catalog is brimming with children's gadgets, holiday accessories, inexpensive jewelry, Santa suits, games, toys, and party supplies. I am not sure that a red musical calculator with a Santa lounging across the top will help a child stay attentive to the homework at hand, but if you think it might do the trick, it is available in the Christmas edition of this catalog for $4.50 each.

Little girls love (and usually lose) jewelry. A 36-piece adjustable birthstone ring assortment for $10.80 is one of the best deals I have seen. Or, step up to an even dozen of the "fancy" adjustable rings for $9.00. A dozen gold-finished, rhinestone-studded bangle bracelets in assorted styles are $10.80 for the dozen. These will make great favors at a birthday party or wonderful stocking stuffers.

Handmade piñatas of a Christmas tree, fat Santa, or a drummer boy are $4.95 each. Wooden toys, soft animals, bike locks, a dartboard and darts for $4.50, and a cookie-and-cake baking set for $4.50 are typical of the fun and low-priced bargains sold here.

■ The Paragon

Tom Harvey Road, Westerly, Rhode Island 02891, (800) 343–3095; in Rhode Island, (401) 596–0134

Free 72-page color catalog

The goods in this catalog are about equally devoted to adult gifts, home decorations, and children's items. Christmas stockings, a toy music box, holiday decorations, small games, stickers, a magic set, origami, and even a couple of kid-sized bean bag chairs have been included for the young crowd.

Kids will love the selection of rubber stamps, which free them of their artistic limitations and allow them to use their imaginations to make a variety of pictures. The Paragon offers good quality stamps and felt ink pads, including a 29-piece set of holiday designs, fish, teddy bears, globes, and shells for $15.00. Another 28-piece set of funny facial features lets kids make hundreds of imaginative face combinations, also for $15.00. Paragon's last fall catalog offered a set of five Inkadinkadoo Christmas stamps for $17.50.

■ Past Times

Guildford House, Hayle, Cornwall, TR 27 6PT, England, Tel: 011-44-736 753 443

Write for current price of 48-page color catalog

This catalog aims to bring you a selection of interesting items reminiscent of every era of English history. The inventory is weighted toward choices for adults, but a dozen or more gifts are especially for children.

A baby book illustrated with forty-five paintings from museums and galleries is $19.95 in hardcover. A Family History Kit for the beginner genealogist of any age includes charts, a document log, helpful addresses, and more for $17.95. Antique paper dolls with thirty Victorian Scraps (paper cut-outs of 200 subjects) can be arranged in a Victorian Scrap Album to provide hours of imaginative fun. Two hundred scraps are $5.95, and a 48-page album to put them in is also $5.95.

You will also find Victorian half-masks, an Advent calendar, some silver charms to hide in the Christmas pudding, and a jack-in-the-box.

Catalog prices are in British pounds but an added price sheet gives all prices in U.S. dollars.

■ The Popcorn Factory

Mail Order Department, P.O. Box 4530, Lake Bluff, IL 60044, (800) 858–1000; in the Chicago area, (312) 362–9600

Free 24-page color catalog

You will find the popcorn here a lot more interesting than the popcorn at the local movie theatre. You can buy, or have sent as a gift, butter, double cheddar, or caramel popcorn in 2- to 6½-gallon decorative cans.

Four gallons of buttered popcorn in a red can decorated with Mickey Mouse is yours for $18.95. For $23.95, one of any number of celebration cans are available with Thank You, Happy Birthday, Nice Going! and such written on them.

If your child doesn't drool over popcorn, they also sell piñatas, jelly beans, Gummie Bears, and more, all packed especially for gift giving.

■ The Prairie Pedlar

Route 2, Lyons, KS 67554, (316) 897–6631

Free black-and-white illustrated information packet

Folk art from the Kansas plains is presented here. Mother Goose's Marionettes are made of pine and include a 36-inch Santa bear, hand-painted and signed by the artist for $75.00. The price is the same for a cinnamon bear, a gander or goose, a teddy, an Annie or Andy, a sad bear, or an old teddy.

Unique toys like standing pine jigsaw puzzles ($25.00 each) and a wooden train whistle are offered. For a touch of whimsy on a sweater, hat, or jacket, you can buy old buttons—a great custom look.

■ Roberta Fortune's Almanac

150 Chestnut Street, San Francisco, CA 94111-1004, (800) 331–2300

Free 43-page color catalog

Featuring unusual gifts and practical products for the whole family, Fortune's Almanac has a smaller 8-page catalog called Fortune's Child stapled in its middle. The appealing merchandise offered here includes useful childcare products and unique clothing and toys. The offerings change completely from season to season.

In one recent catalog a German-made Kettcar looks like a racing car for kids; it is made with a non-tip, tubular-steel frame ($99.00). Walkie-talkies made to last have voice-activated headsets and run on nine-volt batteries. A wooden game case ($49.00) from Great American Trading Company is stocked with five old-fashioned games, such as marbles and jacks.

Parents can encourage finicky appetites with a Flintstone or Jetson plastic dinner set, or confine a curious toddler with a plastic security gate.

■ Ross-Simons Jewelers

Howard Industrial Park, 9 Ross-Simons Drive, Cranston, RI 02920-9848, (800) 556–7376; in Rhode Island, (401) 463–3100

Free 45-page color catalog

Beautiful jewelry and luxury giftware at a good discount have been carefully selected for this catalog. A small collection of children's items will make lovely gifts. A sterling silver baby cup by Towle is sold here for $49.95 (suggested retail price: $70.00). A sterling silver dumbbell rattle by Empire is $33.95 (suggested retail price: $44.00).

A sterling silver 3-piece feeding set by Towle is offered for $74.90 (suggested retail price: $170.00).

Similar discounts are offered on a 5-piece miniature silverplate tea set and a sterling silver porringer. Dear little Beatrix Potter china figurines complete the selection of gifts especially for children. You may consider other offerings suitable for children or adults; picture frames and miniature clocks are lovely baby shower gifts. Whatever you choose, the discounts here make a look at this catalog very worthwhile.

■ The San Francisco Music Box Company

Mail Order Department, P.O. Box 7817, San Francisco, CA 94120-7817, (800) 227–2190

Free 72-page color catalog

This catalog overflows with delightful musical gifts for every taste and budget. Some of the music boxes offer a choice of tunes; you pick the song you want from a list of possibilities. If you are unsure of the tune, you can call the company to hear recordings of each title.

You can choose traditional wooden boxes with beautiful inlaid lids, jewelry boxes in all sizes and styles, musical kaleidoscopes, lucite boxes that allow you to see the movement, and musical ornaments. Seven-inch porcelain sugarplum fairies will hang from your tree and play "When You Wish Upon A Star" for $17.50 each.

A hand-painted porcelain girl or boy will perform Chopin at a lacquered wood grand piano for $64.95. A little porcelain scroll that declares a grandmother's or mother's love plays "Memory" for $29.95. Many musical dolls are stocked; one freckle-faced 9-inch girl plays "Thank Heaven For Little Girls" and is $34.95.

You will also find a great Christmas selection with everything from snow globes to a Daffy Dinosaur that plays "Deck the Halls." Many music boxes are specially designed as gifts for babies, weddings, and a variety of religious ceremonies.

■ Shimbumi Trading, Ltd.

P.O. Box 1-F, Eugene, OR 97440, (503) 683–1331

$3.00 for a 32-page color catalog; a $3.00 coupon is enclosed in your first catalog.

This unique collection of Japanese products includes traditional and decorative items with unusual gifts for children scattered throughout the selection. Parents can choose from silk kimonos, cookware, art prints, and books on Japanese culture. Children will be intrigued by Japanese folk toys, coloring books, Japanese sandals, and more.

Six books of origami instruction are offered, origami paper sets, three calligraphy sets, and three types of rice paper.

Unique and colorful games, puzzles, and toys for younger children and Japanese strategy games for older kids round out the offerings.

Kite collectors might appreciate two Samurai kites hand-painted on paper with bamboo supports; they are $45.00 each.

■ The Smithsonian Institution

Exclusive items based on the museum's collection.
See page 152 under **Museum Shops.**

■ Think Big!

390 West Broadway, New York, NY 10012-9804, (800) 221–7019;
in New York, (212) 925–7300

Free 32-page color catalog

These people obviously feel that bigger is indeed better with their collection of hilariously oversized gifts.

They offer 56-inch waxy plastic crayons with a silkscreened label that looks like the real Crayola's. They stand upright or can be hung from the ceiling. Available in six colors, they are $40.00 each.

Toy chests that look like giant wooden blocks are hand-crafted in maple with a safety hinge on top. Cubes of 16-inch dimensions, they come in three designs ($90.00 each).

A unique desk with a hinged top that looks like a huge black and white notebook can be mounted on the wall ($95.00) or ordered with legs ($125.00). Open your notebook to reveal solid wood construction and ample storage space.

■ U. S. Committee for UNICEF

475 Oberlin Avenue South, Lakewood, NJ 08701, (800) 553–1200

Free 32-page color holiday catalog

This catalog is particularly appropriate for inclusion in this book, because UNICEF has been serving the needs of children since its inception in 1946.

Along with Christmas cards and wrapping paper, you will find a colorful circular UNICEF jigsaw puzzle recommended for children six and up for $6.50. A special calendar brightly decorated with young people's paintings is $5.00. A 48-page coloring book illustrates life on seven islands of the world and is $6.00. A 25-piece puzzle for little hands features children at play, and a 208-piece puzzle for children six and up features "The World's Children." *The World Atlas For Young People* contains maps, drawings, and color photos illustrating the environment, animals, and political and physical features of each continent; it is available in hardcover for $12.50.

Still more puzzles and books are offered, including a delightful title, *Games of the World*, in softcover for $14.00.

■ What on Earth

25801 Richmond Road, Cleveland, OH 44146, (216) 831–5588

Free 64-page color catalog

This is a collection of amusing diversions and fun things to wear for the whole family.

A Pacific Coast Rockfish nightlight will softly illuminate your child's room. The Kremlin Board Game ($19.95) is timely and recommended for children twelve and up. A hand-painted Twelve Days of Christmas puzzle is designed in Britain. Colorful basketballs that look like world globes are available in the official size ($28.95) and miniature versions ($22.95). *The Game of Great Composers* features thirty-two maestros from medieval to modern times. The Kingpin hat, immortalized by Jughead of *Archie* comics fame, is here in black, red, or blue for $19.95; you supply your own buttons. An inflatable Appaloosa or Pinto horse permits your child to make the bronco buck or rear; suggested for children three and up, they are $19.95 each.

PERSONALIZED GIFTS

■ Child Art Studios

6836 Engle Road, P.O. Box 94502, Cleveland, OH 44101-4502

Free color flyer

Makers of Baby's Create-A-Book, Child Art Studios specializes in personalized books for young listeners. We were given a Baby's Create-A-Book when our daughter was born, and it is a beautifully illustrated 36-page book that we treasure.

Printed on high-quality paper with a durable, wipe-clean hard cover, the story is customized for your child with the information you provide. It tells the story of where and when they were born, who delivered them and who came to visit.

This is a nice gift for $14.99, plus $2.00 postage and handling.

■ Historic Newspaper Archives, Inc.

1582 Hart Street, Rahway, NJ 07065, (800) 221–3221

Free black-and-white illustrated brochure

Commemorate the birth of your baby with the newspaper of that date in a beautiful white portfolio, personalized with the baby's name, length, weight, date, time, and place of birth. These are not reproductions or just a front page, but the entire actual newspaper.

Papers from more than fifty cities are available, and most have issues from as far back as forty years. Newspapers alone are $34.50. A newspaper mounted in the Baby Binder Portfolio is $65.00.

■ Initials

409 William Street, P.O. Box 246, Elmira, NY 14902, (800) 782–2438; in New York, (607) 733–9991

Free 48-page color catalog

You can personalize anything for anyone as you will quickly discover here. Loads of items are available for adults, but kids have also been remembered.

A nylon audiocassette or CD case with removable, adjustable shoulder strap can be personalized with the name of your teen across the top ($20.00). A stadium blanket will help keep junior sports fans warm at games and is available in six plaid patterns. Measuring 50 x 60 inches, it is $32.00 with initials.

Eight pages are devoted to young children. Check these cheerful temptations: personalized stationery, wooden puzzles, pencils, bookends, hooded sweaters, sterling silver baby cups, pillowcases, baby blankets, shirts, memory books, porcelain cups and plates, and more.

■ Lillian Vernon

Personalized items like towels, pencils, baseball caps, terry robes, duffel bags, and more. See page 108 under **Gifts.**

■ Livonia

P.O. Box 495, Chester, NY 10918-0495, (800) 543–8566

Free 15-page color catalog

Livonia started its mail-order business more than thirty years ago with one product: NameDate baby shoes. Made of the finest white leather, they have baby's first name and birth date embossed in gold leaf on the soles. They are $13.00 a pair and are made in the United States.

Over the years the company has branched out, and they now offer several other items. A combination picture frame and baby's handprint kit comes with a special pen to write the name and date on the frame. You will also find a few clothes, some gold charms, sneakers, and various styles of socks.

■ **You Name It!**

P.O. Box 134, Medway, MA 02053, (800) 698–6263

Free color brochure

These sixty-two colorful items all can be personalized with a child's name. Prices range from $6.00 for a name spelled out in a soft sculpture to $130.00 for a white rocker painted with heart-shaped balloons and, of course, personalized across the back. Dinosaur, baseball bat, or flowery wall racks for hanging clothes sell for around $25.00. Colorful puzzles, stools, bulletin boards, soft wall hangings, and dolls will make bright additions to a child's room. Hundreds of stock names are available, but special orders are no problem; just allow six to eight weeks for delivery. Understandably, all sales are final.

■ **Young Rembrandts**

P.O. Box 3160, Vero Beach, FL 32964-3160

Free 10-page black-and-white illustrated mini-catalog

Your child's drawing or message can be reproduced in full color on a bonbon dish, tile, lucite paperweight, ceramic trinket box, or dinner plate.

This catalog lists some interesting ideas for gift-giving occasions. Obtain a drawing from the child of your weekend hostess and thank her for her hospitality with a keepsake designed by her own child. Borrow an artwork from a child whose birthday party your child will attend and have a birthday plate made. Young Rembrandt gift certificates are available if the drawings are not easily procured.

Charming mementos of childhood, the designs are permanent and dishwasher-safe. Representative of the cost involved in this art preservation project, the lucite paperweight is $20.00, the 6-inch tile is $14.00, and the 8-inch round dinner plate is $18.00.

SPECIALTY AND ALTERNATIVE GIFTS

■ **Alternative Gift Markets Inc.**

HCR 6682, Lucerne Valley, CA 92356

Free 16-page catalog

"Give the earth a present" with this shopping list for the world. If you share the philosophy that it is better to give than to receive, you and your child can choose a gift to be sent to a worthy cause in your or someone else's name. Worldwide campaigns against hunger, homelessness, and disease are among the issues you will be invited to support. The suggested donations and their anticipated results will remind you of Unicef-type fund-raising campaigns. You may decide to send $1.00 to provide a vaccination to a child in a Third World Country, $25.00 to buy an artificial limb for a war victim in Cambodia, or $5.00 to provide food for one day to one hungry person in the United States. This catalog may provide food for thought for your family on gift-giving holidays.

■ Everything Cows

24 South Water Street, P. O. Box 1219, Edgartown, MA 02539, (508) 627–8072

$1.00 for a 16-page color catalog

If your child is crazy for cows, here is your source for all things bovine. A pair of hand-finished cow bookends are $25.00, a wooden cow bank is $12.50, and a wooden cow light-switch cover is $5.00. A silk-screened herd of cows grazes on a 100 percent cotton bandana; choose from pink, red, green, grey, or blue bandanas for $6.00 each.

An extra-special gift would be a red 100 percent heavyweight cotton "Cow Jumped Over The Moon" sweater. Made in rural England, it sells for $95.00.

Handcrafted stuffed toys made in the Ozarks feature a buxom bovine for $42.00 and her smaller friend for $26.00.

A barnyard baby comforter with matching cow doll is handmade and machine washable and is $55.00 for the set.

■ Finger Prints Catalog

230 West Glebe Road, Alexandria, VA 22305, Voice & TDD, (800) 634–0993; Voice & TDD in Virginia, (703) 683–6389

Free 6-page black-and-white illustrated catalog

Sign language gifts for the hearing impaired are the mainstay at Finger Prints. You can buy T-shirts with your name, "I love you," or "Happy Birthday" in sign language. *Keep Quiet* ($13.95) is a sign language game with crossword cubes for ages 7 to adult.

A soft 19-inch Identabunny with floppy ears wears a yellow T-shirt that you can have printed with any message in finger-spelling sign language.

An I Love You Bear dressed in a bright red cap and sweater printed with the I Love You sign is $25.00.

■ Heifer Project International

216 Wachusett Street, Rutland, MA 01543-9989, (800) 422–0474

$.25 for 18-page black-and-white illustrated catalog

For 45 years HPI has helped to alleviate hunger and poverty worldwide by providing animals and related assistance to those most needy. In their words, "Not a handout, but a hand up."

Your family can choose from twenty-one projects and make a donation in your child's name. This eye-opening exercise in understanding and compassion could change the way your child perceives his or her own good fortune.

In Zaire, $10.00 can help buy a flock of chickens. In India, $30.00 helps to buy a colony of bees. In the United States, a donation can go toward the purchase of a bull or heifer for struggling people in Kentucky or Maine.

When you consider that about 15 million children die of hunger and hunger-related illnesses every year, this could be one of the nicest gifts you ever give.

■ Hog Wild!

the pig store, 239 Causeway Street, Boston, MA 02114, (617) 523–7447

$2.00 for a 19-page color catalog

"Speedy porcelainized service" is Hog Wild's motto, and if your children are pig lovers, they will be in hog heaven here, on "Pork Avenue." Sorry, I couldn't resist that.

Naturally, this is the place to buy a First National Piggy Bank; twenty inches in diameter, it sells for $60.00. Sweatshirts and T-shirts are sold with pig puns. A Superham Bib for the Man of Squeal is $10.00, and a piglet bottle warmer sells for $15.00.

Pig fanciers are sure to love the piglet booties, pig ski hats, Calvin Swine quartz watch, and hogwash laundry bags.

■ Oxfam America

115 Broadway, Boston, MA 02116, (617) 482–1211

Free 44-page color Christmas catalog

Most of the products in this catalog are made by craftspeople in the poorest countries of the world. You help to provide jobs for them with your purchases.

Shoppers will find gifts, books, and toys for the whole family, with four or five pages devoted to children. Dollmakers in Thailand have represented two of several Thai ethnic groups in collector's dolls; the Akha and the Karen doll are $15.50 each.

Published in the United Kingdom, *My Own Christmas Book* has lots of project ideas, presents to make, and games for $4.50. Also from the United Kingdom are a Lace-making Starter Kit and a Games Compendium with more than fifty games in one neat case. An elephant puzzle made in the Philippines and a shell game called Con-gklak from Indonesia are typical of the goods sold here.

The catalog quotes prices in British pounds, but an easy-to-read price list also gives the cost in U.S. dollars.

■ Tonquish Creek

P.O. Box 228, Plymouth, MI 48170, (800) 331–3894

$1.00 for 56-page black-and-white illustrated catalog, refundable with first order

Most children are fascinated with firefighters and fire engines; flashing lights, sirens, and shiny ladders seem to fill kids with awe. If your child wants to be a firefighter or just perks up at the sound of a siren, this very unusual catalog is for you. Tonquish Creek offers gifts and collectibles with firefighter, emergency responder, and police officer motifs. All of the products are offered for the whole family, but some have special kid-appeal.

The ceramic dalmatian bookends ($25.00) will dress up the bookshelf; one of the many embossed or sculptured belt buckles will dress up jeans. Two paperback books will answer the questions of readers nine through thirteen: *A Day in the Life of a Police Cadet* and *A Day in the Life of a Police Detective* are sold for $2.50 each. For the family pet, a "101 Dalmatians" dog bowl is $12.00, and a Christmas stocking for needleworkers to complete in counted cross-stitch features a firefighter, truck, and red hydrants ($20.00).

■ Whale Adoption Project

320 Gifford Street, Falmouth, MA 02540, (508) 564–9980

Free brochure

You and your child adopt one of sixty-six humpback whales that have been pho-tographed, named (Buckshot, Navaho, Othello, and others), and studied, season after season, as they migrate along the coast of the eastern United States. You receive an adoption certificate, a photo of your adopted whale, and a map and calendar of your whale's usual migration pattern. A quarterly newsletter keeps you informed of whale issues and research. Your adoption fee ($15.00 a year) goes to help The International Wildlife Coalition.

■ World Wildlife Fund Catalog

P.O. Box 224, Peru, IN 45970, (800) 833–1600

Free 24-page color catalog

Buy a T-shirt, a book, or a puzzle and help to save the mountain gorillas in Zaire, the snow leopards in Nepal, and giant pandas in China.

Founded in 1961, the World Wildlife Fund is the largest international conservation organization in the world with twenty-seven affiliates on five continents.

Dedicated to saving the world's wildlife, they have special interest in the defense of the tropical forests and their wildlife in Latin America, Asia, and Africa.

WWF has some fine items for children. My favorites are a colorful pair of jungle animal bookends ($29.95), a T-shirtful of friendly animals peeking out from the saying, "It's a Jungle Out There" ($9.95), and a collapsible umbrella with the world globe painted on it ($14.95).

I think the most unique and fun items are the giraffe T-shirt ($13.95) with the head and neck of the tall fellow emblazoned on the front and a pair of matching tube socks ($9.50) printed like the giraffe's hooves and spotted legs. These will be a hit with kids of all ages.

A portion of your purchase price is donated to the conservation efforts of the fund.

Health and
Safety Products

■

■ Allergy Control Products

89 Danbury Road, P.O. Box 793, Ridgefield, CT 06877, (800) 422–DUST;
in Connecticut, (203) 438–9580

**Free 6-page catalog for Mold Spore Allergy and
6-page catalog for House Dust Allergy**

If your child is one of the thousands who suffer from allergies, help is at hand.
Check here for machine washable, dust-proof mattress and pillow casings in comfortable cotton-poly blend fabrics, face masks, electrostatic air filters for hot air heat-
ing systems, room air cleaners, mold control products, and dehumidifiers. All are
designed for those with mold spore and house dust allergies. A bee-sting kit protects
against allergic shock reactions. A book section includes several titles offering allergy advice and information for sufferers and their families.

■ American Foundation for the Blind

Consumer Products, 15 West 16th Street, New York, NY 10011, (201) 862–8838

Free 26-page black-and-white illustrated catalog

The American Foundation For the Blind puts out a very useful catalog called *Products For People With Vision Problems*. Several clocks, timers, and watches are available
with raised dots or large numbers.

A Braille edition of *Monopoly* is $49.50 and a tactile map of the United States is
$21.95. Checkers, chess, cribbage, Othello, tic-tac-toe, bingo, pinochle, dominoes,
and more are all uniquely adapted for the visually impaired.

You can also buy specially designed educational items such as infant learning
blocks, foam letters and numbers, and tuzzles (touch puzzles), as well as everyday
tools and instruments such as a childproofing safety kit, a measuring tape, and a
bathroom scale with a waist-high dial.

■ Anatomical Chart Company

Charts, posters, and books on health and nutrition.
See page 177 under **Science and Nature.**

■ Armchair Shopper

Electronic device that beeps when child wanders away, includes water safety alarm and an emergency call button. See page 102 under **Gifts.**

■ Cycle Goods

Bicycle helmets for children. See page 190 under **Sports Equipment.**

■ Hazelden Educational Materials

Books for older children on AIDS, alcohol abuse, eating disorders, and other health-related topics. See page 33 under **Books.**

■ James Kaplan Jewelers

Children's smoke detector disguised on a wall hanging. See page 107 under **Gifts.**

■ Kapable Kids/The Able Child

P.O. Box 250, Bohemia, NY 11716, (800) 356–1564

Free 20-page color catalog

Founded by pediatric occupational therapists, The Able Child is one section of a larger catalog that offers developmental materials for special needs children. Sign Language Coloring Books teach preschool and elementary kids basic sign language words ($5.95 each). Adapter parts for tricycles encourage independence and include upright handle bars, back supports, and bike boots (wooden stirrups that bolt to pedals and have Velcro straps to secure feet). A hardwood rocking horse with a safety belt, and foot positioner is $165.00 for a 12-inch-high seat and $225.00 for a 19-inch-high seat. The Able Child also offers shape and texture puzzles, multigrip cutlery for those with grasping or arm movement difficulties, a food bumper to help keep food on the plate and assist with self-feeding, and a Universal Cuff (a leather pocket with an elastic strap that slips over the hand and enables function without hand grasp) which helps with such tasks as toothbrushing.

■ Kimbo Educational

Audiocassettes on health and nutrition.
See page 173 under **Records, Tapes, and CDs.**

■ L.L. Bean, Inc.

Child-sized life vests. See page 196 under **Sports Equipment.**

■ Perfectly Safe

7245 Whipple Avenue N.W., N. Canton, OH 44720, (216) 494–4366

Free 32-page black-and-white illustrated catalog

Conscientious parents will appreciate this great source of safety products for your home and children. Along with the standard quick-release gates and cabinet latches, they sell cushions that slip over sharp table corners, doorknob covers that are easy for adults to open but not for toddlers, and easy-reach light switch adaptors that enable small children to turn electrical connections on and off.

Two-way portable nursery monitors, automatic light-sensitive nightlights, and bathtub baby sitters are tried-and-true home safety helpers. Other practical aids are toy chest lid supports, crib warmer thermo-lined mattress pads, bed guard rails, and pool alarms. Kindergaard life vests for infants and children, bicycle helmets, bike seats, Snoopy smoke alarms, and more are offered here for your peace of mind.

■ Piragis' Northwoods Company

Unbreakable sunglasses with UV protection; life vests. See page 80 under **Clothing**.

■ Preventive Dental Care, Inc.

1147 E. Broadway #34, Glendale, CA 91205

$2.00 for a 26-page black-and-white illustrated catalog

If you can help your children develop good oral health habits, many dental problems can be avoided.

This very thorough catalog, presented by practicing dental hygienists and dental consultants, offers dozens of useful products for the whole family. Look for toothbrushes, floss helpers, mouth mirrors, retainer containers, and an orthodontic toothbrush designed for cleaning around brackets and orthodontic bands.

A handy selection of pre-packaged kits includes a Kid's Kit ($4.95) that contains a novelty character toothbrush and paper cups, a floss holder, a mouth mirror, and a tube of fluoridated toothpaste.

Some fun incentives for kids are a combination cup and brush holder with a three-minute timer, a dental game book, a first dental visit book, and a tooth fairy pillow.

■ Practical Parenting

Books for parents on toilet training and ear-tube surgery. See page 38 under **Books**.

■ SelfCare Catalog

P.O. Box 130, Mandeville, LA 70470-0130, (800) 345–3371

Free 39-page color catalog

With the belief that individuals can do more for their own health and well-being than any doctor, hospital, drug, or exotic medical device, SelfCare offers products designed to help consumers help themselves. While this catalog features products for the whole family, parents will be especially interested in items that make child care easier and safer.

You may purchase natural sunscreens made from herbal extracts that double as insect repellents. An earscope ($24.00) will help detect developing ear infections. A babysling infant carrier and matching diaper bag can be purchasd as a set for $80.00 or separately for $44.00 each. Helpful videos include *Parenting, The Miracle of Life, Super Sitters,* and *Baby Basics.*

■ Seventh Generation

310 Farrell Street, South Burlington, VT 05403, (800) 456–1177;
in Vermont, (802) 862–2999

Free 32-page color catalog

Seventh Generation's motto is "Products for a healthy environment," with a focus on healthy alternatives for basic care products. Six pages of the catalog are devoted to items especially for children.

You will find dioxin-free baby wipes, natural-ingredient baby shampoo, talc-free powder, and biodegradable soap. Dioxin-free biodegradable diapers are available at $11.95 per package; the number of diapers per package will vary, depending on their size, from 28 to 60 per box. Cloth diapers, diaper inserts, and Nikky terry pants are also available.

If Earth's Best 100 percent organic baby food is not available in your grocery store, you can buy it by the case ($19.95), or try their sampler pack (six jars of different flavors) for $5.95.

A selection of environmentally sound toys and science kits will please children in the elementary grades. Look for a bug bottle, an ant farm, a lucite birdfeeder, a hydroponic greenhouse, a solar experiments kit, and solar-powered models ($18.95 each), including an airplane, helicopter, and windmill.

Snips and Snails and Walnut Whales ($8.95) is a lively book that presents 100 inventive nature crafts. Leaf-printing, birdhouse building, and daisy-chain construction are just a few examples of the activities in this 288-page book aimed at six-year-olds.

Hobby Supplies

■

■ Hobby Surplus Sales

287 Main Street, P.O. Box 2170, New Britain, CT 06050, (800) 233–0872

$3.00 for 128-page black-and-white illustrated catalog

This catalog is jam-packed with more than 6,000 items for hobbyists of all kinds. Hobby Surplus has been in business for more than sixty years, so you can count on their service and expertise.

They feature model airplanes, cars, and boats, die-cast cars and trucks, ship models, rocket kits, science supplies, slot racing equipment, and radio-control cars. They also offer stamp collecting supplies, baseball cards and collecting kits, coin collecting kits, and several sets of dollhouse furniture kits.

Almost half of the catalog is devoted to model trains and train supplies of all scales, brands, and types, including steam trains. You can buy scenery, signs, decals, buildings, and tracks, plus all sorts of electrical supplies, tools, and replacement parts.

COINS

■ Colonial Coins, Inc.

909 Travis Street, Houston, TX 77002, (800) 231–2392; in Texas, (800) 392–4716

Free 27-page black-and-white illustrated catalog

United States coins, Spanish treasure coins, gold and silver coins of Mexico, gold proofs from bullion, and official Texas bullion are some of the items sold by Colonial.

Because this firm is in the Longhorn State, you will find an especially large number of Mexican and Texan coins.

■ L & C Coins

3215 E. Seventh Street, Long Beach, CA 90804, (800) 533–0790;
in California, (213) 434–0953

Free 49-page black-and-white illustrated catalog

L & C Coins offers a wide selection of U.S. coins sold as singles, sets, proof sets, type coins, and gold coins.

All coins are graded according to ANA standards. A clear, easy-to-read index will help you find the coins you want. Please note that if you plan to pay by credit card, a $50.00 minimum order is required.

■ Littleton Coin Company

253 Union Street, Littleton, NH 03561, (603) 444–5388

Free 68-page black-and-white illustrated catalog

Serving collectors for more than forty-five years, Littleton Coin Company sells copper, nickel, silver, and gold coins, as well as U.S. currency notes and collecting supplies, books, and reference guides. Sets and single coins are offered.

Littleton will send ten bonus coupons for each dollar of your order. Save up these "profit shares" and you can trade them for free catalog merchandise.

■ Trident Coins Ltd.

P.O. Box 335, Maldon, Essex CM9 8UP, England, Phone: 0621 891858

$3.00 for a 24-page black-and-white illustrated catalog

When your coin hobbyist wants something with a continental flair, look here for British gold coins. Perhaps a set of George V sixpences or the silver penny-halfpenny of William IV and Victoria will add a cosmopolitan touch to the collection.

You might want to consider a German-made display system by Linder. The best storage idea I have seen, its quality coin trays are covered in red velour and slide out from a rigid transparent case. A variety of sizes will handle all your needs.

■ Village Coin Shop

Route 125, Box 207, Plaistow, NH 03865, (603) 382–5492

$.25 for 25-page black-and-white illustrated catalog

In business for twenty-eight years, The Village Coin Shop offers a large selection of collector's coins, sets, silver bars and medallions, currency, books, accessories, and supplies.

A Beginners' Kit is available for $12.95 and includes a 208-page question-and-answer book, a Lincoln Cents folder, a Jefferson Nickels Folder, two coin tubes, fifteen coin mounts, a hobby magnifier, and a coin collector's check list of recently issued, popular U.S. coins.

Reference books on Canadian coins, altered and counterfeit U.S. coins and currency, and more are on the catalog's bookshelf.

The Village Coin Shop's approval service allows you to examine selected coins for ten days. Pay for the coins you keep and return the others in the original packing.

MODELS

■ Estes Industries

P.O. Box 227, 1295 H Street, Penrose, CO 81240, (719) 372–6565

$1.00 for a 64-page color catalog

Estes Industries is the world's leading supplier of model rockets and rocketry supplies.

Kits for every skill level are available. Recommended for the beginning model builder is a Rascal Flying Model Rocket; almost 14 inches tall with a 12-inch parachute, it sells for $33.99. With four AA batteries, the finished product can be launched hundreds of feet into the sky. The advanced enthusiast might be interested in a Space Shuttle Orbiter for $21.29.

Among the hundreds of models are replicas of the Space Shuttle and other actual rockets, as well as repair kits, accessories, and launch equipment.

■ Hobby Lobby International, Inc.

5614 Franklin Pike Circle, Brentwood, TN 37027, (615) 373–1444

$2.00 for 103-page black-and-white illustrated catalog

Here is everything you need to make all types of model boats and planes. In addition to dozens of kits for radio-controlled models, you can also order electric and rubber-band powered models. The catalog's parts department includes a tremendous selection of useful tools and hardware.

If you are exploring model building as a novice enthusiast, peruse the catalog's very helpful instructions and advice on how to get started on this popular and exciting hobby.

■ Model Expo, Inc.

P.O. Box 1000, Industrial Park Drive, Mt. Pocono, PA 18344, (800) 821–0200

Free 120-page black-and-white illustrated catalog

Model Expo's manufacturing division is the oldest ship model factory in America and offers superb replicas you can build yourself. Kit materials include premium woods, cotton rigging, and ready-to-use fittings of precision-cast white metal, turned brass, and Brittania pewter.

In addition to ships, you will find models for radio-controlled boats, airplanes, HO-scale Carnival series, HO-scale trains and accessories, and cars.

To make your choice of the right kit easier, Model Expo has rated all the models according to level of difficulty. Look for beginner, intermediate, advanced, and master builder levels.

■ Tower Hobbies

P.O. Box 778, Champaign, IL 61820, (800) 637–4989

$3.00 for 321-page color catalog

Tower Hobbies has been the premier supplier of fine radio-control models for seventeen years. This weighty tome includes hundreds of remote-controlled airplanes, boats, cars, helicopters, tanks, and even fully operational submarines. Considered by some to be the radio-control hobbyist's bible, the catalog also offers extra radios and engine accessories, adhesives, paints, tools, books, and replacement parts.

Satisfaction is guaranteed or you can return the merchandise (in new and unused condition) within ten days for a full refund or exchange.

ROCKS AND MINERALS

■ D. J. Mineral Kit Company

P.O. Box 761, Butte, MT 59703-0761, (406) 782–7339

$1.00 for a 47-page black-and-white illustrated catalog

D. J. Minerals sells dozens of minerals, rocks, and combination kits that use the highest quality specimens available for the price. The rocks and minerals are packaged in heavy cardboard display boxes with cardboard partitions. All specimens are numbered and an identification key provides information on each rock or mineral.

Among the many kits offered, a 16-specimen standard mineral kit with 2 x 2-inch specimens is $12.00. "Minerals of the World" includes 100 excellent specimens for $35.00.

Hundreds of minerals, igneous rocks, sedimentary rocks, and metamorphic rocks are sold individually. You may also purchase storage boxes, tools, and field equipment.

▪ Discovery Corner

Gem and mineral sets. See page 149 under **Museum Shops.**

▪ Greiger's Inc.

Box 93070, Pasadena, CA 91109, (800) 423–4282; in California (800) 362–7708

Free 128-page black-and-white illustrated catalog

Make your own heirlooms with the thousands of treasures available in these pages. Greiger's has been supplying a huge selection of gems, minerals, and jewelry-making equipment for nearly 60 years. Buy the special tweezers and pliers necessary for this delicate work, and choose from hundreds of foundations for pins, rings, bracelets, and necklaces.

The kids will enjoy the selection of crystal-growing kits, prospecting supplies, and rock and mineral and fossil sets. Several books and a few videos will give you advice, instruction, and ideas. Sterling silver and gold chains and settings are among the choices.

▪ Learning Things, Inc.

Rock and mineral kits. See page 181 under **Science and Nature.**

▪ The Penny Whistle

Rock and Mineral Hunt kit. See page 230 under **Toys.**

▪ The Thurston's

385 Central Street, Boylston, MA 01505, (508) 869–2435

Send two $.25 stamps for a 7-page description and price list.

Minerals for the collector are the order of the day in this compact mine of quality specimens. Fair prices and accurate descriptions are the standard here, and every mineral is sold with a mention of its place of origin. You might choose black crystal and syenite, aegerine from St. Hilaire, Quebec, or goethite from Ishpeming, Michigan. Also listed are datolite, eudialite, gahnite, hackmanite, kinoite, margarite, topaz, ulexite, zoisite, and dozens more. The minimum order accepted is $2.00.

SPORTS CARDS

■ Baseball Card World
P.O. Box 970, Anderson, IN 46015, (800) 433–4229; in Indiana, (317) 644–2033

Send two $.25 stamps for a 13-page black-and-white illustrated catalog

BCW, the winner of *The Sports Collectors Digest* quality service award for six years straight, manufactures and sells baseball card supplies.

Double-polished plastic sheets are crystal clear and come in five styles (100 pages for $.12 each).

Three-ring binder albums, clear hard-plastic card holders, and clear lucite holders are offered. Two styles of baseball holders for shelf, desk, or trophy case are $2.00 each. Card sleeves, sorting trays, and boxes are all indispensable collector equipment. Order this catalog and stop saving those shoeboxes.

■ Den's Collectors Den
P.O. Box 606, Laurel, MD 20707

Free 46-page black-and-white illustrated catalog

In the card collector's catalog business for more than twelve years, Den's has amassed an amazing variety of interesting cards and card sets.

The Christmas and Winter 1989-1990 catalog that I have includes the 1989 Football Card Price Guide (football is the latest "hot" item), the Donruss Rookies set, the traded sets (Topps, Fleer, Score), Batman, and the new football card sets, Topps, Swell, Score, and Pro (wax boxes only).

Although some of the dozens of sets available go back as far as 1971, they are mostly more current card sets.

Prices are all in the ball park with a 792-card, 1989 Topps set selling for $27.00 plus postage and a 792-card 1987 Topps set going for $35.00 plus postage.

Among the excellent reference books available are current editions of *Sport Americana Baseball Card Price Guide* ($12.95 plus postage), which is considered the best reference book for collectors. *The Sport Americana Baseball Address List* ($10.95 plus postage) is the autograph hunter's best friend; it lists the mailing addresses of all players who have played in the Major Leagues.

■ Larry Fritsch Cards

735 Old Wausau Road, P.O. Box 863, Stevens Point, WI 54481,
Current card division: (715) 344–8687; Old card division: (715) 344–0821

$1.00 for 71-page black-and-white illustrated catalog

After forty-two years in the baseball card business, Larry Fritsch probably has the card you need.

The print in this catalog is incredibly small, but the inventory is tremendous. You can buy one-of-a-kind cards or you can buy cards in a series.

Football and basketball cards are also stocked.

STAMPS

■ Brooks Stamp Company

P.O. Box 62, Homecrest Station, Brooklyn, NY 11229, (718) 763–6843

$.50 for 47-page catalog (some black and white illustrations)

This is a large selection of both foreign and U.S. stamps. For the collector of foreign stamps, send a list of the countries or areas in which you are interested and they will send you a list from their enormous stock of international sets.

Stamp mixtures are available by the half-pound; a mixture of U.S. stamps is $5.00; a foreign mixture is $15.00. Also, a fair amount of stamp-collecting supplies and accessories are offered, including tongs, magnifying glasses, and mounting papers and corners.

■ Jamestown Stamp Co., Inc.

341-3 East Third Street, Jamestown, NY 14701-0019, (716) 488–0763

$2.00 for a 60-page black-and-white illustrated catalog

Started in 1939, The Jamestown Stamp Company is committed to serving the beginner, intermediate, or advanced collector.

They have a large dealer inventory and they offer sets, singles, first day covers, souvenir sheets and packets. Among the stamps offered are U.S., Canadian, and B.N.A. stamps, foreign stamps and foreign banknotes. Stamp-collecting supplies and accessories are amply stocked; you can buy tongs, watermark detector supplies, magnifiers, glassine envelopes, as well as various sizes and styles of albums.

There is a minimum order of $5.00 but you must be satisfied upon examination or you may return them within three days in the original container for credit or refund.

Some baseball cards and picture postcards are also available here.

■ Mystic Stamp Company

The Catalog for Stamp Collectors, 96 Main Street, Camden, NY 13316, (315) 245–2690

$2.00 for a 104-page color catalog

This huge, very inclusive catalog is definitely worth the money. Mystic claims to be the largest firm in America specializing in medium-priced stamps. After a look at this massive volume, I have no reason to doubt them. Hundreds of stamps, albums, and supplies are listed. Mint or used U.S. commemorative collections are offered at a substantial discount. They pride themselves on fast shipping and have a no-questions-asked, money-back guarantee.

The catalog offers very helpful advice and information to the beginning collector. A list of the terms commonly used and an exploration of the hobby's pleasure and value are especially useful to young collectors. For $9.95 a month, your child can belong to the "Lotta-Stamps-A-Month Club" where he or she will receive at least fifty (and up to 300) stamps from a different country each month.

■ Safe Publications, Inc.

P.O. Box 263, Southampton, PA 18966, (215) 357–9049

Free 56-page color catalog

Safe provides supplies and accessories for collectors of stamps, first-day covers, postcards, and coins.

Dozens of albums will keep your child's stamp collection organized, safe from damage, and easily displayed. Gold embossed labels are available for marking the albums. Specialty albums for coil strips, booklets, mint sheets, and documents are also available.

The Signoscope, the only instrument that will reveal the exact watermark on postage stamps, sells for $119.00.

Several magnifiers, an electric stamp-drying press, tongs, and a perfometer are among the supplies stocked. They also sell several styles of coin cases.

■ United States Postal Service

Philatelic Sales Division, Washington, DC 20265-9980

$5.95 for 327-page color catalog. Request "The Postal Service Guide to U.S. Stamps."

You may not have to send away for this excellent guide, since your local post office should have copies for sale.

This reference is published annually and provides current prices for United States Commemorative and Definitive Stamps, Airmail and Special Delivery Stamps, Souvenir Cards, Pages, and American Commemorative Panels.

Prices are given for unused (mint) and used (canceled) stamps.

A terrific resource for the beginner philatelist, it contains an introduction to stamp collecting, definitions of words and phrases, philatelic organizations, publications, and resources from around the world.

■ Wilton Stamp Co., Inc.

Dept. FB, P.O. Box 850, Wilton, NH 03086-0850

Free 32-page black-and-white illustrated catalog

Another fine resource for the stamp hobbyist, this catalog endeavors to provide diverse, quality selections. They carry sets, singles, covers, collections, and packets of stamps issued in the United States and in dozens of foreign nations and territories.

Wilton's Bargain Boxes sell for $25.00, $50.00, or $100.00 and contain dealer stamps, discontinued circular items, foreign sets, singles, and packets.

Top quality international mixtures imported from Great Britain are called Genuine Unpicked Charity Mix and can be ordered by the pound ($37.50) and half-pound ($19.00).

TRAINS

■ Terminal Hobby Shop

Walthers: The World of HO Scale, Div. of Wm. K. Walthers, Inc., 5619 W. Florist Avenue, Milwaukee, WI 53218, (800) 347–1147; in Wisconsin, (414) 461–1050

$14.98 plus $3.00 handling for a 784-page illustrated catalog.
Some color photographs, but most are black and white.

This catalog costs a lot of money, but you get a lot of catalog. serious collectors and enthusiastic beginners will find current information on 50,000 items for trains made by more than 300 firms.

You will find products by Bachmann, Bowser, Dico, Lionel, Faller, Pactra, Roco, and many more. Fifty pages are devoted just to scenery, 33 others feature only loco-motives. Tools, make-from-scratch building supplies, videos, and books are also sold.

This huge catalog also serves as a reference tool with its tremendous inventory of original equipment and replacement parts. A glossary of terms is helpful to novice railroaders.

Infant Products
and Equipment

■

■ American Bronzing Co.

P.O. Box 6504, Bexley, OH 43209-9988, (800) 423++5678

Free color information sheet

Any parent's resource guide worth its salt must tell you where to get your child's first shoes bronzed. Here goes:

If bronzed shoes are what you want, American Bronzing Company will give them to you. After almost half a century in this business, American Bronzing is so confident of their product that they offer a full twenty-five-year warranty. Shiny copper or antique bronzing finishes are offered, and the process takes about four weeks.

You may have the bronzed shoes mounted in one of seven styles. For example, they can be set on bookends for $24.99, or they can rest on a walnut-finish wood base for $20.99.

The information sheet arrives with a handy mailing bag for your baby's shoes, and American Bronzing Co. pays the postage.

■ Baby Bjorn

c/o Sassy, Inc., 1534 College S.E., Grand Rapids, MI 49507, (616) 243–0767

Free 24-page color catalog

Established in 1961, Baby Bjorn peddles quality Swedish baby products that come with a two-year guarantee. All fabrics are 100 percent cotton and are machine washable.

A neat Carry Cot can be used to bring baby home from the hospital, or as a liner in a carriage (allowing you to lift it and baby out of the carriage without waking baby). At $169, that is the most expensive item. Other useful and well-constructed offerings are a chest-type carrier to keep baby close ($59.00), changing cushions, washing bowls, and a washable travel changing bag ($69.00) in six fashionable colors.

■ baby-go-to-sleep center

Audiocassette with heartbeat and lullaby music.
See page 171 under **Records, Tapes, and CDs.**

■ The Baby's Gallerie

P.O. Box 458, Whitesboro, NY 13492-9976, (800) 446–5951

Free 32-page color catalog

The family that runs this company has been in the juvenile specialty business since 1946 and they offer a wide variety of baby and toddler needs. For baby care, there are Dappi diaper covers, diaper pants, tub toys, and mosquito netting. Helpful feeding time items include an airplane feeding bowl and spoon set for $8.96. Nursery lamps, musical mobiles, strollers, safety gates, and three styles of soft baby carriers will suit most needs and tastes.

Cotton Disney Babies play hats ($5.96) and jackets ($29.96) for infants and toddlers add a bright fashion touch.

A small section of oak and maple bedroom and play furniture includes high chairs.

■ Biobottoms

Diaper covers and cotton diapers. See page 51 under **Clothing.**

■ born to love

21 Potsdam Road, Unit 61, Downsview, Ontario, M3N IN3, (416) 663–7143

Free 23-page black-and-white illustrated catalog

born to love sells a variety of interesting products for nursing, diapering, and child safety. Underwire ($23.95) and soft-cup ($24.95) nursing bras are offered in sizes 34B through 38E. Di-D-Klips ($2.45 per pair) replace safety pins and are rust-resistant stainless steel. A plastic traveling potty seat folds up for easy storage ($6.95).

Neat Sheets are elasticized grippers to keep sheets from wiggling off at the corners (set of four, $9.95). Potty Locks keep your toddler from playing in the toilet or throwing in foreign objects. It fits all standard toilets and automatically locks when you close the lid.

There should be no more tears at bathtime with a Shampoo Halo ($5.95) that fits snugly below the child's hairline. One size fits children 4 months old to 6 years old.

■ CAMPMOR

Frame backpack infant and toddler carriers, soft infant carriers, BabyBag snowsuit. See page 78 under **Clothing.**

■ The Children's Warehouse

1100 Technology Place, Suite 108, West Palm Beach, FL 33407

Free 43-page black-and-white illustrated catalog

The Children's Warehouse sells basic baby products like rocking swings, high chairs, car seats, baby carriers, strollers, and booster seats made by some of the finest quality manufacturers.

Look here for long-lasting equipment by Aprica, Century, Chicco, Evenflo, Graco, Maclaren, Perego, and Strolee. Check the bargain pages that feature sale items by these famous makers.

■ Classics for Kids

Diaper covers. See page 54 under **Clothing.**

■ Claudia Pesek Designs

Patterns for premature infants' clothing; pattern for soft baby carrier. See page 3 under **Arts and Crafts.**

■ The Company Store

Stroller and car seat covers, playpen throw, crib throw in Merino wool. See page 94 under **Furniture and Bedding.**

■ Co-op America Order Service

Diaper liners and diaper covers. See page 263 under **General Merchandise Catalogs.**

■ Crabtree & Evelyn Limited

Scarborough & Co., Box 167, Woodstock Hill, CT 06281, (203) 928–2766

$3.50 for an 88-page color catalog

This is a catalog to drool over with its beautifully packaged toiletries and comestibles from England, Switzerland, and France. A small selection of items for children are lovely and of very fine quality. First, you will find an amazingly soft goat hair Baby Brush ($10.00) and a natural bristle Children's Brush ($10.00) to keep your little ones' hair neat and shiny. Bear-shaped nail brushes ($2.00) in soft pastel colors make handwashing an easy pleasure.

A page of soaps, creams, and lotions for baby's bath time are very mild, with no artificial color and only a gentle perfume. The soaps are offered in the shapes of characters from Two English classics—Lewis Carroll's *Alice in Wonderland* and *The Tales of Beatrix Potter*. Let your children splash around the tub with the likes of Tom Kitten, Peter Rabbit, the Cheshire Cat, Tweedle Dee, and Jemima Puddleduck ($3.00 each).

You will also find gentle sunscreens and lip balms suitable for children, scented drawer liner, sachets and scented powders.

■ The R. Duck Company

Diaper covers. See page 63 under **Clothing**.

■ Family Clubhouse

6 Chiles Avenue, Asheville, NC 28803, (800) 334–0411, Ext. 1207

Free 7-page color catalog

Whether you use disposable diapers, a diaper service, or home laundering, Family Clubhouse will make your work easier.

The full line of Nikky diaper covers will make you toss those scratchy plastic pants, and Velcro closures make them quick, easy, and safe to use.

If you use disposable diapers, try Dovetails brand. They are gel-free, perfume-free, and contain no plastics, and the company claims that they will biodegrade in one month. A box of 100 for size small (under 18 lbs.) is $23.00; size large (over 18 lbs.) is $27.00. You can also buy 100 percent cotton terry training pants and a neat little diaper duffle bag for holding wet diapers or bathing suits.

■ First Step, Ltd.

Hand in hand, Catalog Center, 9180 Le Saint Drive, Fairfield, OH 45014, (800) 543–4343

Free 36-page color catalog mailed in the fall and spring

These people have done a fine job of selecting both traditional and innovative products at reasonable prices. Choose from safety gadgets, books, toys, and a wide range of products that will make meals, bath, and travel easier on parents and more fun for kids. Infant products abound, but many items are offered for toddlers and children up to about ten years of age.

The catalog's bookshelf is filled with fun and educational titles, many of which allow children to interact with the story. Cloth books, board books, picture books, songbooks, and cookbooks are sold along with many audiocassettes and videos of stories and music.

The toy selection includes hard rock maple building blocks, hand puppets, musical instruments, shape sorters, car seat entertainment centers, sand and bath toys, moldable soap dough, face paints, a training tricycle, an easel, and such educational products as a teaching wristwatch, travel games, and a United States map puzzle.

A large inventory of child-care products form the third category of merchandise here. Buy a canopied infant seat, a stroller, changing table, portable potty, diaper bags, sun hats, safety gates, lambskins, infant utensils, and much more. Of the many health and safety products offered here, my favorite was a set of three terry cloth Boo Boo Bunnies for $21.95. Just put an ice cube in the bunny's back and apply to bruises, scrapes, or cuts.

■ High Peaks Cyclery
Child carriers, backpacks, toddler sled, BabyBag outerwear.
See page 199 under **Sports Equipment.**

■ Huggies Toyland Catalog
P.O. Box 3370, Maple Plain, MN 55348

Free 25-page color catalog

Huggies Toyland Catalog features Playskool brand baby and preschool toys. By collecting proof-of-purchase points from Huggies disposable diaper packages, you can purchase items at prices below the average retail price.

A deluxe baby monitor that works with or without electrical outlets is $35.00 plus twelve Huggies points. A Li'l Busy Box that attaches to crib, playpen, or stroller is $5.00 plus six Huggies points. A pink or blue musical rocking pony is $16.00 plus nine Huggies points.

If you fill out a special request card, you will recieve valuable coupons and various offers throughout the year.

■ I Love You Drooly Products
Corporate Office, 109 W. Pippin Drive, Islamorada, FL 33036, (305) 852–8967

Free 6-page catalog

If you are looking for a musical item to help soothe a crying infant, try these musical bibs, playpen sheets, or crib sheets.

A small electronic musical unit is concealed in the bib or sheet; when baby presses the "Music Spot," a tune will play once through until completion. They claim that the unit will play 10,000 times and can only be removed by an adult.

Choose from *It's A Small World, Brahms' Lullaby, Love Me Tender,* or *The Teddy Bears' Picnic.*

You can also change the selection of tunes in the sheets and bibs by ordering additional musical units for $5.95 each.

■ Ingi

P.O. Box 6111, Westerville, OH 43801-6111, (800) 344–6908

Free 16-page color catalog

This is the original European Nursery Collection created by designer Ingi de la Sorret. The entire collection of bedding, bath accessories, plush toys, and baby carriages is handmade in Belgium, Holland, France, Italy, and West Germany. The quality is reflected in the prices, so unfortunately Ingi is not for those with a careful eye on the checkbook.

A beautiful quilted diaper bag opens to a chamois changing surface and has pockets and compartments for all baby's accessories ($94.00).

A handmade bassinet with a white wicker basket covered with luxurious fabric comes complete with mattress and matching fitted sheet, its own comforter and pillow, and satin appliqué covers and handles in pink or blue ($365.00).

A combination carriage, stroller, and bassinet has a mattress with fitted matching sheet, outside over-hood, rain cover, stroller seat, and removable grocery basket ($795.00).

■ Lillian Vernon

Infant toys, safety gadgets, towels, gifts. See page 108 under **Gifts.**

■ The Mother Nurture Project

Breast pumps, breastfeeding books. See page 75 under Clothing.

■ One Step Ahead

P.O. Box 46, Deerfield, IL 60015, (800) 274–8440

Free 36-page color catalog

This superb collection gathers wonderfully convenient products for baby and toddler care. Feeding, travel, and playtime all will be made easier with the innovations and improvements offered in these pages.

Versatile baby or child carriers, car seats, strollers, security gates, bottle coolers and warmers, and a tote sleeping bag are just some of the items you will find. A folding portable bath tub would be great for apartment dwellers with little space ($17.95).

I found myself saying every few pages, "Now that's a good idea." This is a winning catalog resource for parents and parents-to-be.

■ Racing Strollers, Inc.

516 N. 20th Avenue, Yakima, WA 98902, (509) 457–0925

Free 6-page color brochure

Want to get into shape but not leave baby at home with a sitter? Well, you and baby can jog together with these well-made racing strollers. A child weighing up to 50 pounds sits in the stroller seat while Dad or Mom pushes the three-wheeler as they run. There are three styles. The Baby Jogger is the ultimate all-terrain stroller. Its big wheels and light aluminum frame allow it to roll smoothly over any kind of ground ($279.95). The Walkabout has the advantages of The Baby Jogger but is more portable ($279.95). The Twinner can carry two children up to 75 lbs. of combined weight and is 31½ inches at its widest point. It sells for $349.95.

Racing Strollers, Inc. can usually modify the Baby Jogger for special needs children. Write to them for their Special Needs information if you need this option.

■ Rubens & Marble, Inc.

Cotton crib and bassinet sheets. See page 64 under **Clothing.**

■ Sears, Roebuck & Company

Infant bedding, strollers, car seats, furniture, layette, toys.
See page 266 under **General Merchandise Catalogs.**

■ Sensational Beginnings

Crib toys, mobiles, teethers, parenting books, lullaby audiocassettes, sheepskins, more. See page 232 under **Toys.**

■ Seventh Generation

Biodegradable diapers, organic baby food, more.
See page 126 under **Health and Safety Products.**

■ Wimmer-Ferguson Child Products, Inc.

P.O. Box 10427, Denver, CO 80210, (303) 733–0848

Free 8-page black-and-white illustrated catalog

The focus here is on infant development and sensory stimulation products.

Wimmer-Ferguson began its collection with the Infant Stim-Mobile when the idea of high-contrast black and white toys for babies was practically unknown. Now research has shown that babies are more attracted to high-contrast patterns than to color or brightness alone.

The Stim-Mobile consists of four black and white designs and three faces; it comes with mounting hardware and sells for $12.50.

A two-sided mirror features a large 12 x 16-inch shatterproof mirror on one side and an eye-catching "see-scape" of black and white graphics on the other side.

All fourteen products here are washable, durable, and portable. Choose from a plastic ball rattle, squeaky toys, an activity center, a ring rattle, and a few lullaby cassettes.

Magic, Jokes, and Novelties

■

■ Abracadabra Magic Shop

Catalog Dept. 11, P.O. Box 711, Middlesex, NJ 08846-0711, (201) 805–0200

Free 16-page black-and-white illustrated catalog

A large selection of magic tricks and gag items are crammed into Abracadabra's "Fun Catalog." If you are searching for 5-in-1 Miracle Coins, a magician's cape and top hat, a 5-in-1 Miracle Wand, or the famous cups-and-balls trick, you have come to the right spot.

Kids will love to amuse or frighten their guests (or yours) with a variety of gags and practical joke items. Some tricks, such as the Color Change Flower, are easy enough for a three-year-old to perform. With a pass of the hand, a white flower changes to red. They sell for $3.99 each; buy two and get one more free.

Magic that will interest older kids is sold too. A floating-dancing handkerchief can be made to waltz, fox trot, and even rock 'n' roll; $4.95 includes a free bonus trick.

The inventory includes some practical joke items like itching powder, stink bombs, and the shocking hand shaker ring (two for $3.99).

The holiday edition features a catalog-within-a-catalog with Halloween costumes from Allstar Costumes.

■ Bethany Sales Company, Inc.

P.O. Box 248, Bethany, IL 61914, (217) 665–3395

Free 16-page color catalog

Bethany Sales Company is a direct importer and distributor of a wide selection of fireworks. All merchandise is sold and shipped with the assumption that the buyers understand their own state laws governing the use of fireworks. Obviously, only the adult purchaser should have the matches; the kids should only participate as an audience at a safe distance.

Bethany Sales offers hundreds of cones, rockets, wheels, fountains, firecrackers, spinners, and Roman candles. Merchandise is sold in case lot quantities only. Assortment packages are also available.

Along with their regular fireworks catalog, they also send two smaller catalogs of "Safe and Sane" non-fireworks items. They offer novelty snakes, paper caps, trick noisemakers, and toy smoke devices.

■ Hank Lee's Magic Factory

Mail Order Division, P.O. Box 789, Medford, MA 02155, (617) 482–8749

$6.00 for a 350-page black-and-white illustrated catalog

The outstanding feature of this jam-packed catalog is that every trick and gimmick it offers is explained. Beginners and experts alike will understand exactly what they are buying.

Hundreds of amusing and easy-to-perform tricks will appeal to youngsters. Magic Frogs, Floating Dollar Bills, Super Spikes, and Lucky Bucks all make an appearance (and sometimes a disappearance) in these pages. The prices vary widely, but the simpler gags and tricks are all in the low range, beginning at around $2.00.

■ Johnson Smith Co.

4514 19th Court East, P.O. Box 25500, Bradenton, FL 34206-5500, (813) 747–2356, Extension 2

Free 96-page color catalog

The subheading of this catalog is "Things You Never Knew Existed.... And Can't Possibly Live Without!" It is filled with hundreds of gag items, novelties, and gadgets for older children. An automated laughing mirror lets out a loud, raucous laugh every time someone picks it up to admire themselves ($13.98). For fun finger play, ten Chinese finger masks ($5.98 for the set of 10) are hand-painted and slip on the finger tip.

There is something here for most budgets, starting with a $.98 enchanted bottle that will not lay on its side for anyone not in on the secret. On the practical side, a roll-a-coin bank automatically stacks coins and is $9.98.

A deluxe magic set with thirty tricks plus a book called *50 Magical Miracles* sells for $19.95. Moving up the price scale, $99.50 will buy a deluxe gorilla suit, and $110.00 will buy a chicken suit; both are suitable for teens.

■ The Juggling Arts

612 Calpella Drive, San Jose, CA 95136

Free 12-page brochure

Since 1979 these folks have been providing juggling books and props for beginners as well as for experienced performers. The selection is reasonably priced and guaranteed against breakage in normal use. Six books on the art of juggling teach all the basics; if your coordinated youngster masters the skills in these books, there are others that proceed to more sophisticated tricks. Books sell from $5.50 to $14.95. As for props, you can buy plates and dowels for spinning, beginner or professional clubs for flipping, and a variety of balls to bounce and toss. Music to juggle by is offered on 60-minute audiocassettes. Circus themes, calliope tunes, Big Band sounds, and banjo music ($10.95 each).

■ Maher Studios
Box 420, Littleton, CO 80160, (303) 798–6830

Free 48-page black-and-white illustrated catalog

Maher is one of the largest supplies of ventriloquist products and services. Lightweight Knee Pal dummies have turning heads, opening and closing mouths, and eyes that move from side to side. All are fully guaranteed.

They also offer ventriloquist action puppets (parrot or lion for $52.95), dolls, custom carrying cases, performance stands, and how-to books.

The back of the catalog features juggling instruction and equipment, various games, magic tricks, and visual puzzles.

■ Phantom Fireworks Company
P.O. Box 66, 12900 Columbiana-Canfield Road, Columbiana, OH 44408, (800) 777–1699

Free 36-page color catalog

Aerial repeaters, shells and comets, jumbo rockets, crazy bees, and cloud dragons are among the sky-brightening wonders of the Phantom Fireworks Company. They have been in business for eighteen years and offer more than 1,000 selections.

Assortments of many different pyrotechnic devices are probably the best buy. Phantom offers packages such as the Jumbo Mid-America Assortment ($29.95) for those who want sparkling fountains, sparklers, and non-explosive fireworks. A tremendous variety is stocked at all times, but the Fourth of July is their high season. If you wait until June to order, you may get caught in the rush.

As with all fireworks, these are an exciting entertainment in the hands of a responsible adult and extremely dangerous in the hands of children. Keep all fireworks away from the youngsters.

■ U.S.T. Magic Company

2008 W. 103rd Terrace, Leawood, KS 66206, (800) 255–6124;
in Missouri, (913) 642–8247

$2.00 for a 70-page black-and-white illustrated catalog

U.S.T. Magic Company carries all those fun magic tricks that every generation of kids seems to love.

Their magic shop in Missouri is 10,000 square feet full of magic, juggling, and clown items. As you can imagine, they offer hundreds and hundreds of products.

"Be a Juggler" or "Be a Magician" kits include video cassettes and juggling or magic accessories for $19.95 per kit.

Remember the ball and vase trick? The ball is removed from the vase and put into the magician's pocket. Suddenly, the ball reappears in the vase, and then vanishes again—only to reappear in your pocket. You get the picture. You can also get the trick for a mere $2.50. You can wade through page after page of fickle nickels, floating dollar bills, vanishing coin-in-glass tricks, flying fish, and the like. Many of the tricks are designed for beginners and all come with instructions. A variety of juggling and clown accessories are also available.

■ Winkler's Warehouse of Wonders

24 Doyle Road, Oakdale, CT 06370, (203) 895–3474 (for inquiries);
(800) 223–9465 (orders only)

$2.00 for a 73-page black-and-white illustrated Professional Magic Catalog
$1.00 for a 23-page black-and-white illustrated Magic Books Catalog.
These charges are refundable with the customer's first order.

Your kids can dazzle and amaze their friends with the Bionic Card Trick, Rabbit in a Wallet, a locked card deck, coin wand, rainbow water illusions, or any of the hundreds of magic tricks and novelties available here for all skill levels. The clearly written catalog entries describe each illusion but not the secret of how it works.

The book catalog features many titles on every area of magic as well as a few more on clowning and balloon sculpturing.

Choose carefully—Winklers does not give exchanges or refunds for any reason, except for a defect in manufacturing.

Museum Shops

■

■ The Children's Museum

3000 N. Meridian Street, Indianapolis, IN 46208, (317) 924–5431

Free 16-page color catalog

Welcome to the world's largest children's museum. If you are unable to go to Indianapolis, you can have a taste of the museum's bounty on its catalog pages.

Turn any darkened room into a planetarium with the Super Star Machine ($29.95). It projects stars, exploded star fields, and constellations onto the ceiling or wall. An audiocassette tour of the night sky and the *Discover the Universe* book are included. Other weather kits and space exploration packages allow children eight and up to construct a model solar system, build a weather station, or learn about living in space.

A Shake, Rattle and Rhythm set will head your child in the right direction for Carnegie Hall. Its professional quality instruments include a tambourine, wrist bells, rhythm sticks, maracas, and gong. A cassette tape and carrying case complete the set ($49.95).

Children will also enjoy craft and science kits such as a Make-A-Mask set, a volcano kit, and a Discovery Pak that includes a gyroscope, a prism, and magnets.

Lots more books, novelties, puzzles, and games are included in this terrific catalog.

■ Discovery Corner

University of California, Lawrence Hall of Science, Berkeley, CA 94720-0001, (415) 642–1016

Free 16-page color catalog

"Toys, tools, and games for exploring the world" are yours from this innovative science center. This is a rich source of imagination builders and creative play fun. Bubble Wands create giant bubbles and even bubbles inside of bubbles. A simple recipe for bubble solution is included. For your next car trip, squelch the "Are we there yet?" questions with a lap-top Travelling Scientist that contains everything a child needs to calculate travel times, compute fuel economy, and read maps. Travel Trivia cards are included.

Wonderful for gift-giving occasions are kaleidoscope kits that are easily assembled, gem and mineral sets, a dinosaur fossil kit, and a fantastic sandscape sculpture where solids, liquids, and gases combine to create new worlds of mountains, clouds, and valleys. Your child can sleep under the stars for $27.50 with the Night Sky Star Stencil that includes an 8-foot stencil, non-toxic, glow-in-the-dark paint, brush, and simple instructions.

Discovery Corner also sells a dishwasher-safe space shuttle table setting and a construction set called a Googolplex that was a 1988 Parents' Choice award winner.

■ The Metropolitan Museum of Art
Special Service Office, Middle Village, NY 11381, (800) 635–5355

Free 32-page black-and-white illustrated catalog; also a seasonal 32-page *Presents for Children* catalog and a *Posters* catalog, both in color.

A small section of the Met's regular catalog features some lovely newborn gifts with a baby book, note cards, a calendar, and two activity books decorated with colorful illustrations from Le Journal de Bébé, an early twentieth-century French baby book in the Museum's collection.

International Circus Pop-Up Book unfolds to reveal several daring acts reproduced from a nineteenth-century original. A three-dimensional construction set called Pablo has unlimited possibilities and sells for $35.00.

About twenty titles are offered in the Books For Children section and they lean toward classics. Each 7½ by 9½-inch book has full-color illustrations and is bound with bonded leather on the spines. Pages are deckle-edged. Such beauties are quite reasonably priced at $8.95 for well-loved treasures like *Andersen's Fairy Tales*, *Anne of Green Gables*, *Heidi*, *Just So Stories*, *King Arthur and His Knights*, *Little Women*, *Peter Pan*, and *The Wind in the Willows*.

The seasonal *Presents for Children* catalog features a changing selection of books, kaleidoscopes, origami sets, puzzles, games, science kits, quality musical instruments, audiocassettes, and more.

■ Museum of Fine Arts, Boston
Catalog Sales Department, P.O. Box 1044, Boston, MA 02120-0900, (800) 225–5592

Free 96-page color catalog

This beautifully prepared catalog provides seventeen pages of delightful gifts for children.

Your children will play Beethoven or Mozart on a letter-coded keyboard that is part of a book about the great masters' lives. There are nine musical pieces and twenty-one pages of text in each book.

The Snowman Game is a board game for ages 4 to adult; players move snowman playing pieces through all sorts of winter fun on the toss of the dice ($19.95).

A charming Victorian Christmas Advent calendar is $18.95 and an educational Egyptian mummy doll adapted from one in the Museum's collection sells for $12.00.

A set of four mummy masks is $14.95; a make-your-own kaleidoscope is $20.00. Card games, illustrated books, a xylophone, a kaleidoscope, and a box of more than 100 marbles are among the treasures here.

■ Museum of Modern Art

Mail Order Department, 11 West 53rd Street, New York, NY 10019-5401, (800) 447–6662

Free 40-page color catalog

Within the colorful pages of modern designs offered as gifts for adults are five pages devoted to children. A "Paint Factory" for $27.00 begins with a sturdy bright-red carrying case that holds three 8-ounce squeeze bottles of tempera paints, three flip-top cups for mixing, and three paintbrushes; the set is completed with a plastic apron and a vinyl drop cloth in case your budding Picasso has any spills.

26 Letters and 99 Cents is a fun picture book that also teaches. A mask kit sells for $19.50 and is a *MOMA* exclusive. Materials and instructions for six animal masks leave room for your kids to express their own creativity.

Mobiles, a How to Build an Alligator Kit, a bucket of blocks, and unique puzzles are all part of the collection.

■ Museum of the Rockies

Gift Shop, Montana State University, Bozeman, MT 59717, (406) 994–6611

Free 15-page black-and-white illustrated catalog

Museum of the Rockies has a small but well-thought-out selection for children. For $33.95, a Junior Astronomer Planetarium projects groups of stars on the ceiling so that kids can learn to locate and identify thirty-one constellations.

A good selection of dinosaur items includes wooden skeleton kits to make accurate reproductions of eleven different dinosaurs for only $4.95 each. *Maia: A Dinosaur Grows Up* by John R. Hormer is a wonderful book and can be purchased in hardback, paperback, or with a read-along audiocassette. Your children might be more inclined to scrub behind their ears if they can use the Museum's Dinosaur Egg Soap.

■ The Norman Rockwell Museum at Stockbridge

Stockbridge, MA 01262, (413) 298–5231

Free 32-page color catalog

Dozens of prints by this master illustrator are suitable to hang in a child's bedroom or playroom. Rockwell's inimitable style is evident in prints of children experiencing first love, Santa, fishing, a favorite dog, a doctor's visit, and more.

Two books written by Norman Rockwell's son, Thomas, are lively children's fare: *How to Eat Fried Worms* and *How To Fight a Girl*. The only other item specifically for children is a pop-up book with eight full-color movable action scenes and six double-page pop-ups. All illustrations are by Norman Rockwell; this hardcover edition is $12.95.

■ San Francisco Museum of Modern Art

Museum Books-Mail Order, P.O. Box 182203, Chattanooga, TN 37422, (800) 447–1454

$1.00 for 39-page color catalog

Interesting treats for children are scattered throughout this especially well done catalog. Kids will have hours of fun with creative books of paper crafts such as *Spooner's Moving Animals*, with designs to be cut out and assembled into a menagerie.

Wonderful watercolor or pastel handbooks are for older children and sell for $10.95 and $11.95, respectively. Boxes of pastel crayons or watercolor paints alone are also offered. A *Rainy Day Adventures* activity book includes treasure hunts, interviews, fill-in narratives, fun facts, and a sturdy case roomy enough to hold the activity book, crayons, pencils, marbles, and more. An SFMMA exclusive is a solid cherry puppet stage for $27.50. Finger puppets are extra.

Most of the toys and gifts are art-related, as are the many other books, selected especially for their illustrations or unique design.

■ The Smithsonian Institution

Dept. 0006, Washington, DC 20073-0006, (703) 455–1700

Free 64-page color catalog

A look through these lovely pages reveals many items children will love. A pretty child's wicker rocker like the one in the Ice Cream Parlor in The National Museum of American History is 21 inches high and sells for $45.00. Lovable stuffed animals from the Smithsonian's Wild Heritage Collection include a snowshoe hare, black-footed ferret, tassel-eared squirrel, and more. A pack of Presidential Playing Cards for $15.00 features official portraits of the presidents, plus other people and events in American History. A teddy bear tea set, so important for those rainy afternoon tea parties, is made of white porcelain. The most unusual items are those inspired by the madcap characters from *Alice in Wonderland*. An "Alice" croquet set includes six wooden wickets of Lewis Carroll characters, two balls, and 18-inch mallets for $22.00. There are "Alice" figures, gloves, a collector's edition of the well-loved story, and the Museum's exclusive hand-embroidered "Alice" sweater of 100 percent acrylic in sizes 2T through 6X ($42.00). You can buy astronaut and baseball uniforms in child sizes for great dress-up play and trick-or-treating.

Music

■

MUSICAL INSTRUMENTS

■ Accordion-O-Rama

16 West 19th Street, New York, NY 10011, (212) 675–9089

Free brochures

Established in 1950, Accordion-O-Rama has a tremendous selection of new and expertly rebuilt accordions. If you know the tone, size, and feature that you want, they are sure to be able to help you. Specific information can be sent to you upon request.

For a fully refundable $25.00 deposit, the company will send you a VHS or Beta videocassette tape of the top electronic accordions available. Several non-electronic choices are also shown on the videocassette and are stocked at Accordion-O-Rama.

■ Black Mountain Instruments

P.O. Box 779, Lower Lake, CA 95457, (707) 994–9315

Free 6-page black-and-white illustrated catalog

Black Mountain has been making hand-crafted dulcimers for sixteen years. Besides the traditional mountain dulcimers, they also have paper-tune, electric, and wooden variations.

If you are handy and want to save some money, they also offer some of these instruments in kit form.

A special beginner's package includes a finished dulcimer, chipboard carying case, instruction books by David Cross with companion audiocassette, and an extra set of strings.

■ Chaselle, Inc.

Musical instruments for young children. See page 87 under **Educational Materials.**

■ Children's Book and Music Center

Musical instruments for young children. See page 24 under **Books.**

■ The Children's Museum

Shake, Rattle, and Rhythm set of instruments for young children.
See page 149 under **Museum Shops.**

■ Constructive Playthings

Rhythm instruments for young children. See page 218 under **Toys.**

■ Eddie Bell Guitar

Jan Mar Inc., P.O. Box 314, Hillsdale, NJ 07642, (201) 664–3930

**$1.00 for annual 72-page black-and-white illustrated catalog,
refunded with first order**

Eddie Bell is a picker's dream-come-true with its stock of instruments, accessories, parts, and supplies available at discounts up to 40 percent off list prices. Guitars, mandolins, ukuleles, banjos, and harmonicas are among the inventory of more than 800 products.

They also repair fretted instruments and will give you a free estimate if you call (212) 594–8124. Neil Young, Bo Diddley, Emerson, Lake and Palmer, Blondie, and many others trust their guitars to Eddie Bell—you can count on these folks to do a great job.

Eddie Bell also stocks original replacement parts for Gibson and Fender guitars.

■ General Music Store

50741 US 33 North, South Bend, IN 46637, (800) 348–5003; in Indiana, (219) 271–9444

Free 38-page catalog

General Music directs its catalog to school music teachers but parents can also buy from its stock of instruments and supplies for education and entertainment. Glockenspiels and xylophones, timpani, mallets, agogo bells and bongos, omnichords, pan flutes, tambourines and ukuleles are waiting to fill the air in your house with sound, if not music.

The company employs professional musicians so if you need help in making a selection, they can offer advice.

Most items are kept in stock and can be shipped immediately.

■ Hammacher Schlemmer

Kid-scaled electric guitar with amplifier. See page 223 under **Toys.**

■ International Violin Company

4026 W. Belvedere Avenue, Baltimore, MD 21215, (301) 542–3535

$1.00 for a 56-page catalog

Established in 1933, International Violin Company's staff includes a concert violinist-violist, a resident violin maker-restorer, and a music educator. The catalog offers violins, violas, cellos, basses, guitars, and kits as well as many accessories and a huge variety of strings.

■ Lark In The Morning

P.O. Box 1176, Mendocino, CA 95460, (707) 964–5569

$2.50 for an 87-page black-and-white illustrated catalog

Anything that can carry a tune or sound a beat is carried here. Lark travels the world to offer you some of its most unusual instruments as well as those more common.

Harps, hammered dulcimers, strings, free reeds, bagpipes, winds, and percussion instruments of all kinds await you.

International musical instruments will enrich the sound of your family orchestra. Look here for African, Burmese, Chinese, Indonesian, Indian, and many, many other fascinating choices.

■ Lone Star Percussion

10611 Control Place, Dallas, TX 75238, (214) 340–0835

Free 48-page price list

The text is spare in this catalog, but if you know what you want, definitely give this large discount supplier a try. Lone Star specializes in percussion equipment and accessories and they stock every item listed.

Thousands of instruments from snare drums and timpanis to tom-toms and triangles are listed here at discount prices.

■ Mail Order Music

P.O. Box 310, New Berlin, WI 53151, (414) 784–2223

Free 24-page color catalog

Casio keyboards for the whole family are sold through the M.O.M. catalog. A colorful Muppet Baby Keyboard, on which each note on the board is represented by its own color, is $99.00. Matching music books are included. Lightweight and durable with four preset sounds and ten preset rhythms, it includes a pre-recorded demonstration tune and a 100-note built-in memory.

To begin on a smaller scale (literally), three Sesame Street songbooks with their own 8-note keyboard attached are sold for $12.95 each.

If you need note-reading help, ABC Key Stickers can be applied to your keys for $.99 a pack.

■ Mandolin Bros. Ltd.
629 Forest Avenue, Staten Island, NY 10310-2576, (718) 981–3226

Free 46-page black-and-white illustrated catalog

Mandolin Bros. carries a large stock of guitars, banjos, and mandolins, including Martin, Gibson, Taylor, Santa Cruz, Guild, and Ovation models. More than 600 models are kept in stock, and a good supply of banjo heads, even in odd sizes, are on hand as well.

They have recently added sheet music, books, audiocassettes, and videos to their inventory.

Staffed by people experienced in music education, Mandolin always has a knowledgeable person available to answer your questions.

■ The Metropolitan Museum of Art
Quality instruments and songbooks in the *Presents for Children* catalog.
See page 150 under **Museum Shops.**

■ National Educational Music Co. Ltd.
P.O. Box 1130, Mountainside, NJ 07092, (800) 526–4593;
in New Jersey, Alaska, and Hawaii, (201) 232–6700

Free 32-page color catalog

With its large selection of band and orchestra instruments, NEMC has provided over thirty years of service to schools and parents.
Look for a full line of woodwinds, brasswinds, marching and concert percussions, drum sets, cymbals, string instruments, guitars, amplifiers, recorders, and accessories.

They also carry Passport MIDI software, winner of the 1989 Music and Sound Award, which lets you connect your musical instrument to your computer, creating a recording studio of sorts in your home. The software is compatible with MacIntosh, IBM/C1, Atari ST, Apple IIGS, Apple IIe, and Commodore 64 and 128 machines.

■ Peripole Inc.

Brown Mills, NJ 08015-0146, (609) 893–9111

Free 31-page catalog

Peripole is a manufacturer of distinctive musical instruments for education and recreation and is the exclusive North American distributor of Orff Schulwerk instruments.

A truly wide variety of glockenspiels, metallophones, resonator bells, cymbals and gongs, bell-tone instruments, tambourines, and more are sold here. They also carry accessories and some books.

For the younger child, there are five musical rhythm zoo animals. Who could resist a Big Bear Drum, a Pinto Pony Drum, a Duck Guiro, a Tom-Tom Cat, and a Bull Frog Guiro? These are all musical instruments of excellent tone and quality.

■ Philip H. Weinkrantz Musical Supply Company

870 Market Street, Suite 1265, San Francisco, CA 94102, (415) 399–1201

Free 38-page black-and-white illustrated catalog

This musical supply company specializes in strings and all accessories. They have a complete line of German strings, violins, cellos, and violas as well as cases, stands, bags, and more.

A 14-day trial period offers customers a money-back guarantee on any instrument or bow in stock. Expect to pay a five percent restocking charge for any returns.

They also sell a wide selection of quartz, electric, or non-electric (keywound) metronomes.

■ Shar Products Company

2465 S. Industrial Highway, P.O. Box 1411, Ann Arbor, MI 48106-9978, (800) 248–7427; Local, 665–7711; in Michigan, (800) 482–1086

Free 56-page color catalog

For 28 years Shar has been a leading supplier of violins and quality accessories.

Their catalog offers Lothar Seifert bows, violins by Otto Ernst Fischer, Mustang cases, Cushy bags and covers, plus many new videos, compact discs, and books.

An interesting item for children is *Musopoly*, a game designed for learning and reviewing fundamentals of music theory ($14.95). Also designed for children, "I Love To Practice Kits" are available for violin or cello.

A special Children's Music Series features supplementary books for kids three and up.

SHEET MUSIC, SONGBOOKS, AND INSTRUCTION

■ The Boston Music Company

116 Boylston Street, Boston, MA 02116, (617) 426–5100

Free; four different catalogs

The Boston Music Company is a venerable Boston institution founded in 1885 by the G. Schirmer family. They carry one of the largest selections of sheet music and books anywhere; they stock music of all publishers and have resources for obtaining any domestic or foreign music in print.

A 48-page Instrument Music catalog features piano, choral, organ, and instrumental music. You can order instructional materials, such as the well-known Williams piano series and the Tune-A-Day instrumental series.

The 48-page Organ and Choral catalog features organ music books and other organ publications as well as choral music, choral arrangements for Christmas, and choral publications from other publishers.

The 47-page Schirmer's Library of Musical Classics catalog is a complete listing of the piano, organ, vocal, and instrumental works available in the world-famous Schirmer Library.

Lastly, the 48-page Piano Vocal catalog lists music for voice and keyboard plus some teaching aids. Look here for Christmas and Easter themes, jazz, electronic keyboard, and Broadway and movie themes as well as secular and sacred vocal solos and anthologies.

■ Davidsons Music

6727 Metcalf, Shawnee Mission, KS 66204, (800) 782–SONG

Free 54-page black-and-white illustrated catalog

Davidsons Music guarantees that you will learn to play the piano, organ, or guitar with their teach-yourself method that combines books and audiocassettes. Each cassette follows the outline of the course book.

All styles and skill levels of music are offered; *Play Gospel By Ear, Beginnings for Keyboard, Patriotic Songs, Christmas Time, Hawaiian Songs, Polkas and Marches, Disney Dazzle, Songs for Children, The Medley Way Piano Method,* and *Sunday School Songs for Children* are among the many instruction books and songbooks.

The Children's Corner section has a special piano course for young children called *Music Is For Everyone*. Level 1 through Level 5 are $4.95 each. For $1.95 you can buy self-sticking decals with note names that will attach to any keyboard. They come with an 8-page booklet of instructions and song excerpts. *Sesame Street A-B-C Music For Beginners* ($5.95) contains thirty favorite songs from the popular PBS program.

Three other books for youngsters are *Christmas Songs You Like, Mother Goose Music*, and *Rhymes For Children*.

Instruction books for guitar, ocarina (a whistle-type instrument that is included), dulcimer, and harmonica are also available for children.

■ Mandolin Bros. Ltd.

Sheet music and books for banjo, mandolin, and guitar. See page 156 under **Music**.

■ Museum of Fine Arts, Boston

Letter-coded keyboard songbook of great masters pieces.
See page 150 under **Museum Shops**.

■ Shar Products Company

Games and books for music theory. See page 157 under **Music**.

■ Willis Music

7380 Industrial Road, Florence, KY 41042, (800) 354–9799;
in Kentucky, (606) 371–5050; in Cincinatti, 371–5050

Free 65-page black-and-white illustrated catalog

This large catalog is filled with sheet music and teaching materials for the piano and guitar. A special section entitled "Kindergarten Books" lists song collections.

A good selection of Christmas and Easter music can be used for vocals and instrumentals.

They publish their own teaching materials, and they can get any music in print that you request.

Several fine books can teach piano to youngsters. *Teaching Little Fingers to Play* ($2.95) and *John Thompson's Easiest Piano Course* ($2.25) are two choices. These books are also available in French or Spanish editions.

■ World Around Songs, Inc.

5790 Highway 80 South, Burnsville, NC 28714, (704) 675–5343

Free 8-page pamphlet

This neat little catalog offers pocket songbooks. Particularly aimed at schools, camps, churches, or whoever needs songbooks in quantity, they are less expensive when purchased in bulk, but you can also buy just one copy at an extremely reasonable price.

From their International Songbooks collection they offer titles like *Aloha Sampler, Songs of Hawaii* (24 pages for $1.30 each), *Amigos Cantando*, a collection of forty South and Central American folk songs with English verses, and *Come Friends Let's Be Merry,* thirty-one songs from Middle Europe. Many more include songs of Africa, the Middle East, Germany, Guiana, Czechoslovakia, Poland, Japan, India, Hungary, Spain, Burma, Sri Lanka, Armenia, Turkey, and others.

A 72-page songbook called *Very Favorites of the Very Young* is aimed at those 3 to 6 years old. *A Little Book of Carols, Let's Sing* (compiled for the Girl Scouts), and *Tent and Trail Songs* (a popular camp song book) are fun and happy collections especially good for kids.

MUSICAL SUPPLIES AND GIFTS

■ Friendship House

29313 Clemens Road, Suite 2G, P.O. Box 450978, Cleveland, OH 44145-0623, (216) 871–8040

Free 40-page color catalog

Since 1961 the Friendship House has been providing musical games, teaching aids, party supplies, and gifts to both teachers and individuals.

A wide assortment of pens, pencils, rulers, and notebooks are decorated with musical notes and various instruments. Colorful, acrylic pins are shaped as clefs, pianos, eighth notes, or sixteenth notes.

Friendship House sells umbrellas, sweatshirts, T-shirts, acrylic sweaters, tote bags, posters, rubber stamps, and party supplies—all with a musical motif.

You will find dozens of reference books, biographies of the great composers, musical games, and coloring books. Statuettes of the famous composers, postcards, bookmarks, playing cards, and even bracelet charms are all sold here.

■ Stewart MacDonald's Guitar Shop Supply

21 N. Shafer Street, Box 900, Athens, OH 45701-0900, (800) 848–2273

Free 96-page black-and-white illustrated catalog

MacDonald's has been supplying instrument repair services since 1968, offering a tremendous supply of parts and tools for building and repairing guitars, banjos, mandolins, violins, and dulcimers.

If you are in the business or a do-it-yourselfer, look here for blueprints, instrument bodies, cases, fingerboards, finishing supplies, fretwire and fretting supplies, straps, and more—all at fair prices. If you need guidance, you can order videocassettes with repair instruction.

■ The Woodworker's Dream

The 1833 Shop, 510 Sycamore Street, Nazareth, PA 18064, (800) 247–6932;
in Pennsylvania, (215) 759–2064

Free 62-page black-and-white illustrated catalog

Published by The Martin Guitar Company, this catalog contains souvenirs, memorabilia, accessories, and parts for the renowned Martin guitar. Called the 1833 Shop because that is the year the company was founded, this firm takes justifiable pride in their product. The only Martin product you cannot buy through this catalog is the actual guitar—you will have to see an authorized dealer for that.

They also sell a large variety of exotic hardwoods for those ambitious souls who want to build their own instruments.

Party Supplies

■

■ Friendship House

Party supplies with a musical motif. See page 160 under **Music.**

■ Just For Kids!

Paper goods, loot bags, trinkets, cake molds. See page 226 under **Toys.**

■ La Piñata

No. 2, Patio Market, Old Town, Albuquerque, NM 87104, (505) 242–2400

Free 6-page color catalog and price list

Fill a colorful piñata with small presents for your child and start a beloved Mexican tradition in your own family.

Available in five sizes, they range in price from $3.50 for a 9-inch miniature to $20.00 for 24-inch or 37-inch design.

Piñatas can be made in a number of styles including a bull, burro, sleeping Pedro, elephant, unicorn, penguin, ghost, Disney characters, Sesame Street characters, Santa Claus, a snowman, a witch, a pumpkin, and more.

La Piñata will also do custom orders but these have to be ordered eight weeks in advance of your party date.

■ Lillian Vernon

Holiday decorations, giftwrap, gifts. See page 108 under **Gifts.**

■ Little League Baseball, Inc.

Party supplies with Little League insignia, awards, banners. See page 189 under **Sports Equipment.**

■ Maid of Scandinavia

3244 Raleigh Avenue, Minneapolis, MN 55416-2299, (800) 328–6722; in Minnesota, (800) 851–1121; in the Twin Cities Metro Area, 925–9256

Free 96-page color Special Occasion Catalog; $1.00 for 200-page complete catalog.

You can make beautiful, professional-looking cakes for birthdays and holidays with the books and equipment sold here. The truly ambitious can even make a wedding cake.

Maid of Scandinavia sells dozens of shapes and sizes of cake molds, edible cake decorations, candy-making equipment and molds, paper doilies, and more than sixty hues of food coloring.

Among the how-to books offered is a *Children's Party Cake Book*. Many of its cake designs are based on children's fairy tales and nursery rhymes. Check other chapters for numbers, animals, and sports and hobby themes.

Paperware sets containing napkins, tablecover, plates, hats, loot bags, and invitations are available in about a dozen children's designs. Balloons, streamers, party signs, candles, and much more will be a boon to party-giving parents.

■ Oriental Trading Company Inc.

Balloon Book, P.O. Box 3407, Omaha, NE 68103,
(800) 327–8904; in Nebraska, (402) 331–5511

Free 48-page catalog

Oriental Trading Company sells balloons in thousands of styles for all occasions along with other party supplies. Halloween balloons with pumpkin faces, black cats, smiling ghosts, and friendly mylar bats will add cheer to any All Hallows' Eve party. For Christmas celebrations, choose a red-nosed Rudolph, Santa, a filled stocking, or a decorated tree.

Choose from an amazing variety of birthday, get well, thank you or sorry balloons, or pick a theme—nearly any theme—like football or baseball, and they have a balloon for you.

If you get winded just thinking of blowing up all these incredible balloons, Oriental Trading can also sell you air inflators or helium tanks.

■ The Paper Wholesaler

795 N.W. 72nd Street, Miami, FL 33150, (800) 237–6280; in Florida, (800) 367–1643

Free 43-page color catalog

The Paper Wholesaler offers more than 2,000 coordinating disposable and non-disposable party and catering supplies. Fun children's birthday ensembles come with paper plates, cups, napkins, table cover, invitations, centerpiece, party hats, blowouts, lootbags, and balloons. Designs include Sesame Street, Bobo Clown, Bunnies and Bears, Transformers, Princess of Power, Mickey and Minnie, and more.

Cake decorating supplies are also offered, and many designs are suitable for children. Banners and pennants make this a one-stop shopping place for your paper party supplies.

■ Paradise Products, Inc.

P.O. Box 568, El Cerrito, CA 94530, (800) 227–1092; in California, (800) 433–6266

$2.00 for a 72-page color catalog

Hundreds of party supplies and decorating kits are indexed here by theme for easy selection. You can throw a theme party with kits and accessories for auto racing, pirates, Halloween, nautical, Jewish, Oktoberfest, fiesta, circus, luau, France, baseball, railroad, and Western, just to name a few. You can buy cowboy hats, tiaras, pilgrim hats, and other headgear in bulk and at low cost, so all your party guests can be festively attired. Favors, posters, and dozens of accessories complement each theme. Crêpe papers, pennants, garlands, and balloons will add color and fun to the whole setting.

There is a bounty of Thanksgiving, Valentine, St. Patrick's Day, Independence Day, and Easter decorations, as well as two Santa suit outfits in economy and deluxe styles. Also look here for Bingo supplies. If your total order is less than $60.00, a $4.00 service charge will be added.

■ The Party Basket Ltd.

734 Nashville Avenue, New Orleans, LA 70115, (504) 899–8126

$2.00 for a 16-page color catalog

These party goods and favors in dozens of themes and designs will have special appeal to children. Trains and planes, clowns and cowboys, puppies, teddy bears, Big Bud, Barbie, Mother Goose, Peter Rabbit, dinosaurs, horseback riding, football, gymnastics, and baseball will add zip to your child's next party.

Invitations in packages of eight range in price from $1.50 to $2.85 per pack.

Party favors purchased by the pack offer a savings. A package of four colorful plastic sunglasses is $2.00; twenty-four jelly bracelets are $1.30, many other small gifts are available.

Party Basket also offers twenty-seven designs of piñatas for $16.99 each, with a special handling charge of $5.95 each. Double this charge if you are in a hurry and need UPS Second Day Air.

■ Stumps

Box 305, South Whitley, IN 46787-0305, (800) 348–5084; in Indiana,
(800) 342–5644; in Alaska and Hawaii, (219) 723–5171

Free 89-page color catalog

Stumps has been providing party supplies and decorations for school functions for
more than sixty years, and while you may not be planning a prom, lots of these
products can add fun to your children's parties.

Stumps has separated its catalog by month, so in the January section you will
find Happy New Year hats, noisemakers, and fringed horns; in February there are
heart balloons, centerpieces, miniature gift boxes, and lighted silk roses for Valentine's Day and cutouts of Washington, Lincoln, and Martin Luther King (with red,
white, and blue streamers) for the Presidents' holidays.

Leprechauns and shamrocks abound on the March pages, while a corrugated
paper 7-foot lighthouse rotates a battery-powered beam in the July section of nautical motifs. You get the picture—now just plan your party.

■ U.S. Toy Company, Inc.

1227 E. 119th Street, Grandview, MO 64030, (800) 255–6124;
in Missouri, (816) 761–5900

$3.00 for a 157-page color catalog

U.S. Toy Company is a wholesaler of carnival, decorating, and party supplies with a
guarantee that they will not be undersold.

Lots of theme ideas will make your parties a splash. Patriotic, Pirate, Feista, Baby
Shower, Graduation, School Days, Birthday, Halloween, Thanksgiving, Christmas,
and Chanukah are among the festivities.

Many of the goods are inexpensive, so your party doesn't have to require a bank
loan. Eighteen-inch pirate balloons are $7.50 for 10, sheriff's badges are $4.50 for 144,
party hats are $.90 for a dozen, and colorful tissue shakers are $6.25 for a dozen.

A school carnival or a carnival-theme party can be easily stocked from this catalog. Casino games, bingo supplies, other games of chance, and tickets, balloons,
prizes, and hundreds of novelties will turn your backyard into a street fair.

Pet Products

■

■ Animail Pet Care Products

2525 East 43rd Street, Box 23547, Chattanooga, TN 37422-3547, (800) 255–3723

Free 48-page color catalog

Animail has hundreds of useful and/or fun items for dogs and cats and their owners. From Crocmatic of France comes a wonderful automatic pet-feeding system for $165.00. You program it to dispense dry food once or twice a day, and it keeps fresh water available continuously. It requires six AA batteries and comes with a one-year warranty.

A green or red acrylic yarn reindeer sweater for the dog with holiday spirit is $25.00. A plush pink bed with rosebud-print canopy will provide a world of luxury for a small dog for $65.00. The Sit-'n'-Stay car seatbelt and harness system ($28.00 to $34.00) comes in three sizes and can be used with any seatbelt to keep Spot safe. Traveling cages, doghouses, retractable leashes, collars, tags, pet doors, sweaters and coats, grooming aids, and a few hundred more items from the extravagant to the practical can be found in these pages.

■ Cats, Cats & More Cats

Bull Mill Road, P.O. Box 270, Monroe, NY 10950, (914) 783–7697

$1.00 for a 20-page color catalog

This cat lover's treasure chest is filled with puzzles, switchplates, rubber stamps, candies, Christmas cards, calendars, notecards, jewelry, coasters, and more, all with a feline motif.

A set of alphabet stamps has a cat intertwined in each letter, and a self-inking stamp-wheel rolls out pawprints. Your child will be protected from April showers with a 24-inch cat face umbrella for $22.95.

■ Echo Aquarium Supplies

Box 145, Westland, MI 48185, (313) 453–3131

Free 38-page black-and-white illustrated catalog

Want to buy a fish? Echo sells aquariums and the fish to put in them. Discounts are offered on dozens of aquariums, water filters, lights, water pumps, air pumps, heaters, and other accessories. They also offer information and directions for setting up a freshwater aquarium.

An interesting variety of catfish, sharks, cichlids, tetras, swordtails, and other fish can be purchased. A $15.00 minimum order is required for fish orders.

The catalog's bookshelf includes titles of interest to pet and aquarium owners.

■ J-B Wholesale Pet Supplies, Inc.

289 Wagaraw Road, Hawthorne, NJ 07506, (800) 526–0388;
in New Jersey, (201) 423–2222

Free 95-page black-and-white illustrated catalog

The products you find in this catalog have been tried by its dog-breeder owners or by their breeder friends. Among the hundreds of offerings are dog toys, grooming aids (including several hair dryers), flea-and-tick control solutions, medications, vitamin supplements, breeding and whelping accessories, and travel crates. White rawhide bones are sold here at $.55 each for a dozen or more 3–4 inches long and $1.05 each for a dozen or more 5–6 inches long. Take it from me, that's a bargain. Our Labrador puppy casually chews on the *house* if we forget to give her a bone. More sizes and shapes of chew treats are also sold.

Peruse the book section for training guides and care and feeding advice for a variety of breeds.

■ Our Best Friends

79 Alberston Avenue, Albertson, NY 11507, (800) 852–7387

Free 20-page color catalog

Lady and the Tramp opens with this quote: "To date, there is but one thing that money cannot buy... the wag of a dog's tail." Well, if you have cash to play with, there are a few things here that may prove Walt Disney wrong. Soft dog and cat beds come in a variety of styles, including an orthopedic mattress that provides comfort for older pets and those with hip problems.

Wee Wee Pads are specially treated to attract your puppy when Nature calls. To give puppies something to chew on besides the legs of your grandmother's coffee table, twenty-five rawhide bones are $22.95.

Feeding stations, litter boxes, scratching posts, grooming aids, leashes, collars, and toys will please the pets at your house. Books for owners give advice and information on the care and feeding of many breeds of dogs and cats.

■ Patio Pacific, Inc.

24433 Hawthorne Boulevard, Torrance, CA 90505-6506, (800) 826–2871

Free color brochures and price sheet

Patio Pacific is one of the foremost suppliers of pet doors. Rover and Princess can now go freely in or out when Nature calls or inclement weather strikes. There are several models, some of which can be used on garage doors or sliding glass doors. Prices range from $69.95 for a 7 x 13-inch Instant Pet Door to $259.95 for a 16 x 28-inch Giant Security Door.

■ That Fish Place

237 Centerville Road, Lancaster, PA 17603, (717) 299–5691

$2.00 for a 129-page black-and-white illustrated catalog

The fish hobbyist shopping here will find a tremendous selection of aquarium accessories and related products at reasonable prices. To make your selection easy, they have listed the Table of Contents by both product and manufacturer. Aquarium Pharmaceuticals, Aquarium Products, Aquatronics, Blue Ribbon, Eheim, Hagen, and Penn Plax are just a smattering of the many name brands represented here.

That Fish Place does not send actual fish through the mail. Gift certificates are available and there is a minimum order of $15.00.

■ United Pharmacal Co., Inc.

P.O. Box 969, St. Joseph, MO 64502-0969, (816) 233–8800

Free 161-page black-and-white illustrated catalog

Like a "complete pet store in your mailbox," Upco offers more than 5,000 pet products at wholesale prices. Grooming aids, training equipment, first aid supplies, and many other products are available for your horse, dog, cat, bird, and other small animals.

Upco prides itself on being a leader in new product introductions and its very helpful staff welcomes your questions.

Records, Tapes, and CDs

■

■ Alcazar Records

P.O. Box 429, Waterbury, VT 05676, (800) 541–9904

Free 88-page catalog; be sure to request the Children's Music Catalog.

In business for 12 years, Alcazar is a distributor for independent label recordings. Labels aside, many of the recording artists and titles are well known. Meryl Streep and George Winston narrate *The Velveteen Rabbit*, Robin Williams and Ry Cooder bring *Pecos Bill* to life, and Pete Seeger is the voice on *Stories and Songs for Little Children*. Other artists include Raffi, Cathy Fink, Tom Paxton, Mister Rogers, Bill Harley, and Linda Arnold. Wee Sing and Sesame Street cassettes are also here.

Storytelling titles, music anthologies, and lullabies are all offered in this catalog, jam-packed with children's music.

■ baby-go-to-sleep center

P.O. Box 1332, Florence, AL 35631, (800) 537–7748

Free color brochure

This color brochure features classic and contemporary favorites of children's picture books, but the real star of the show is the *baby-go-to-sleep* tape. An actual human heartbeat recording provides the rhythm for ten beautiful lullabies. The brochure claims that in newborn nursery tests at The Helen Keller Memorial Hospital in Sheffield, Alabama, 94 percent of crying babies fell asleep without a bottle or pacifier as the tape played. Suggested for newborns and children up to six years old, it sells for $12.95, shipping included.

The bookshelf includes fairy tales, folk stories, and myths, along with titles like *The Secret Garden* and Van Allsburg selections. It too is worth a look.

■ Children's Recordings

P.O. Box 1343, Eugene, OR 97440, (503) 485–1634

Free 31-page black-and-white illustrated catalog

Here you will find the familiar music of Elephant Records, Raffi, Mister Rogers, Barry Polisar, Hap Palmer, and many other children's favorite artists. Several holiday recordings, lullabies, music from other countries, and activity songs for creative movement, ballet, and kids' aerobics will appeal to every taste.

Read-alongs feature the voices of well-known persons reading classic tales, and the poetry selection includes Shel Silverstein reciting his own poems.

The catalog lists the Notable Children's Recordings of the American Library Association from the year 1975 to 1989, and many of the ALA's choices are kept in stock. A handy preschool guide lists all the titles suitable for children under 5 years of age.

■ The Children's Small Press Collection

Learning titles for preschoolers and up. See page 25 under **Books.**

■ Educational Activities, Inc.

P.O. Box 87, Baldwin, NY 11510, (800) 645–3739; in New York, (516) 223–4666

Free 23-page color catalog

The complete Hap Palmer series, fairy tale classics, Ella Jenkins, Mother Goose favorites, and more are presented in this catalog of early childhood records, audiocassettes, and videocassettes.

Educational Activities sends this catalog to schools and day-care centers, so some choices have a sort of institutional flair. For instance, Patriotic & Morning Time Songs features kindergarten favorites like *This Land is Your Land, My Country 'Tis of Thee, America,* and *God Bless America.*

■ Educational Record Center

472 East Paces Ferry Road, Atlanta, GA 30305, (800) 438–1637; in Georgia, (404) 233–5935

Free 64-page color catalog

With 2,500 records, cassettes, read-alongs, videos, and film-strips in stock, ERC has something to keep everyone from baby to pre-teens entertained. The album cover of each item is displayed in color and is accompanied by a clear description and, thank heavens, age level recommendations. Grandparents and other gift givers are often unsure of age-appropriateness, and this feature is a boon to easy selection. The Table of Contents lists the titles by artist or subject; the extensive index lists all the titles.

Raffi, Greg and Steve, Mister Rogers, Shel Silverstein, Joe Scruggs, Ella Jenkins, Cathy Fink, Rosenshontz, and other popular artists are here, as are Wee Sing, Sesame Street, and Disney. Dance music, Christmas and other holiday music, musical plays, soundtracks from favorite children's films, and classical treats such as the *Nutcracker Suite* offer something for everyone in the family. Stories read aloud by celebrity artists are great listening at lunchtime or in the car. Foreign language cassettes for Spanish, French, German, and Italian complete the list.

■ A Gentle Wind

P.O. Box 3103, Albany, NY 12203, (518) 436–0391

Free 15-page black-and-white illustrated catalog

This fine little catalog of carefully selected children's music cassettes includes beloved classics and many new favorites. Favorably reviewed in *Parents Magazine*, *Working Woman*, *School Library Journal*, and *The Mother Earth News*, A Gentle Wind has come up with an excellent idea called Audio Catalog. If you are not sure which recording artist or what type of music your child likes best, for $4.95 each you can get a sampler tape that includes selections from many artists. Your children can become familiar with these wonderful performers and choose full-length cassettes of their favorites. There are five samplers available. You can also choose recordings of stories, both contemporary and classic.

Count on A Gentle Wind to carry many of the Parents' Choice and American Library Association's award winners.

■ Kimbo Educational

P.O. Box 477J, Long Beach, NJ 07740, (800) 631–2187; in New Jersey, (201) 229–4949

Free 40-page color catalog

These records and cassettes with a strong emphasis on educational material will make wonderful additions to a child's audio library. Such topics as science, health and nutrition, basic skills, aerobic fitness, and safety may sound dry, but you will be misled if you pass up the chance to enjoy these lively selections. Dance music, games, and nursery rhymes help teach the lessons, and the colorful companion books offered with read-along titles are sure to capture a child's attention. Filmstrips and videos are also offered, and since most items are in stock at all times, you can count on fast delivery.

■ LibertyTree

Tapes on our heritage and practice of Liberty. See page 35 under **Books**.

■ Linden Tree

170 State Street, Los Altos, CA 94022, (415) 949–3390

$1.00 for a 39-page catalog listing records and cassettes plus a 16-page color children's book catalog. The $1.00 is refundable with the first order.

Linden Tree started their children's record business six years ago and have compiled a varied, quality list. For your convenience, the recordings are listed both alphabetically by artist and alphabetically by title.

All the favorite standards are here—Raffi, Romper Room, and Wee Sing among them. The collection also features some more uncommon fare, and the titles alone should make your child giggle: *Horse in My Pocket, I'm A Delightful Child, Chickens in My Hair,* and *Milkshake, Moustaches and Bubbly Baths* sound irresistible.

With the music catalog, you will also receive their smaller book catalog. Many classic titles, with color photos of the book jackets and brief descriptions of the stories are listed.

■ Music for Little People

Box 1460, Redway, CA 95560, (800) 346–4445

Free 32-page color catalog

This beautiful and delightful catalog is filled with classic and contemporary records and cassette titles and dozens of wonderfully fun musical instruments.

Recording artists include Raffi, Rosenshontz, Pete Seeger, and many others. Taj Mahal's folksy, bluesy, sunshiney tunes on *Shake Sugaree* won the American Library Association's "Notable Children's Recording Award" in 1989 and sells here for $9.95. Carefully selected videos offer such treats as The Bolshoi Ballet's *Nutcracker*, a collection of songs the whole family will enjoy called *Just In Time For Chanukah*, the fanciful winter classic *The Snowman, Raffi's Christmas Album*, and *Raffi's Baby Beluga*.

When your youngsters are so inspired that they want to do more than sing, flip to the second half of the catalog for a terrific variety of child-appropriate instruments. A Pueblo Tom Tom is $32.00, a West African Mbira is $21.50, and easy-to-play Pan Pipes with a simple instruction book are $19.00. Guitars, recorders, harmonicas, kazoos, a ukulele, and a lap harp nearly guarantee the success of a joyous backyard orchestra.

■ Pocket Songs

50 S. Buckhout Street, Irvington, NY 10533, (800) NOW-SING

Free 64-page color catalog

These cassette tapes contain only one song on each tape, but they are a shower singer's dream. By turning the balance adjustment on your cassette player, you can remove the original vocals and sing solo with the music. Side one contains the complete performance with band and singer. Side two contains the same performance in stereo except that the vocal track is entirely removed. There are thousands of songs to choose from and each tape is $12.98.

The choices include all the superstars of past and present, plus movie songs from hits like *Carousel* and *Top Gun*. Jerry Lee Lewis, Chicago, and The Beach Boys rock away on other tapes.

Young children will enjoy a Christmas album with songs like *Rudolph the Red-Nosed Reindeer* and *White Christmas*.

FOREIGN LANGUAGE INSTRUCTION

■ Audio-Forum

96 Broad Street, Guilford, CT 06437, (800) 243–1234; in Connecticut, 453–9794

Free 31-page black-and-white illustrated catalog

Audio-Forum is one of the largest suppliers of self-instructional foreign language cassettes for children and adults. More than sixty languages from Afrikaans to Zulu are offered, and only native speakers are used in the full-length courses.

Children's tapes are fun as well as instructional and make use of stories and songs to teach the lessons. *Story Bridges* repeats foreign words and phrases in the context of familiar stories such as *Little Red Riding Hood* ($19.95). You can choose from many tapes that will help youngsters learn French, Spanish, Italian, or German.

Polyglot, a board game for two to six players, offers a fun way to build vocabulary at beginning, intermediate, or advanced levels. The game ($29.98) can be played in French, German, Yiddish, Spanish, or English.

One cassette teaches the basics of sign language. A small selection of audio equipment and supplies includes audiocassette player/recorders, a lightweight cassette player, a belt pack for carrying a compact cassette player, and a cassette organizer.

■ Berlitz Publications

P.O. Box 506, 900 Chester Avenue, Delran, NJ 08075, (800) 228–2028, ext. 434

Free 6-page black-and-white illustrated catalog

If Junior needs more help with his language studies than you can give him, maybe you ought to let Berlitz take over the job.

Leaders in foreign language instruction, Berlitz has cassettes for Spanish, French, Italian, German, Chinese, Russian, and dozens of other languages. A new audio cassette is uniquely structured to allow students to play an active part in spoken dramas.

The full-length courses, offered at a wide variety of prices, assume that the listener has no familiarity with the language. These comprehensive courses containing fifty taped lessons, workbooks, a dictionary, and a verb finder study aid are available for French, Spanish, German, and Italian ($145.00).

Travelers will have hundreds of useful foreign travel phrases at their fingertips with Cassettepaks that contain a cassette, a pocket phrasebook, and a written script of the tape. Available in fifteen languages, they are $14.95.

■ Claudia's Caravan

Multicultural, multilingual records and tapes. See page 26 under **Books**.

■ The Mind's Eye

Foreign language instruction tapes for children and parents.
See page 46 under **Books**.

Science and Nature

■

■ American Camping Association, Inc.

Nature books and nature activity books, some videocassettes.
See page 19 under **Books.**

■ Anatomical Chart Company

8221 N. Kimball Avenue, Skokie, IL 60076, (800) 621–7500;
in Illinois, (312) 679–4700

$6.00 for a 242-page color catalog

While researching this book, I thought I had seen it all until I found The Anatomical
Chart Company. This amazing catalog has a collection of more than 5,000 innovative
educational products on health and human anatomy.

You can buy plastic human skeletons and nylon anatomical body suits that show
the central nervous system, vital organs and bones, muscles, and intestines. Charts
and posters illustrate either healthy or diseased organs, nutrition guidelines, and exercise programs. Models of every part of the body include the teeth, which come
with a giant toothbrush (excellent for teaching children how to brush and floss). Although the models are a bit pricey for parents, dozens of inexpensive books explore
topics like braces, wisdom teeth, nutrition, and cocaine.

This company is clearly geared to the medical and teaching community, but
some of the charts and models may be of interest to older kids and helpful in teaching good family health habits.

Since explicit models of all body parts and organs are illustrated, some parents
may want to review the catalog before the kids do.

■ Animal Town

Nature card games, board games, and audiocassettes. See page 215 under **Toys.**

■ The Butterfly Company

50-01 Rockaway Beach Boulevard, Far Rockaway, NY 11691, (718) 945–5400

$2.00 for a 20-page color catalog

If butterflies, moths, miscellaneous beetles, and pupae are your child's thing, then this catalog with more than 800 specimens is a must. Insects arrive daily from all over the world, so this company has an ever-changing inventory.

The Creepy Bug Kit is a fine starter kit for all those interested in insects and is an excellent value at $5.00.

Mounting boards and other accessories for the collector are available, but for those who prefer their butterflies flying free, they also offer live cocoons and pupae. The cost per cocoon ranges from $2.00 to $4.50 each, but they are significantly cheaper by the dozen. Order now and watch cecropia, Imperial, Regalis, and Papilio Troilus pupae become beautiful butterflies in your yard this summer. Instructions for care and storage are included.

For craft work, paper-bodied butterflies with real wings are available in packs of 100.

■ Chaselle

Science kits. See page 87 under **Educational Materials.**

■ Childcraft

Science kits. See page 217 under **Toys.**

■ The Children's Museum

Super Star Machine, weather kits, space kits, science books.
See page 149 under **Museum Shops.**

■ Cuisenaire Co. of America, Inc.

12 Church Street, P.O. Box D, New Rochelle, NY 10802,
(800) 237–3142; in New York, (914) 235–0900

Free 110-page color catalog

This tremendous resource for math and science materials is aimed primarily at educators but is available to parents as well.

Arithmetic models, calculators, puzzles, and workbooks will please the budding mathematicians in your house; science kits and nature labs include hydroponic greenhouses, hot-air balloon kits, and chemistry sets. Microscopes, test tubes, stethoscopes, compasses, and magnets crowd the catalog's instrument section.

■ The Developing Child/Winnetka Square

The Fossil Hunt Kit with authentic fossils. See page 219 under **Toys.**

■ Dinosaur Catalog

Dinosaur models authenticated by the British Museum of Natural History. Dinosaur books. See page 219 under **Toys.**

■ Discovery Corner

Travelling Scientist, Night Sky Stencil, volcano kit, gem and mineral sets, and a dinosaur fossil kit. See page 149 under **Museum Shops.**

■ D.J. Mineral Kit Company

Minerals, rocks, and combination kits. See page 130 under **Hobby Supplies.**

■ The Dragon's Nest

Fossil and rock collection, science kits, and a star machine planetarium. See page 105 under **Gifts.**

■ Edmund Scientific

101 E. Gloucester Pike, Barrington, NJ 08007-1380, (609) 547–8880

Free 80-page color catalog

This is a must-see for the technical hobbyist and a goldmine for the child who enjoys science projects.

Much more than just microscopes, binoculars, and magnifiers, this company has terrific science projects and science novelties including solar equipment, specialty magnets, lasers and fiber optics, special effects photography items, star maps, gyroscopes, meteorological equipment, dissection instruments, prisms, holograms, and more.

■ Geode Educational Options

Science books for children from preschool through high school.
See page 31 under **Books.**

■ The Gifted Children's Catalog

Science kits, a flower press, nature and science books. See page 222 under **Toys.**

■ Greiger's Inc.

Crystal-growing kits, prospecting supplies, and rock and mineral and fossil sets.
See page 131 under **Hobby Supplies.**

■ Hobby Surplus Sales

Rocket kits and science supplies. See page 127 under **Hobby Supplies.**

■ The Home Library

160 South University Drive, Plantation, FL 33324, (800) 367–7708

Free 16-page color catalog

This catalog is devoted exclusively to fine world globes at discount prices. With
more than fifty styles to choose from, they range from $47.00 for the Lenox, a 12-
inch globe in raised relief on a solid wood base, to $4,200.00 for the 48-inch Diplo-
mat with fingertip-touch light control, an example of which is found in The White
House.

■ Hubbard Scientific Company

P.O. Box 104, Northbrook, IL 60062-9976, In Illinois, (312) 272–7810;
Outside Illinois, (800) 323–8368

**Free color catalogs: "Health/Fitness" 16-page catalog; "Weather Watch" 39-page
catalog; "Raised Relief Topographic Maps," 5-page brochure.**

Hubbard has been working with science and health educators for more than twenty
years and stocks more than 3,000 science products. The Health/Fitness catalog features items like an inexpensive yet reliable stethoscope ($7.95), board games that
focus on good health habits, and anatomical models (a bit more pricey at about
$65.00).

Weather Watch offers star charts; study prints for minerals, geology, and meterology; weather-map plotting charts; rainmaker models; globes; maps; solar energy devices; and games that deal with stars and ecology. Software and books focus on seasonal star demonstrations, oceanography, astronomy, and geology.

Raised relief topographic maps include regional maps of mountainous areas of the United States and other regions throughout the world.

■ Ideal School Supply Company

Nature and dinosaur study kits, weather and science kits.
See page 89 under **Educational Materials.**

■ Imaginative Inroads

A volcano kit, a solar energy lab, Grow-A-Frog kits, butterfly gardens, weather stations, and more. See page 225 under **Toys.**

■ Judy/Instructo

Science and nature kits. See page 90 under **Educational Materials.**

■ Learning Things, Inc.

P.O. Box 436, Arlington, MA 02174, (617)646–0093

Free 49-page black-and-white illustrated catalog
There is a minimum order of $15.00 before shipping and tax.

Learning Things, Inc. specializes in high quality, reasonably priced products designed to help educate children in the fields of science, mathematics, and technology. The company is geared to schools, but individuals may order also.

For the young scientist there is a wonderful assortment of excellent instruments, kits, and projects, some of which I have seen only in this catalog.

The equipment and kits will provide hours of educational play and can also be used for terrific school science projects. You can buy microscopes (starting at $18.00), handheld pocketscopes (starting at $2.50), a miniature pond life aquarium, stethoscopes, anatomical model construction kits, a star finder kit, magnets, prisms, binoculars, rock and mineral kits, telescopes, solar energy experimentation kits, compasses, periodic element charts, and a marvelous collection of books.

■ Miller's Fossils

1219 Glenside Avenue, Wilmington, DE 19803, (302) 478–7382

$1.00 for 6 pages of black-and-white illustrated information sheets.

If you have a dinosaur lover in your house, Miller's is the place to buy a rubber nose of a tyrannosaurus, stegosaurus or other prehistoric creature. You can order colorful embroidered dinosaur patches to sew on jackets, sweaters, or book bags, and plastic masks ($3.50 each) of several dinosaurs, a tiger, an elephant, and a fox.

Moving on to the more sophisticated stuff, resin casts of dinosaur fossils include a 10-inch tyrannosaurus tooth ($16.00), a 5-inch Allosaurus claw ($8.00), and a dinosaur skin impression ($5.00). You can also purchase a 140,000,000-year-old piece of dinosaur bone from the Jurassic Period for $1.00 each. Dinosaur erasers, pencil sharpeners, adjustable rings, and magnets are also reasonably priced for under $2.00 each.

■ Museum of the Rockies

Dinosaur items and a Junior Astronomer Planetarium.
See page 151 under **Museum Shops.**

■ National Geographic Society/Books

Science and nature books for all age groups. See page 36 under **Books.**

■ The Nature Company

P.O. Box 2310, Berkeley, CA 94702, (800) 227–1114

Free 40-page catalog

The Nature Company endeavors to share their "vision of love for the natural world," and as you look through this wonderful catalog for children and adults, you are bound to be impressed with their results.

Mom or Dad will like the 100 percent cotton T-shirts and sweatshirts, birdfeeders, nature-theme jewelry, and outdoor gear such as compasses, thermoses, flashlights, and more.

Children can choose from T-shirts, nature puzzles, globes, kaleidoscopes, posters, books, and nature kits. You can buy two boxfuls of the best-selling toys from The Nature Company's retail stores for $24.95 each. Every box includes seven toys and contains useful and educational items like an optical illusion toy, compass pen, dinosaur ruler, or tele-microscope.

A colorful cardboard mobile of an archoeopteryx, the controversial "missing link," is $16.95, and a beautiful tropical fish mobile is $16.95. A set of ten assorted magnets and an accompanying leaflet show the budding scientist about invisible lines of force.

■ The Penny Whistle

Science and nature kits such as a Giant Ant Farm or a Rock and Mineral Hunt™ kit. See page 230 under **Toys.**

■ PlayFair Toys

Science kits. See page 230 under **Toys.**

■ Rand McNally & Company

Animal videos including titles from National Geographic, National Parks Videos, and Readers Digest. See page 39 under **Books.**

■ Schoolmasters

745 State Circle, Box 1941, Ann Arbor, MI 48106, (800) 521–2832

Free 96-page color catalog

Your child can boil water and cook an egg with solar energy, identify hidden finge prints, or track weather patterns with the many fun science kits from Schoolmasters.

Lab equipment, models of anatomy, botany, and dinosaurs, earth science kits, charts, books, and videos will add a learning dimension to creative play.

Accurate models of the human heart, ear, eye, brain and skull, or nose and mouth are $10.95 each and will be a wonderful aid to understanding biology lessons.

Ant farms start at $8.95, but real estate moguls may want to purchase a deluxe six-module ant city for $21.95.

■ Seventh Generation

Science kits and nature activity books.
See page 126 under **Health and Safety Products.**

■ URSA Major

P.O. Box 3368, Ashland, OR 97520, (503) 482–1322

Free color brochure

Transform your darkened room into a dramatic home planetarium with an accurate Night Sky Star Stencil. The sizes of the stars on your ceiling correspond to the brightness of the actual stars in the sky. You can buy a winter or summer sky stencil in 8- or 12-foot sizes. The kit includes adhesive, luminous paint, brush, instructions, and a hand-held Star Map and Constellation Finder. The 8-foot stencil is $25.00 and the 12-foot design is $30.00.

The special paint glows in the dark for up to an hour, but is invisible in the light.

■ Wind and Weather

The Albion Street Water Tower, P.O. Box 2320, Mendocino, CA 95460-2320, (800) 922–9463

Free 36-page black-and-white illustrated catalog

Wind and Weather's fourteenth annual catalog is devoted in large part to weather instruments. With worldwide concern about chlorofluorocarbons endangering the atmosphere, this is a timely area of science.

Kids can measure and record the six weather elements with the instruments offered here. Most of the items are professional quality tools too expensive for purchase by parents, but a careful look will reveal instruments that will not endanger your finances. An EZ Read jumbo rain gauge is $15.00, a fold-up thermometer and humidity gauge is $13.00, a soil thermometer is $12.00, and a hand-held windmeter is $13.00. A 5-way weather watch ($7.00) that shows temperature, wind speed, wind directions, and rainfall is probably the best buy for your junior meteorologist.

■ World of Science

Merrell Scientific, Division of Educational Modules, Inc., 1665 Buffalo Road, Rochester, NY 14624, (716) 426–1540

$2.00 for a 184-page black-and-white illustrated catalog

Can butterflies smell? Where do you find a grasshopper's ears? Why does the moon shine? The answer to these and thousands of other questions can be discovered in this absolutely terrific catalog with an amazing variety of science and nature items.

Merrell Scientific provides kits, chemicals, and labware for the study of chemistry, biology, earth science, solar energy, astronomy, and more. Parents may be especially interested in these products kids can enjoy: ant farms, microscopes, chemistry sets, dissection instruments, volcano kits, crystal-growing kits, dinosaur models, minerals, star charts, terrariums, weather maps, whale posters, and much, much more.

The catalog's bookshelf is filled with titles exploring many earth sciences and includes identification guides, project books, coloring books, and reference texts.

■ World Wildlife Fund Catalog

T-shirts, books, puzzles, and more in nature motif. See page 122 under **Gifts.**

Sports Equipment

■

■ Passon's Sports

P.O. Box 49, Jenkintown, PA 19046, (800) 523–1557

Free 52-page color catalog

Passon's Sports has good values in physical education equipment for children in the elementary grades. Badminton, basketball, baseball, croquet, bocce, hopscotch, horseshoes, football, hurdles, tetherball, tennis, toppleball, and more are all sold here.

Many noncompetitive products are also available. Look for hula hoops, jump ropes, pogo sticks, and rock and balance boards.

Game tables, water trays, building toys, playground balls, and even early childhood furniture for play kitchens are sold here.

■ Strokemaster

5130 Boyd Boulevard, Rowlett, TX 75088, (800) 527–7187; in Texas, (800) 441–0061

Free 16-page black-and-white illustrated catalog

Strokemaster sells all the accessories (some basic, some fancy) that you might need on or near the tennis court—all, that is, except rackets. Expect to find scorecards, Tidy Masters to hold drinks and trash, water brooms, water coolers, balls, and ball machines.

■ Things From Bell

P.O. Box 206, 230 Mechanic Street, Princeton, WI 54968, (800) 543–1458

Free 100-page color catalog

Cricket anyone? Bring a little European flair to your backyard with this or any of the hundreds of physical education products for early childhood.

Hours of fun can be had with Softee baseball, lacrosse, Bataca, balance boards, broomball, Do-Nut Rings, Feather ball, tetherball, miniature table tennis, jacks, and juggling equipment. Softee Hockey combines elements of polo, floor-, field-, and ice-hockey with stick heads made from safe, soft urethane foam.

Bell also supplies some storage units and wooden play tables and chairs.

This catalog is directed to educators, so a $4.00 service charge is added to orders under $25.00

ARCHERY

■ Anderson Archery Catalog
Box 130, Grand Ledge, MI 48837

Free 74-page black-and-white illustrated catalog

Archery buffs will hit the bull's-eye if they search for equipment in this catalog. Aim here for archery accessories as well as bows and arrows.

All of Anderson's arrows are custom fletched on Bitzenburger Fletching tools and are dipped in Bohning clear Fletchlac. They use Trueflight feathers, Marco vanes, and Plastinocks. Easton Aluminum makes the aluminum shafting.

You can buy youth bows and sets for young archers. A set with a 50-inch Glass-flex bow, three 26-inch target arrows, a side quiver with belt loop, tab, a multi-colored target face, and instructions sells for $22.99.

They also sell bowsights and targets.

■ Bow Hut
2214 S. Mooney Boulevard, Visalia, CA 93277, (209) 734–2882

Free 103-page black-and-white illustrated catalog

This great big catalog presents an incredible array of bowhunting supplies and is a valuable source of useful information and practical advice. Along with its hundreds of bows, quivers, bow arrow cases, points inserts, vanes, and feathers, Bow Hut also offers advice on how to choose the right bow and how to make arrows.

■ The Sport Shop Inc.
P.O. Box 340, Grifton, NC 28530, (800) 334–5778; in North Carolina, (800) 682–6264

Free 64-page color catalog

After thirty-four years in business, The Sport Shop knows its bows and quivers. Choose from dozens of bows, bow cases, shafts, arrows, arrow decals, nocks, arrow straighteners, points, sharpeners, and more.

BASEBALL, BASKETBALL, FOOTBALL, AND SOCCER

■ Athletic Supply

10812 Alder Circle, Dallas, TX 75238, (800) 635–4438

Free 48-page NFL color catalog, or 16-page NBA color catalog

Athletic Supply offers two gift catalogs—one for NBA items and the other for NFL items, so be sure to ask for the one you want. If basketball is your child's game, the NBA catalog has authentic starter jackets, uniforms, logo-embossed sneakers, sweats, hats, warm-up pants, and 100 percent cotton jams. All these items will be hits with teens. Younger kids will like the T-shirts ($13.95) with official team insignia for such popular clubs as the Celtics, 76ers, and Knicks.

The NFL catalog has authentic jackets, winterwear, sweats, jerseys, workout clothing, caps, practice shimmels, license-plate frames, mug sets, and more.

■ Little League Baseball, Inc.

P.O. Box 3485, Williamsport, PA 17701

Free 60-page color catalog

Little League is the world's largest youth sports program and the organization's own catalog offers everything young sluggers might need.

Party supplies with Little League insignia are great for parties, banquets, and meetings. Embroidered caps, banners, seat cushions, rule books, helmet and face-guard systems, pitching machines, approved awards, and batter's gloves will please players, parents, and coaches.

Several companies advertise their baseball equipment in this catalog, and of those, several have their own catalogs that you may request.

■ Soccer International, Inc.

P.O. Box 7222, Arlington, VA 22207-0222, (703) 524–4333

$1.00 for a 15-page color catalog

Does your child want to read about soccer? Watch soccer on videotapes? Set up a playing field? Everything you need to please a soccer fan can be found in these pages.

Uniforms, balls, cork-handled referee and linesman flags, first aid supplies, room decorations, and gifts with soccer motifs are all offered at reasonable prices. Soccer balls range from $6.75 for a size 1½ mini-ball to $79.75 for a size 5 handsewn leather Mitre Multiplex ball.

BIKING

■ Bike Centennial

P.O. Box 8308, Missoula, MT 59807-8308, (406) 721-8719

Free 24-page color catalog

Bike Centennial specializes in maps and products for bike touring. They have developed several biking maps that will guide cyclists on trips from Canada to California, along the California coast, from Maine to Virginia, and from Virginia to Florida. To make these treks easier, they also sell panniers, racks, rain covers, small packs, raingear, tents for touring, sleeping bags, transam wheels, and guide books for shorter distance riding.

■ Cycle Goods

2801 Hennepin Avenue South, Minneapolis, MN 55408,
(800) 328-5213; in Minnesota, (612) 872-7600

$2.00 for a 107-page color catalog

Some rather extraordinary bicycles as well as every kind of part and accessory imaginable are shown in this "Handbook of Cycl-ology."

Ten pages of bikes include specialized models such as Team Stumpjumper, Rockhopper Comp, Hardrock, Sirrus, Allez Epic, Guerciotti, Tommaso, Masi, Gitane, and Rossin. A large inventory of bicycle parts will help you rebuild or repair your machine.

Look also at the serious cyclist's apparel, shoes, helmets, gloves, glasses, and carriers. Helmets for children, now widely recommended by healthcare professionals, are available as well.

■ Mountain Bike Specialists

340 S. Camino Del Rio, Durango, CO 81301, (800) 255–8377

Free 32-page black-and-white illustrated catalog

In recent years, cycling enthusiasts have been praising the versatility of mountain bikes. More rugged than the slim-line ten-speeds we have been riding, they have three chainrings in the front instead of the traditional two. Great for off-road cycling, they are available with up to twenty-one gears.

Assembled bikes by Brave, Fat Chance, Fisher, Klein, LiteSpeed, Merlin, Off Road, and Ritchey are offered. If you wish to customize, you can choose your own components from their wide selection. Dozens of frames, forks, pedals, brakes, handlebars, seatposts, and more are available in many traditional and spunky color choices. Prices generally start around $500 for an assembled bike.

Look here for shoes, helmets, T-shirts, gloves, duffles, roof racks, bike mounts, and more.

■ Performance

One Performance Way, P.O. Box 2741, Chapel Hill, NC 27514, (800) 727–2453

Free 64-page color catalog

Performance offers cycling accessories and gear that will appeal to the older enthusiasts in the family.

Colorful wind jackets and pants, jerseys for summer and winter, vests, turtlenecks, and hats come in stylish designs to fit teens and adults.

Thermax long underwear, Gore-Tex outerwear, cycling shorts, shoes, socks, helmets, waterbottles, cages, and training equipment are well stocked and backed by a 100 percent guarantee. Look here also for many good quality bicycle parts.

DANCE, GYMNASTICS, AND FITNESS

■ Ballet Barres

P.O. Box 261206, Tampa, FL 33685, (800) 767–1199

Free color brochure and price list

If your own prima ballerina wants to practice at home, you may want to invest in a ballet barre for your playroom or basement.

For twenty-four years, this company has been providing durable, quality barres to customers like the Chicago City Dance Theater, the Charleston Ballet, the Metropolitan Ballet of St. Louis, and the Philadelphia Performing Ballet.

Traditional models that fasten to the wall are available in several styles, or you may prefer their sturdy, all-steel portable barres.

■ Hoctor Products for Education

P.O. Box 38, Waldwick, NJ 07463, (201) 652–7767

Free 88-page black-and-white illustrated catalog

A treasure trove of music, records, and videos for dancers, this catalog presents a special section devoted to dance music for pre-school and the early grades. The music for complete children's ballets (*The Magic Garden, Mother Goose Ballet, Westward Ho, The Ballet of The Enchanted Dolls,* and *Color Me Ballet*) is arranged especially for easy use with young children. Tap, jazz, and gymnastics music are also on the program.

A minimum order of $50.00 is required, and there are no refunds or exchanges on records and educational material.

■ Taffy's-By-Mail

701 Beta Drive, Cleveland, OH 44143, (216) 461–3360

$3.00 for a 98-page color catalog that comes with a $5.00 gift certificate.

A must for dancers, gymnasts, cheerleaders, and exercise buffs, this catalog holds a huge, quality inventory of leotards, tights, and shoes for pointe, gamba, ballet, tap, jazz, and gymnastics. Clothes and accessories are offered by Capezio, Bal Togs, Body Wrappers, Danskin, Baryshnikov, and others. The pretty dance costumes alone will make your feet start tapping. You can also order dance and exercise videos, records, and cassettes.

If you want more costumes, ask for the Showstoppers Costume Catalog for $5.00. It offers a beautiful selection of costumes in adult and children's sizes, for use in dance programs, parades, and other festivities, including trick-or-treating.

EQUESTRIAN

■ The Elegant Equine

225 East Deerpath, Lake Forest, IL 60045, (708) 234–6901;
(800) 624–9415 (for orders only)

Free 33-page color catalog

The Elegant Equine features luxury gifts for the horse lover in your family. After thumbing past the $10,000 hand-carved horsehead necklace made from 70-carat rubellite tourmaline, I came upon some reasonably priced fare. A plush bear and fox dressed for the hunt are nineteen inches tall and cost $52.00 each. Black, gray, or chestnut horses are fourteen inches tall and are $35.00. A hobby horse with a plush black or brown head and mane mounted on a 33-inch pole is ready to ride for $15.00. Children's pajamas with hunt scenes are made of flame-retardant flannel, and a sweatshirt with a horse on the front can be personalized with your child's name.

■ J. Eiser's

P.O. Box T, Huzleton, PA 18201-0096, (800) 526–6987; in Pennsylvania, (800) 626–8139

Free 120-page color catalog

Everything for the horse and rider is pictured in this huge catalog of equestrian supplies. You will find finely crafted saddles imported from England, France, and Australia and a new "feeling" saddle ($398.00) that allows subtle body language messages to pass through a polymer foam core. Western and English saddles, halters, bridles, bits, crops, stirrups, pads, blankets, groom aids, and more are offered in many styles and models.

Riding apparel for both adults and children includes hats, coats, jodhpurs, boots, and protective gear. Riding experts and students, as well as horse enthusiasts of any kind, will find titles of interest among the selection of books and videos.

■ Miller's

235 Murray Hill Park, East Rutherford, NJ 07073, (216) 673–1400

Free 147-page color catalog

From the most fashionable in equestrian clothes to a revolutionary "Lastic" figure 8 noseband for your horse to Korsteels "itty bitty pony bits," it is difficult to imagine that the horse lover could want anything that cannot be found here.

One of the world's largest suppliers of riding equipment and clothing, Miller's designs many of its products and imports others from around the world. The quality is good and the variety is tremendous.

Handsome children's breeches and jods in a variety of colors start at size 6. Equestrian II riding coats are $73.95 in girls' even sizes 8-16. Boots, shirts, and stock ties can outfit every member of your family.

Once your child is appropriately attired, choose gear for your horse. Dozens of saddles, bits, muckers, muzzles, neck cradles, polo equipment, runs, valet brushes, and other supplies will fill all the needs of horse, stable, and tack room. Videotapes and books are also stocked, and your complete satisfaction is guaranteed or your money is refunded.

■ Schneiders Saddlery and Western Wear

1609 Golden Gate Plaza, Cleveland, OH 44124, (800) 365–1311

Free 136-page color catalog

In business for more than thirty-five years, Schneiders carries basic equestrian necessities, as well as distinctive extravagances.

Your child will definitely make a splash with a limited edition saddle with silver trim and hand-tooled detailing for $3,395.00. If that price worries you, be assured they also carry quality basics at reasonable prices and oh, what a selection.

Arabian show equipment, pages of saddles, coordinated show equipment, training and using bits, snaffles, and halters and halter accessories are all here. Also offered are suits, hats, hat carriers, jod boots, show and work gloves, and a good selection of novelties for the horse lover.

■ State Line Tack, Inc.

P.O. Box 428, Route 121, Plaistow, NH 03865, in New Hampshire, (603) 382–4718; outside New Hampshire, (800) 228–9208

Free 140-page black-and-white illustrated catalog

You will be ecstatic at the terrific savings you can realize at this discount tack store. Children's Brentwood breeches that retail for $37.95 are listed here for $29.90. An Olympic velvet helmet listed for $89.95 is offered for $67.80. A children's paddock shoe by Savoy that retails for $64.95 is $49.90.

Look for similar discounts on other quality items such as saddles, bits, reins, stirrups, neck cradles, manure forks, muzzles, blankets, gifts, gloves, and hundreds of other products for the horse and horse lover.

FISHING

■ Bomber Bait Company

P.O. Box 1058, Gainesville, TX 76240, (817) 665–5505

$.50 for 30-page color catalog and price list.

Bomber Bait Company has been designing and improving lures since the late 1930s, and they offer hundreds of them here, photographed in full color.

They sell their own painstakingly designed "crank bait" in eight performance variations. Minnow Type lures and sound-vibrating lures are also available. Custom-build your own Bushwacker lure by choosing any combination of skirt and blade.

You will also find dozens of spoons and jigs. So thumb through this interesting, colorful catalog, and as they say, "Tie one on!"

■ Capt. Harry's Fishing Supply

100 NE 11th Street, Miami, FL 33132, (800) 327–4088

$3.00 for a 41-page color catalog

Captain Harry's has long been one of the largest suppliers of salt water fishing tackle, and with the recent addition of a complete saltwater fly fishing department, this is truly one-stop shopping.

Professional fishermen from more than a hundred countries have bought their custom rods and reels here.

You will find dozens of reels, swivels, scalers, knives, hooks, gaffs, and jiggs, plus lures by Boone, Porter, Moldcraft, and Rapala. Salt water flies and other fly fishing supplies are available if you want to tie your own. Capt. Harry's also offers gift certificates.

■ Eppinger Mfg. Co.

6340 Schaefer, Dearborn, MI 48126, (313) 582–3205

Free 24-page color catalog

Eppinger began it all when they made the now-classic red and white Daredevil fishing lure. Now, thirty years later, they carry more than 4,000 sizes, shapes, and colors of lures.

Spinners, Midgets, Skeeters, Klickers, Bucktail Flies, and hundreds more are shown here in full color. On the back of the price list, a lure guide recommends those lures most irresistible to bass, trout, salmon, panfish, and other species.

■ Fishing Hot Spots

1999 River Street, P.O. Box 1167, Rhinelander, WI 54501-1167, (800) 338–5957

Free 48-page color catalog

A good fishing book, an instructional fishing video, a fish art print, or a lure-making kit all can be found here. Fishing Hot Spots has lots of how-to and guide books, fishing equipment, cookbooks, and much more.

Check here for an extensive line of fishing maps and lake reports from all over the United States, and peruse the list of magazines that will be of interest to fishing enthusiasts.

■ L.L. Bean, Inc.

Freeport, ME 04033-0001, (800) 221–4221

Free 56-page color catalog. Request Fly Fishing Catalog.

When you see the L.L. Bean name, you can be sure that you will be ordering functional, good-quality products at a no-nonsense price. Well, it turns out that old "L.L." himself was an avid fisherman, and the staff of his original store included experienced local fishermen and professional guides. The tradition continues. Look for a large selection of fresh and/or saltwater fly rods in standard sizes or a 4-piece packable travel size, and dozens of reels, downriggers, carrying cases, traveling bags, fly lines, leaders, tackle, waders, hippers, flies, vests, and other gear. Many of these are Bean's own brand.

L.L. Bean clothing catalogs offer a few clothing and sports items for children. Look for child-sized life vests for fishing, boating, and swimming, child-sized sleeping bags for camping and sleepovers, and infant outerwear for winter; ask for the Outdoor or Winter catalogs.

■ The Netcraft Company

2800 Tremainsville Road, Toledo, OH 43613, (419) 472–9826

Free 163-page black-and-white illustrated catalog

Established in 1941, Netcraft built its reputation as suppliers of fishing tackle, but they now offer that and a great deal more. As you would expect, they sell dozens of nets and net-making kits, lures, hooks, jigs, and spinners. You will also find thousands of other items like boots, wading shoes, horns, taxidermy kits, and boat covers.

■ Reed Tackle

Box 1250, Marshalls Creek, PA 18335, (717) 223–7044

Free 45-page black-and-white illustrated catalog; minumum credit card order is $25.00.

Fly tying is a relatively simple but rewarding art of the sportsman. The basic requirements for the beginning as well as the expert flytier are offered here. Tools such as vises, hackle pliers, scissors, tweezers, and dubbing needles are part of the inventory. Lure making parts and instruction books are also listed.

Hundreds of flies are offered as well as kits in a variety of materials and prices.

GOLF

■ Austad's

4500 East 10th Street, P.O. Box 1428, Sioux Falls, SD 57196-1428, (800) 759–4653

Free 46-page color catalog

Austad's is chock-full of everything a golfer could need or want. While most of the selection is best suited to teens and adults, the youngsters have been remembered with a few items. Junior Senator woods and irons are designed in two sizes for children five to nine and ten to fourteen. Left-handed clubs are also available in one size designed for children ten to fourteen. You can buy individual irons for $13.00 each, woods for $16.50 each, or you can buy them as a set with a Junior golf bag and head covers included.

For children two to five, the Lil' Duffer Golf Set for $32.00 includes two irons (5, 9), a driver, a putter, a red or blue golf bag, and head covers.

Lastly, best-dressed little golfers can order a white sweatsuit with the Lit'l Golfer design screened on the shirt and right leg of the pants.

■ Lefties Only

A Golf Specialty Shop, 1972 Williston Road, South Burlington, Vt 05403, (800) 533–8437

Free price list

Left-handed golfers will be thrilled to find this catalog of putters, woods, wedges, and more designed especially for southpaws. Dozens of name brand clubs are available for men and women with a half dozen starter sets for kids.

The least expensive set is a Junior Northwestern, recommended for kids ten to fourteen; it sells for $79.95 and includes a #3 wood, 5-7-9 iron, a putter, and bag. The most elaborate is the MacGregor CG1800, in two sizes designed for children five to ten or eleven to fourteen. A #3 and #5 wood, putter, 3-5-7-9 irons, wedge, bag, and head covers are sold for $184.95.

SKATEBOARDING AND SNOWBOARDING

■ California Cheap Skates

4035 S. Higuera Street, San Luis Obispo, CA 93401, (800) 841–4476; in California, (800) 327–5283

Free 30-page color catalog

Serving skateboarders since 1975, California Cheap Skates offers nearly 100 styles of decks. You can buy the decks alone if you have wheels, or you can buy a complete unit with the wheels.

You can also buy the wheels separately. Choose from names like Rat Bones, Toxic Poison, Santa Cruz, Hosoi Sky Rocket, and Vision Shredder. Dozens of trackers, helmets, knee pads, and wrist guards are also available.

If it begins to snow, skateboarders have no need to become couch potatoes—Cheap Skates also sells thirteen styles of snowboards.

Videos, banners, fingerboard keychains, and T-shirts are also sold here.

■ Skully Bros.

4629 N. Blythe, Fresno, CA 93722

$2.00 for a 15-page black-and-white illustrated catalog and six stickers

You choose the deck truck and the wheels, and Skully will build a custom skateboard for you. If you have a deck already, you can buy wheels and hardware separately; or, if you want to forego the custom look, choose from dozens of ready-made, complete boards for $89.00 each.

Keep Skully in mind for other skateboarding gear as well. "Skate rags," as they call their clothes, include pants for $29.95 and T-shirts for $9.95. Shoes, caps, and safety equipment are also available. Banners and decals provide a decorative touch, and videos may help you learn a few more tricks.

SKIING AND SKATING

■ High Peaks Cyclery

18 Saranac Avenue, Lake Placid, NY 12946, (800) 446–6HPC;
in New York, (518) 523–3764

$2.00 for a 41-page black-and-white illustrated catalog

Established in 1983, High Peaks Cyclery has put together an excellent list of functional gear for cross-country skiing, skating, snowshoeing, rollerskating, and other sports.

Most of these products are best suited to adults and teens, but a four-page section is devoted to younger children's gear. Versatile and very functional child carriers from ToughTraveler start at $49.99 and rise to $109.99 for The Kid Carrier, considered by some to be the Cadillac of baby backpacks. A hardwood sled with steel runners is $49.99. Children's cross-country skis, boots, bindings, and poles come as a set for $79.95.

Extra-warm Baby Bag booties, Babymitts, snowboots, shellpants, socks, gloves, and hats round out the selection of functional yet fashionable items.

■ New Moon Cross Country Ski Shop

P.O. Box 132, Hiway 63 North, Hayward, WI 54843, (715) 634–8685

$1.00 for 32-page color catalog

I see more and more kids shooshing over cross-country ski trails these days, and New Moon is a good mail-order source for the gear needed to enjoy this great sport.

A clear, easy-to-follow guide for sizing children's skis, boots, and poles simplifies the task of getting the right fit. Many of the skis for adults are also offered in junior sizes, including a Micros junior racing ski in sizes 150-180 centimeters for $95.00. A package deal for Micros skis, Salomon 101 Jr. boots, SNS Auto Jr. bindings, and Exel Active poles is $185.00.

Rollerblades, which are trainer skates specifically designed for Nordic skiers, are also available in junior sizes 1-6.

Liliputs are offered here as a first set of cross-country skis for very young children. Recommended for skiers 18 months to 3 years, they are 70 centimeters long and sell for $25.00. Also, check out Kinderbindings, designed to fit any child's snow boot, they sell for $14.00 a pair. Youngsters may enjoy the story of *Cross Country Troll*, a children's book about a little troll's first expedition on skis ($5.95).

■ Rainbo Sports Shop

4836 North Clark Street, Chicago, IL 60640, (312) 275–5500

$2.00 for a 28-page black-and-white illustrated catalog

Skaters will hit the ice in fine fashions and top-of-the-line equipment when they select from the wonderful assortment of supplies and accessories from Rainbo Sports.

Skates in dozens of boot styles are offered here; you can even order custom skates. They also offer skating bags, speed skates, scribes, boot covers for warmth, and rollerblades, as well as skating costumes, and T-shirts or sweatshirts with fun skating designs.

You will find jewelry with skating motifs, including enamel pins for $3.95, and gold and silver earrings, charms, and necklaces.

To assist you in dressing up your skating costumes they sell sew-on beadwork and iron-on beadwork. You will also find books, a board game called Ice Skating Trivia, mugs, videos, stationery, and stickers.

WATER SPORTS

■ Armstrong Wetsuits

Trenant Ind. Est. Wadebridge, Cornwall, PL27, 6HB, England, Phone: 0208 81 4919

Write for current price of an 8-page color catalog, measurement brochures and fabric samples.

Believe it or not, Armstrong Wetsuits will custom-tailor a superior quality wetsuit for you—or your dog. Their motto is, "You design it—we make it!"

In business for 10 years, they offer brilliant colors and designs that can be mixed and matched at your whim.

The growth of this remarkable and unique company is in large part due to its commitment to personal service, and Armstrong urges you to call them if they can be of assistance.

■ Bart's Water Ski Center, Inc.

Highway 13, P.O. Box 294, North Webster, IN 46555,
(800) 348–5016; in Indiana, (800) 552–2336

Free 48-page color catalog

With more than eighteen years in the business, Bart's knows what the water ski enthusiast is looking for, and the whole family is likely to find it in this catalog.

A pair of Kidder Junior Trick Skis are 38 inches long and retail for $270.00, but are available here for $189.98. Jobe Shark Jr. Combo skis are designed for the beginner and are 57 inches long; the usual retail price is $195.00, but you can get them at Bart's for $139.98.

Also look for children's life vests and wetsuits. Kneeboards and dozens of water skis and accessories are all available here.

■ JSI Discount Sailing Source

P.O. Box 20926, St. Petersburg, FL 33742, (800) 235–3220

Free 12-page black-and-white illustrated catalog

This newspaper-like catalog features lots of bargains. They keep more than 12,000 parts and products in stock (far more than they could begin to show here), so they encourage you to give them a call if you want something you have not found in these pages.

Life rafts by Plastimo, Viking, Switlik, and Avon come in a variety of sizes. Dozens of winches are stocked, and you will be allowed a 10 percent discount off the already low prices if you buy two.

See also cruising apparatus, furling systems, sails, canvas, and more.

■ Sailboard Warehouse, Inc.

300 South Owasso Boulevard, St. Paul, MN 55117,
(800) 992–7245; in Minnesota, (612) 482–9995

Free 83-page color catalog

Every conceivable product for the sailboard enthusiast is offered here. The catalog is divided into two parts: Section A is devoted to light to moderate wind boards, and Section B covers moderate to high wind boards, race boards, and accessories.

Sailboarding is easier to learn than ever before with a combination of the products offered here. Videos, books, stabilizing devices, and learning rigs will have you windborne in no time. Sailboard Warehouse carries almost every line of board on the U.S. market, and experienced salespersons are ready to help with any questions.

Among the other products carried are sails, masts, booms, bases, extensions, harness systems, wetsuits, drysuits, boots, helmets, gloves, car racks, and fins.

Stationery and Birth Announcements

■

■ Babygram Service Center
201 Main Street, Suite 600, Fort Worth, TX 76102, (800) 345–BABY

Free color samples and price list

The Babygram birth announcement comes in the form of a 8½ by 11-inch telegram with a photo of your child posted in the center of the page. You send your own message and a negative of a color photograph to Babygrams, and the negative and your announcements will be returned to you.

These prices include handling and photo processing: under 25, $2.00 each; 25 to 100, $1.50 each; 100 or more, $1.00 each.

With a fifty percent deposit, Babygrams will send you the envelopes ahead of time so that you can address them before baby's arrival.

■ Baby Name-a-Grams
P.O. Box 8465, St. Louis, MO 63132, (314) 966–BABY

Free black-and-white illustrated brochures with a sample card

Baby Name-a-Grams offers original, hand-personalized birth announcements and matching thank-you cards in twenty-six designs. Your baby's name is hand-scripted on the announcement again and again to form the outline of the design you have selected. Choose a rocking horse, teddy bear, sailboat, toy soldier, bunny, lamb, stork, or any of the fourteen designs offered. You have a choice of three hand-scripted type styles on either flat cards or the slightly more expensive fold-down cards. The cards can also be used as invitations to christenings or other celebrations.

Envelopes can be mailed to you early so that addressing and stamping can be done before baby arrives.

Chocolate cigars, bubble gum cigars, and "It's a he/she" Hershey's chocolate bars are also sold to add a spoonful of sugar to the festivities.

■ A Baby's Secret Garden
Elegant birth announcements. See page 103 under **Gifts.**

■ Birth-O-Gram Company

1825 Ponce de Leon Boulevard, P.O. Box 140398, Coral Gables, FL 33114-0398, (305) 446–6015

$.50 for a 66-page black-and-white illustrated catalog and one sample announcement

Birth-O-Gram has hundreds of original birth announcements and matching thank-you cards.

In business since 1946, they print in large quantities and sell their product at low prices.

The index lists dozens of themes for your cards, many designed to reflect the careers or interests of the parents. If either parent is a banker, there is a card that reads" "Announcing a new high in family interest by the Birth of _____. Counting our blessings: legal, tender, loving, care. Adding a balance of happiness."

Similar cards announce births for accountants, artists, data processors, farmers, golfers, hairstylists, teachers, and others. Several special announcements are available for adopted babies.

■ Cats, Cats, & More Cats

Notecards, calendars, and Christmas cards with a feline motif.
See page 167 under **Pet Products.**

■ Current

Express Processing Center, Colorado Springs, CO 80941-0001, (719) 593–5900

Free 94-page color catalog

Current offers a tremendous selection of stationery products for the whole family. Hundreds of choices of colorful gift wraps, ribbons, tissue papers, bows, note cards, and writing tablets are staples here. Birthday cards for tots and teens, children's stationery sets, calendars, memo pads, and much more are scattered throughout these pages. A Christmas card kit for kids includes blank cards, envelopes, stickers, Christmas stencils, colored paper, foil paper, and instructions. Hundreds of stickers, rubber stamps, puzzles, books, small gifts, and a few craft items are great for party favors and stocking stuffers.

Quantity discounts are offered on all the products.

■ Earth Care Paper, Inc.

Recycled Paper Catalog, P.O. Box 3335, Madison, WI 53704, (608) 256–5522

$1.00 for 32-page color catalog

The purpose of Earth Care is to explain the uses and benefits of recycled paper and to give people the opportunity to purchase recycled paper. Choose from note cards, holiday cards, postcards, stationery sets, ruled paper, envelopes, writing tablets, birthday cards, and office and printing paper. Truly unique and pretty gift-wrap paper is offered with designs of dancing dinosaurs, penguins, constellations, caribou, flamingos, and more.

A special section of Books and Games has a neat book entitled *Paper by Kids*. It shows you how to make real paper in your home by recycling your junk mail. Recommended for kids in fifth grade and up, it is offered in hardcover for $11.00. The *World Awareness Game* is an educational board game that has directions for six games that are designed for various skill levels. Recommended for children eight and up, it is $35.00.

Earth Care also offers educational and fundraising programs for interested groups.

■ Green Tiger Press, Inc.

Hand-tipped note cards, birthday and special occasion cards, Christmas cards. See page 32 under **Books**.

■ H & F Products, Inc.

3734 W. 95th Street, Leawood, KS 66206, (800) 338–4001

Free 6-page color catalog

H & F Products sells beautiful personalized birth announcements with more than thirty designs and several colors of ink.

All of their announcements include a matching ribbon at the top in pink, yellow, or blue. All announcements plus envelopes are priced as follows: 25 for $21.00; 50 for $32.00; 75 for $45.00; 100 for $60.00.

Matching thank-you notes are available in all thirty styles; your baby's name is printed at the top of each note. They also offer a photo announcement made from your 35mm negative or color print.

Call H & F with your baby's weight, birthdate, and name, and they will ship your order to you within 24 hours. If you really want to get a head start, you can ask them to send your envelopes early so you can address them in advance of the birth. They will send the envelopes at no charge with a small, refundable deposit.

■ Heart Thoughts

6200 E. Central, Suite 100, Wichita, KS 67208, (316) 688–5781

Free black-and-white illustrated brochure and sample

Carefully drawn black and white birth announcements and thank-you cards have illustrations of dear little babies' heads and shoulders, footprints, or tiny hands. Among the twenty-four designs for birth announcements are cards for grandparents to send and a card to announce twins. Five of the designs are offered as thank-you cards. These cards are not personalized, so they can be ordered with no delay for printing. You fill in your baby's vital information on enclosed insert cards.

Baptism and christening invitations are also offered (25 cards for $3.25).

■ Initials

Personalized stationery. See page 117 under **Gifts.**

■ Joy Bee Designs

3650 Greenfield Avenue, #7, Los Angeles, CA 90034

$3.00 for 16-page birth announcement catalog and samples, plus a 9-page Kiddie Kards catalog. A coupon worth $3.00 will be sent to you and discounted on your first order.

Dozens of birth announcements, personalized note cards, party invitations, and baptism invitations are available on several hues of colored paper. Name cards done in custom calligraphy are lovely for your child's first thank-you notes and gift enclosures. They come in a variety of styles and are $25.00 for 50 cards, plus $3.50 for postage and handling.

The birth announcements are often whimsical or quotable; some are designed to reflect the interests of pilots, cooks, campers, joggers, and others. You can choose a message from those listed in the catalog, or you can request that they print your own message.

My favorite announcement reads, "Oh Boy, Oh Boy, Oh Boy . . ." on the outside, and then the inside declares, "It's a Girl."

■ The Metropolitan Museum of Art

Note cards, postcards, Wizard of Oz blank cards. See page 150 under **Museum Shops.**

■ Miles Kimball Company

Personalized notepads, memo pads, name stickers. See page 109 under **Gifts.**

■ New Moons

530 Rhodora Heights Road, Lake Stevens, WA 98258-9708, (206) 334–6403

Send a long, stamped, self-addressed envelope for a black-and-white illustrated brochure

This family-run business offers fifteen original designs of birth announcements and postcards. Seasonal cards announce the birth of a Christmas baby or a fall, winter, spring, or summer baby. Other cards celebrate the homecoming of an adopted child or twins. The illustrations are detailed pen-and-ink drawings with an earthy, simple quality.

The cards include blanks for you to fill in vital statistics, so they can be ordered without delay, in advance of the birth or quickly thereafter. Prices include envelopes and postage and handling costs: 12 for $8.00; 25 for $11.50; 35 for $14.75; 50 for $19.00.

■ Printed Personals

138 Magnolia Street, Westbury, NY 11590, (516) 977–6906

Free 8-page black-and-white illustrated brochure and sample

A selection of seven hand-lettered birth announcements includes one celebrating the birth of twins. Three designs of thank-you cards are also available.

Sweet pen-and-ink illustrations of a rocking horse, teddy bear, rattle, or bonnet and booties decorate each card. Envelopes may be ordered before your child's birth so you can get a jump on your mailing. Fifty announcements or thank-you notes are $30.00; an order of fifty of each kind of card is discounted at $45.00 per set.

■ A Star Is Born

6462 Montgomery Avenue, Van Nuys, CA 91406, (818) 785–5656

Free color brochure

Announce the premiere (translation: birth) of your own newest rising star with a genuine black and white Hollywood movie scene clacker.

Each clackerboard is $12.00 and is personalized with the names of Mom, Dad, and baby, baby's date of birth, time, weight, length, and birthplace.

A real "scene" stealer, this keepsake is made of tempered masonite with a workable hardwood top and silk-screened lettering in glossy enamel.

Clackers can also be personalized for birthdays, anniversaries, bar mitzvahs, graduations, and the like.

■ The Writewell Company

215 W. Michigan Street, 898 Transit Building, P.O. Box 6112,
Indianapolis, IN 46206-6112, (317) 264-3730

Free 56-page color catalog

Established in 1942, Writewell is a major manufacturer of personalized stationery, with a generous inventory of gaily decorated children's cards, writing tablets, and stationery sets. They also sell rubber stamps and three designs of washable, heavy plastic children's growth charts. One of their best ideas is a child's washable placemat that is printed with a color map of the United States; a second placemat features a map of the world; you can order both map placemats for $7.95. You can also order personalized stationery and address labels; twenty personalized pencils with your child's name hot-stamped in gold are $6.95.

Your child's original artwork drawn on a dishwasher-safe plate is sure to be appreciated by grandparents or as a keepsake for you or your child. The Make-A-Plate Kit includes materials, instructions, and a 10-inch melamine plate for $9.95.

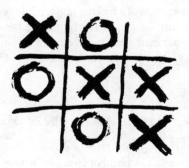

Stickers and Rubber Stamps

■

■ Alaska Craft

Rubber stamps with an Alaskan theme. See page 101 under **Gifts.**

■ All Night Media, Inc.

Box 10607, San Rafael, CA 94901, (415) 459–3013

**$2.00 for a 45-page black-and-white illustrated catalog, refundable with
first purchase**

If there is a rubber stamp enthusiast in your house, you should not miss this mar-
velously fun and varied collection. Hundreds of single stamps, stamp wheels, and
stamp sets will make an impression on serious stamping fans.

Winnie-the-Pooh stamp sets include six stamps of Pooh illustrations and quota-
tions. Dozens of single stamps are based on the original E. H. Shepard illustrations
of Pooh and his friends.

A new *Wizard of Oz* set offers faithful recreations of Dorothy, the Yellow Brick
Road, the Tin Man, and all the characters of Oz.

Name stamps, alphabet sets, farm animals, teddy bears, marine animals, flowers,
silly messages, musical notes, cartoon characters, and dozens of other designs are
among this fabulous inventory.

You may also purchase ink pads in many colors, colored pens, glitter glue, and
embossing powders. Bookplate stamps can be used to personalize your child's library. Holiday stamps, birthday stamps, invitation stamps, and thank-you stamps
can be used to create original stationery products.

■ Childcraft

Silly faces rubber stamp set. See page 217 under **Toys.**

■ Circustamps

P.O. Box 250, Bolinas, CA 94924

$1.00 for a 17-page black-and-white illustrated catalog

This entertaining collection of rubber stamps revolves around the cast of characters, animals, and props that you would find in a circus. Children can, of course, combine and position them in any number of positions to make pictures, stationery, invitations, and more.

Available singly or as a set, these stamps are beautifully drawn, and each one is scaled to proportion with the rest of the collection. Any child's imagination is sure to be stimulated with this complete cast of clowns, tigers, lions, animal tamers, jugglers, elephants, trapeze artists, and others. Prices for single stamps range from $2.50 to $10.00. Boxed sets are $17.00.

Circustamps also offers a variety of pads and inks to use with their rubber stamps.

■ Current

Stickers and stamp sets. See page 204 under **Stationery and Birth Announcements.**

■ Dinosaur Catalog

Rubber stamp sets with a dinosaur motif. See page 219 under **Toys.**

■ The Disney Catalog

Disney characters, including Pooh and friends. See page 105 under **Gifts.**

■ Good Impressions

P.O. Box 33, Shirley, WV 26434, (304) 758–4252

$1.00 for a 26-page illustrated catalog, refundable with first order.

If there is such an animal, these are heirloom-quality stamps. Made from the highest quality rubber and solid hardwood mounts, they feature finely detailed impressions of hearts, moons, cupids, farm animals, skyscrapers, trains, cats, children, fairies, bears, cars, and much, much more.

You will also be treated to a variety of alphabet sets and holiday phrases. Fine felt stamp pads are offered in eight single colors; a rainbow pad allows you to create multi-color impressions with a single blow.

■ Kidstamps

P.O. Box 18699, Cleveland Heights, OH 44118

$1.00 for 36-page black-and-white illustrated catalog, but mention the name of this book and they will send you one free!

Kidstamps has put together the largest collection of quality rubber stamps created by children's book illustrators. What fun to recreate the characters of Joan Walsh Anglund, Eric Carle, Arnold Lobel, Beatrix Potter. H. A. Rey, William Steig, and dozens of others. Babar, Amelia Bedelia, Curious George, Strega Nona, and Jemima Puddleduck are just a few of the hundreds of characters available. Most stamps cost $4.00 to $6.00.

Kidstamps are created of fine gum rubber, mounted on hand-finished hardwood blocks, and then stamped on top for easy identification.

For every five rubber stamps you purchase, you are entitled to choose a sixth at no charge. A variety of non-toxic ink pads are available, as are re-inkers. Kidstamps welcomes your request for custom stamp designs.

Kidstamps also prints a six-page color catalog of T-shirts for kids and their parents. Most of the shirts feature the works of the artists mentioned above.

■ The Learning Factory

Stickers by the yard, sixty designs. See page 91 under **Educational Materials.**

■ Lillian Vernon

Stickers and stamp sets. See page 108 under **Gifts.**

■ The Paragon

A variety of stamp sets and ink pads. See page 111 under **Gifts.**

■ Personal Stamp Exchange, Inc.

345 South McDowell Boulevard, No. 324, Petaluma, CA 94954, (800) 782–6748; in California, (800) STAMP-IT

$3.00 for 49-page color catalog. Be sure to request the retail catalog.

More than 550 original rubber stamp designs fill the pages of this wonderful catalog. Pigs dance, dogs laugh, ducklings waddle, and cows jump over moons in some of these wonderfully executed designs.

Each stamp's handle is made from a hand-cut block of hard maple. The stamps themselves are carefully crafted and give a clean, crisp image. Ink pads in many colors will enliven your artwork, as will colorful markers with flexible brushes for painting the stamped image.

Children will spend hours creating their own stationery, Christmas cards, Valentines, birthday cards, and lunch bags. Several "how to" pages are filled with instructions and creative ideas. Borders, bookplates, alphabets, and invitations will produce such sharp designs that you may leave store bought goods on the shelf and go into the stationery business yourself.

■ PlayFair Toys

Stamp sets and sticker books. See page 230 under **Toys.**

■ Rubber Stamps of America Catalog

P.O. Box 567 - GLOBE, Saxtons River, VT 05154, (802) 869–2622

$2.00 for a 33-page black-and-white illustrated catalog, refundable with first order

These high-quality rubber stamps are mounted on beautiful hardwood handles with the image stamped on top. An abundance of wonderfully clear designs include sea life, toys, food, hearts, bears, fantasy creatures, Halloween and other holidays, and much more.

All kinds of dinosaurs thunder about, while cavemen carve images on rocks. Autumn leaves float down the page, spiders weave webs, and a Bengal tiger stalks his prey.

Cheerful designs print happy and silly messages such as Thank You, Happy Birthday, U.S. Snail, OOPS!, AAAAHH, Congratulations, and I've Moved. A beautiful selection of alphabet and number sets, invitations, and stamp pads in a variety of colors will make stationery productions a snap. A blue sheet of paper, a few marine life stamps, and a little imagination will make a wonderful mural.

■ Stamp Magic

358 Merriweather Drive, P.O. Box 60874, Longmeadow, MA 01116

$2.00 for a 28-page black-and-white illustrated catalog, refundable with first order

Kids (and some adults I know) love making pictures and stories with rubber stamps. In addition to the stationery ideas mentioned elsewhere, children can also design their own lunch bags, envelopes, book covers, and wrapping paper.

Stamp Magic offers several hundred rubber stamps and a variety of ink pads. Choose from a whimsical array of teddy bears, barnyard and fantasy animals, dinosaurs, funny faces, pets, balloons, Indians, sports, and dancing motifs as well as sorcerers, dragons, witches, castles, and unicorns.

This firm also does custom work if you send a clearly drawn design. Self-inking stamps can be provided for custom designs.

■ Stick em Up, Inc.

P.O. Box 9108, Pleasanton, CA 94566, (415) 426–1040

Free 24-page black-and-white illustrated catalog

A good source for literally hundreds of pressure sensitive stickers, this company offers cards of assorted prism stickers for $.70 per card. Some designs are suitable for young children: butterflies, clowns, rainbows bears, pigs, flowers, and kites are among the choices. Most of the hundreds of others are meant for your teenagers to put on skateboards, bikes, notebooks, and motorcycles. Stickers that read, "Killer Ramp," "Awesome," "Super Kid," and "Lookin' Good" are popular, as are ones with brand names like "Camaro," "Moroso," "Champion," "Honda," and "O'Neal USA."

■ Toys to Grow On

Stickers and rubber stamps. See page 234 under **Toys.**

■ Wordsworth Ltd.

Paint-and-peel kit for kids to make their own stickers. See page 235 under **Toys.**

Toys

■ American Foundation for the Blind

Toys, games, and puzzles for the visually impaired.
See page 123 under **Health and Safety Products.**

■ Animal Town

P.O. Box 2002, Santa Barbara, CA 93120, (800) 445–8642

Free 40-page color catalog

Animal Town presents "cooperative venture" toys, games, outdoor play equipment tapes, and books based on the concept that people can play *with* one another and leave competition out of the game. This twelfth annual catalog also features many items to encourage children to appreciate and care for nature. Educational card games called "Predator" and "Pollination" are two such offerings. Some audiocassettes identify bird songs and one called *Hug the Earth* includes fourteen toe-tapping songs to celebrate the riches of the planet. Their most requested board game is *Save the Whales.* At $33.00, it is recommended for two to six players, ages eight to adult. Dozens of interesting books include *Carpentry For Children, Drawing With Children,* and a fun title, *Handmade Secret Hiding Places.* The prettiest card game comes from England: Garden Rummy is beautifully illustrated and imparts such nature tips as mint repels ants, peas improve the soil with nitrogen, and more. A lively little 36-page book of jump-rope rhymes called *Anna Banana* sells for $7.00.

■ Aristoplay, Ltd.

P.O. Box 7529, Ann Arbor, MI 48107, (800) 634–7738; in Michigan, (313) 995–4353

Free 14-page color catalog

Parents Magazine cited these games in an article on the best board games for families. Aristoplay does indeed offer colorful, exciting games that just happen to teach as well. *By Jove* brings alive the world of classical myths and is the winner of a 1984 Parents' Choice Award. Designed for ages ten through adult, it sells for $20.00. Authorized by the Winterthur Museum, *Made For Trade* ($22.00) is a board game of early American life with four levels of skill.

Where In The World? has been recommended by *Games* and *Ms.* magazines and can be played in a variety of ways; each approach helps your child to memorize geography in an exciting, fun way.

Beautifully illustrated rummy card games involve classic fairy tales; each deck is $4.00.

■ The Ark Catalog

4245 Crestline Avenue, Fair Oaks, CA 95628, (800) 872–0064; in California, (916) 967–2607

Free 22-page color catalog

The Ark has just celebrated its tenth anniversary in the catalog business, and their goal remains to offer a little fantasy, a dash of common sense, and a touch of whimsy to your child's early years. The business is run by mothers and grandmothers, and they have stocked the shelves with many of the books and toys their own children have enjoyed.

Your youngster will love to help you during planting and raking seasons with a sturdy steel and hardwood child's wheelbarrow for $25.00. Or perhaps the kids could care for their own garden planted with A Child's Collection of Seeds ($9.85). Included are seeds for pumpkins, blue lake beans, cosmos, cucumbers, sunflowers, and more.

A bag of fifty marbles comes with a booklet of games to play ($5.00). Beatrix Potter fans should look for Peter Rabbit's Puzzle Game. It is $12.00 and is suggested for children four through seven.

Highly recommended for kids four through ten is *Kids on Stage*, a kind of charades game in which the players pretend to be animals or actions.

The catalog also features a kite, a bubble wand, a kaleidoscope kit, a pillow for the tooth fairy, and a wonderful collection of books.

■ B.C. Playthings

1065 Marine Drive, North Vancouver, BC V7P 1S6, Canada, (800) 663–4477

Free 44-page black-and-white illustrated catalog

While you will find many of the same games and toys here that you see in American catalogs, this Canadian import also presents lots of different and interesting offerings. A unique little toy invented and manufactured in British Columbia is called a Skwish; a round maze of wooden connectors and knobs, it fits baby's hand and is recommended for baby's finger exploration.

Flexible rubber Locktagons that hold together with friction sell for $13.90 for 100 pieces.

Award-winning Brio-Mec hardwood slats, blocks, and plastic connectors are popular. They also sell puzzles, puppets, great storybook villages and cities, sand and water tables, and much more.

Owner Patrick Gallaher, a parent and teacher, has been in business for thirteen years and has studiously avoided Barbie dolls and Cabbage Patch Kids in his search for non-sexist, non-violent products. The editors have thoughtfully provided approximate appropriate ages in brackets for all the items.

■ Cherry Tree Toys, Inc.

Plans and kits for whirligigs, ride-on toys, and wooden boats and cars.
See page 2 under **Arts and Crafts.**

■ Childcraft

20 Kilmer Road, P.O. Box 3143, Edison, NJ 08818-3143, (800) 367–3255

Free 64-page color catalog

Childcraft has hundreds of "Toys That Teach," as well as dozens that are just plain fun, including special holiday items such as an Easter Bunny Piñata and Halloween costumes.

Art supplies include a set of 46 rubber stamps depicting silly ears, eyes, noses, and more for kids to create zany pictures ($12.95); creative modeling wax that becomes soft and pliable in the warmth of a child's hands ($5.75 for six colors or $9.95 for a dozen); fabric pens for designing T-shirt art; and many other art books and craft kits.

Look here for a child's first camera ($7.95), a dinosaur cake pan, Make Your Own Movie kit, dollhouse furniture, outdoor play equipment, kid-sized furniture, walkie-talkies, science kits, and more.

■ Children's Factory

505 North Kirkwood Road, St. Louis, MO 63122, (314) 821–1441

Free 24-page color catalog

Children's Factory designs and manufactures preschool equipment for kids six months to six years.

A very large selection of indoor play products and a smaller number of outdoor swing sets make up the inventory.

For $44.95, you can own a 6-foot Tyrannosaurus or an 11-foot Brontosaurus that you construct from heavy-duty, double-wall corrugated board. Each piece is numbered or lettered for easy placement and child participation.

A 30-inch red, white, and blue cardboard mailbox ($14.95) is a special favorite of children. Many letters to pretend friends or Santa could pass through these slots. Look for 12-inch soft foam blocks, a cardboard dollhouse, and a corrugated puppet stage.

Many of these items are designed for the rugged use of schools and daycare centers and as such may be more expensive than an individual family would be interested in paying. The sturdy construction may be cost-effective in the long run, but if you are on a budget, choose some of the other kid-pleasers available at more reasonable prices.

■ Constructive Playthings

2008 W. 103rd Terrace, Leawood, KS 66206, (800) 255–6124;
in Kansas, (913) 642–8244

Free 44-page color catalog for home use; $3 for larger school catalog.

For more than three decades, Constructive Playthings has been servicing schools and daycare centers; now they are offering their toys, games, and creative materials through this catalog.

They offer costumes for the prospective bride, princess, race-car driver, and cheerleader, as well as dress-up duds in assorted animal designs. A roomy hardwood theatre comes with an assortment of puppets. Plastic fruits and other goods are available for fantasy play in the little kitchen or the market stand. Brio train sets and accessories, maple building blocks, cardboard bricks, and other construction sets are also great for imaginative play.

Six pages are devoted to first playthings for infants; Noah's Ark Fun Center, Walk-a-Long Activity Train, Baby Activity Rocker, and knobbed wooden puzzles will keep baby happy.

Creative toys are given special attention here. Needlepoint kits, stencilling projects, beadwork, and more offer something to please most children. You might choose a Build-A-Bonnet kit or a puppet factory set. You will also find travel games, storage ideas, bath toys, a small selection of books and audiocassettes, musical instruments, and a few scientific toys such as magnets and periscopes.

■ Crate and Barrel

A seasonal variety of quality toys. See page 94 under **Furniture and Bedding**.

■ The Developing Child

Winnetka Square, 19956 Ventura Boulevard, Woodland Hills, CA 91364,
(800) 621–2468; in California, (818) 346–6200

Free 12-page color catalog

The proprietors of The Developing Child aim to provide educational toys and books
for children from preschool through the elementary grades. Their catalog includes
arts and crafts, building blocks, and a nice selection of games.

The Fossil Hunt Kit ($24.00) comes with over twenty authentic fossils buried in a
box of volcanic sand; each specimen is guaranteed to be 100 to 550 million years old.
The kit includes a dual-power magnifier, cleaning brushes, and the 160-page *Golden
Guide to Fossils* book with 481 illustrations.

A set of ten natural wood Nesting Blocks are great for building castles and rockets and they provide their own storage solution: They nest inside each other. Each
block is colorfully painted with pictures, numbers, and letters that stack up to create
a total picture ($30.00).

A neat idea is the Kiddoworks Playhouse ($27.00) from Danica. Made from rein-
forced cardboard, it is plain white so kids can decorate and paint it themselves. It
could be a school house, puppet theatre, store, spaceship, or even the candy house in
the tale of Hansel and Gretel.

■ Dinosaur Catalog

P.O. Box 546, Tallman, NY 10982, (914) 634–7579

$2.00 for 24-page color catalog

What a terrific idea considering the continuing popularity dinosaurs enjoy. This catalog is *the* source for hundreds of dinosaur models, including replicas authenticated
by the British Museum of Natural History, stuffed soft sculptures, finely detailed
pewter figurines, hand-painted plastic figures, three-dimensional paper designs to
cut and assemble, and more.

A dinosaur party set includes gift wrap, balloons, invitations, plates, loot bags,
and napkins. *The New Dinosaur Dictionary, Prehistoric Monsters Did the Strangest
Things,* and *Dinosaur Days* are just a few of the books available.

Dinosaur cookie cutters ($5.50) are on the shelf, as are a walking wind-up
dinosaur skeleton ($4.95) and an 80-piece hand-cut wooden puzzle with
stegosaurus, tyrannosaurus, and the like ($6.95). Six members of a Neanderthal
tribal family will spark a child's imagination for $13.95.

You can find dinosaur mugs, dinnerware, wooden banks, rubber stamps, puzzles, dinosaur rummy cards, bingo, stencils, and coloring books.

■ The Enchanted Forest

P.O. Box 24, Republic, MO 65738, (417) 732–7060

$1.00 for 16-page black-and-white illustrated catalog

Heirloom quality toys, some handmade by American crafters in traditional, often nostalgic designs are the trademark of this lovely collection.

Two gorgeous European wood puzzles feature Alice in Wonderland and Love Birds; each has 16 square pieces and sells for $12.50.

A solid wood rocking horse with legs that pivot creates a clippety-clop sound as it rocks; it sells for $129.00.

A combination puppet theatre and chalkboard ($89.00) includes crayons, colored chalks, and eraser as well as two chalkboards in bright red and blue.

Wooden blocks, letter puzzles, some cute table and chair sets, many adorable stuffed animals, and books are also sold here.

■ Family Pastimes

RR 4, Peth, Ontario, Canada K7H 3C6

Free 31-page black-and-white illustrated catalog

Family Pastimes is the maker and distributor of games of cooperation. Their philosophy is that children can learn from and be happier playing together and not against each other. A very helpful index indicates the age-appropriateness of each game, so it is easy to choose the games that will match your child's skill level.

You will find games in which players help each other climb a mountain, build a community, or bring in the harvest—all in a spirit of cooperation. The games can be played without the tears and frustration of other competitive board games.

This Canadian firm offers dozens of games and puzzles, as well as games manuals that describe the rules of play clearly and have an accompanying picture with each entry. Look here for new play ideas that are fun for the whole family.

■ F.A.O. Schwarz

P.O. Box 182225, Chattanooga, TN 37422–7225, (800) 426–TOYS

Free 56-page color catalog, mailed once yearly in August

The ultimate toy store is, of course, F.A.O. Schwarz. Millions of kids (of all ages) are taken to this palace of delights just to gawk at its wonders.

If you are too far from New York City or one of Schwarz's smaller stores, take a mini-tour through these glossy pages. You will behold such luxuries as the Mini 325i, the ultimate driving machine for kids four and up. The powerful 2.3 HP gas engine fuels it to 13 mph, and it will only set you back $3,500.00. Am I showing my age to tell you I remember when you could get a real car for not much more than that? If you were not lucky enough to win the lottery this year, for $40.00 you can have a sleek, silver-radio controlled Corvette; just $140.00 will buy a set of kids' electronic digital drums by Kawasaki; a mere $32.00 will buy a bead loom to make beaded bags, belts, and bows; a motorized potter's wheel with two pounds of air-dry clay, plus tools and four non-toxic paints, is only $20.00.

The catalog also displays beautiful dolls, board games, electric trains, costumes, and stuffed animals. There are lots of choices for all pocketbooks and much that will inspire the holiday dreams of your children.

■ Fisher-Price Bits & Pieces Catalog

Consumer Affairs, 636 Girard Avenue, East Aurora, NY 14052-1880

This catalog from Fisher-Price *is* a mail-order source and a veritable warehouse of replacement parts for hundreds of current and older Fisher-Price toys. A slim parts list and order form gives you the name and model number of the toy and a list of its loose or replaceable parts. Each entry includes prices but no photographs. you can order Little People, furniture, cars, wheels, dishes, shape sorter and puzzle pieces, animals, tools, or whatever they can offer to help you complete your toy set. You must send payment with your order.

■ Fisher-Price Toy Catalog

P.O. Box 97902, Dallas, TX 75397

$1.50 for a 66-page color catalog

While this is a great idea guide where you can find every Fisher-Price toy currently available, you cannot buy anything through this catalog. Meant to be a guide for you before you visit your local toy store, it includes full-color photographs and descriptions of function and size.

Prices are not included, so it may be difficult to make a real decision about what you want to buy. Give it to your kids in early November, though, and they will not have any trouble at all.

■ Gail Wilson Duggan Design, Inc.

Folk dolls and accessories. See page 8 under **Arts and Crafts**.

■ The Gifted Children's Catalog

Drawer 11408, Phoenix, AZ 85061-1408, (800) 828–3303; in Arizona, 272–1853

Free 44-page color catalog

The Pied Piper Collection offered here is a subsidiary of Pied Piper Schools, Inc., providers of child development materials since 1966. The selection of toys, games, books, and educational materials has been chosen to help encourage children's creative and intellectual potential—while they have fun.

The Build Your Own Alphabet set for $17.95 uses bright, patterned letters as sculptures so kids can create their own names, initials, school names or whatever for their rooms, doors, and other artwork. The Creative Woodworking set contains absolutely everything needed to complete fifty-five woodworking projects. It comes with a 30-minute instruction cassette that explains how to make a truck, boat, tiny helicopter, birdhouse, napkin-holder, key chains, and more. Recommended for children ten and up, it is $28.00.

Books include guides to the stars and weather, a first dictionary, an innovative atlas, pet handbooks, myths, and more. A wooden loom, a flower press, outdoor play toys, science kits, birdfeeders, mini hydroponic greenhouses, mask and puppet projects, pour-and-paint plaster kits, and musical instruments give you an idea of how well rounded and diverse this catalog is. If the title of the catalog conjures up images of stuffy, intellectual fare designed for "smart" kids only, order a copy today—you will be pleasantly surprised.

■ Hamleys

Freepost 35, London, W1E 5PQ, England, Phone: 01-287-7866

1.50 British pounds for a 96-page color catalog

First opened in 1760 under the name Noah's Ark, Hamleys has grown to a magical six-floor toy store on Regent Street in London—even the Royal Family shops here.

The catalog is divided into eight sections: Dolls and Soft Toys, Large Toys, Action & Models, Arts and Crafts, Books, Pastimes, Magic, and Executive Games for the child in every adult. Many items can be found in American stores and catalogs, but unique English toys are offered here as well.

A Scots Piper Band with ten hand-painted soldiers or a red double-decker London bus and a London taxi are just a few of the model-sized toys. You can also order a policemen set and several other vehicles.

Hamleys' Arts and Crafts section is quite imaginative with some items I have not seen elsewhere. The Snowman Plaster Casting kit contains all you need to make a trio of snowpeople. A Plaster and Paint kit allows you to create miniature English cottages.

A coloring contest and other competitions are sprinkled throughout the catalog; winners may receive merchandise prizes or credit vouchers worth up to 250 British pounds.

You need the latest exchange rate to determine the cost of the items in this catalog. Hamleys gladly accepts overseas orders, but request that you use Visa, American Express, Access, or Diners Club to charge your order.

■ Hammacher Schlemmer

147 East 57th Street, New York, NY 10022, (800) 543–3366

Free 72-page color catalog

Hammacher Schlemmer has prided themselves as purveyors of innovation and quality for more than 140 years. Catering to the whole family, they scatter a fair number of children's items throughout the pages. Prices may be steep for some budgets, but the products are top-of-the-line and fully guaranteed.

A child's professional-quality electric guitar is approximately two-thirds the size of a standard model. Its precision-cut maple neck and fretboard fit smaller hands, so that a child can become more accomplished and less frustrated; it comes with a 2-watt RMS amplifier and sells for $169.50. An accurate Mickey Mouse electronic bathroom scale has imprints of Mickey's feet on the platform so your child knows exactly where to stand; it has an easy-to-read LED display and is $79.95. An electronic dartboard, limited-edition Flexible Flyer sled, an English-style rocking horse, a log cabin playhouse, a redwood outdoor play center, and a young explorer's space station building set are all offered here and give you an idea of the innovative products you might find. The inventory changes seasonally.

■ Hancock Toy Shop

97 Prospect Hill Road, Jaffrey, NH 03452-1123, (603) 525–4033

$.50 for an 8-page black-and-white illustrated catalog

Hancock is a small New England company producing toys and children's furniture from hardwood—principally rock maple.

These handcrafted designs are simple, unadorned, safe, and rugged. A dollhouse sells for $130.00, a pull-toy dog for $12.00, a helicopter for $15.00, and a rocking chair for $35.00.

Of the twenty-one items offered, five of them are children's play kitchen equipment made from premium birch plywood. Your junior chef can select a stove, a sink, a combination sink and stove with a removable stainless steel sink, a hutch, and a refrigerator. All of the pieces have operative doors and self-closing latches.

You can also buy doll furniture, trucks, block sets, a toy chest, and table and chair sets.

■ HearthSong

P.O. Box B, Sebastopol, CA 95473, (800) 325–2502

Free 40-page color catalog

I never can make it through this charming catalog without finding several items I want for my children. I continually find unusual, quality merchandise that is not available anywhere else. Creative play with non-sexist, noncompetitive toys is the primary focus here. The most frequently ordered item in 1987 was Stockmar modeling beeswax. Because the beeswax is clean and colorful and can be shaped with warm hands into animals, flowers, people, and more, it is ideal for children's projects.

Specially cut maple block sets with red roof accessories allow your children to design their own castles. They will also enjoy two- or three-story pine and birch dollhouses. Dollhouse furniture is available in several sets and colorfully dressed dollhouse dolls from Germany are $9.95 each. Finger puppets, hand puppets and a puppet theater will also provide hours of imaginative play.

Carefully chosen books encourage creative play, old-fashioned games, and time-honored skills like gardening, cooking, knitting, painting, and more. Beautiful editions of folktales, bedtime stories, Chanukah tales, and Christmas stories comprise an especially exquisite collection of books.

The catalog also includes many kits and books that guide adults in making items for children. Kits for making ornaments, hand-dipped candles, baskets, and stuffed toys share catalog space with books on doll-making, playhouse-building, and toy-making.

A child's lyre, a tom tom and mallet, a pentatonic pitch pipe, and a couple of simple song books help round out this imaginative catalog.

■ Heir Affair

Toys and crafts for indoor and outdoor play. See page 107 under **Gifts.**

■ House of Tyrol

P.O. Box 909, Alpenland Center, Helen Highway, Route 75 North, Cleveland, GA 30528-0909, (800) 241–5404

Free 52-page color catalog

House of Tyrol was established in 1970 so you could shop the Alps from the comfort of your armchair. You will probably expect the large selection of detailed cuckoo clocks, expensive and unique nutcrackers, and Tyrolean fashions for adults, but look beyond those items for six pages of interesting choices just for children.

Russian Babushka nesting dolls with inlaid straw detailing sell for $29.95. Three lifelike dolls from Bätz of Germany include soft-bodied boy or girl baby dolls ($39.00) or a girl toddler ($98.00); the dolls have hand-painted features on their vinyl faces.

My favorite is the Hansel and Gretel Mini Chalet Clock ($19.95); made in West Germany, it has a one-day key-wind movement and a black cat on its chimney.

■ Huggies Toyland Catalog

Features Playskool brand toys for babies and preschoolers.
See page 141 under **Infant Products and Equipment.**

■ Imaginative Inroads

169 Lafayette Road #1, Portsmouth, NH 03801

Free 7-page black-and-white illustrated catalog

Let your kids build their own volcano and watch it erupt. They'll have a real blast!

I loved this little catalog with toys, kits, and crafts that involve hands-on activities. With the Volcano Kit, your children build the papier-mâché volcano, and then they add baking soda and vinegar to make the mountain erupt; the volcano can be used repeatedly. The set ($10.95) includes papier-mâché, a work tray, and an interesting booklet of information about volcanoes.

A Make-A-Mask kit comes with one face form, one roll of quick-dry sculpting gauze, five colors of non-toxic paint, a paintbrush, and a 16-page step-by-step instruction guide. It is recommended for children six and up and is $9.95.

Kids can build a timer that really tells time, a finger-powered wooden record player, and a solar energy lab. There are shirt-painting kits, butterfly gardens, Grow-A-Frog kits, weather stations, and more.

■ John Deere Catalog

1400 3rd Avenue, Moline, IL 61265, (800) 544–2122

Free 36-page color catalog

Who would expect to buy toys from the purveyors of farm plows? If you find your-self in need of some help in the fields, take a look at their easy-pedaling John Deere tot-size tractor with optional trailer. Both pieces feature chassis of steel, plus rubber tires. Once your little farm hands have finished up those chores, they can practice inside with toys like the radio-controlled tractor, a faithful mini-replica of a forage wagon, round baler, and forage harvester. Road builders are priced from $26.00 for a loader to $47.00 for a articulated turning motor grader. All their small-scale vehicles are replicas of the real thing and built to last.

Only about five pages of this catalog are devoted to children's items, but if you need some help out in those fields . . .

■ Johnson and Johnson Child Development Toys

Toy Catalog Program, P.O. Box 45113, Jacksonville, FL 32232-5113, (800) 223–8916

Free 24-page color catalog

Concentrating on developmental toys for newborns to preschoolers, Johnson and Johnson has brought together lots of colorful, stimulating toys in a subscription pro-gram that brings two new toys to your door about once a month. Each toy arrives with a booklet of suggestions to parents for the best use of the product. Choices like the Spinner Rattle, Red Rings, and Balls-in-a-Bowl are *de rigueur* in the nursery and durable enough to last through two or more children.

Through microchip technology, Johnson & Johnson has also designed a voice-activated crib mobile. It will provide hours of visual pleasure and stimulation for $29.95. Babies love to look at themselves, and the Johnson & Johnson shatterproof plastic mirror is ideal for crib use. It sells for $15.95.

Teething and grasping toys, rattles, bathtime items, colorful board books, and tapes with songbooks are some of the infant and toddler pleasures found here.

■ Just for Kids!

75 Paterson Street, P.O. Box 15006, New Brunswick, NJ 08906-5006, (800) 654–6963

Free 96-page color catalog

Just for Kids sells a nice variety of kids' toys, dolls, games, costumes, and art equipment. Arts and crafts, baby toys, books, Disney slippers and suspenders, building blocks, watches, plastic farmyard and jungle animals, science kits, Sesame

Street playsets, videos, and outdoor activity centers abound.

Pretend items for a kid's kitchen are here: plastic food, dishes, aprons, cleaning equipment, and more. Wonderful costumes ensure Halloween fun; choose from an astronaut suit, gladiator armor, an aviator outfit, or a Fire Chief helmet complete with working siren and rotating emergency light. Other dress-up clothes include feather boas, wing sets, play jewelry, hat-decorating kits, and washable face paints.

Holiday and seasonal products change with each catalog. Party supplies such as paper plates, napkins, candle holders, party favor holders, cake molds, and trinkets for filling loot bags are always on hand.

The furniture selection is small (an easel, a plastic toddler's "school" desk, a few stools and booster seats), but includes two unique items: A dinosaur-shaped chair flips open to convert to a sleeping area for naps or guests; and a table and chair set features a table top that flips up to reveal a storage compartment for crayons or games.

■ Learn and Play For Kids

Troll Associates, 100 Corporate Drive, Mahwah, NJ 07498-1053, (800) 247–6106

Free 48-page color catalog

While I have not noticed many price bargains here, several unique offerings still make this a worthwhile read. A Partytime Floor Piano (a takeoff on the one featured in the movie "Big") can liven up your home with its 17-note range for $88.95. A menacing plastic pirate ship will float and pillage in your tub for $74.95.

A picture frame and handprint kit allows you and your child to created a special keepsake for parents and grandparents. Wooden puzzles, books, a very good selection of crafts, cook and bake sets, and educational videos fill the catalog pages. Loads of dinosaur items include great dinosaur craft kits for constructing wood models of Brachiosaurus, Triceratops, and the like. No tools or glue are necessary and the kits range from $7.95 to $9.95.

■ Learning Materials Workshop

58 Henry Street, Burlington, VT 05401, (802) 862–8399

Free color information sheets and price list

Learning Materials Workshop makes a variety of brightly colored wooden building systems designed with modular, interchangeable units that provide unlimited possibilities for creative play. Toddlers and teens will enjoy these equally.

Made in Vermont from the finest maple and birch hardwood available, each piece is carefully sanded and painted in non-toxic enamel paint. The sets are durable enough to last for years, but if you should lose a piece, replacement parts are available.

The Thingamabobbin system was the recipient of the 1976 Public Action Coalition on Toys Award and sells for $35.00. Recommended for children from three through eight, it consists of a base, four bobbins, six dowels, and four rubberbands. Cubes, Bobbins, Beams won the 1981 Parent's Choice Award and, like the other toys offered here, it is a colorful, open-ended construction toy. Arcobaleno, winner of the 1986 Parent's Choice Award, is a puzzle and a construction toy rolled into one.

■ LEGO Shop at Home Service

P.O. Box 640, Enfield, CT 06082, (203) 763–4011

Free 37-page color catalog

For fifty years, this family-owned company has provided some of the best known and loved childhood toys. LEGO products are available for kids from toddlers to teens. Truth is, you often see parents sitting on the floor with their kids playing architect with LEGO bricks and LEGO construction sets.

In this shop-at-home catalog, parents of infants and preschoolers can choose from well-constructed Ring McRabbit Telephones, Bathtub Buddies, 46-piece farms, DUPLO block sets, train sets, and playhouses.

You will find hundreds of products and accessories for LEGO Town, LEGO Space, LEGO Boats, and more of these durable toys.

■ Lillian Vernon

Large selection of games, puzzles, toys. See page 108 under **Gifts**.

■ Little Folk Felts

80975 Indio Boulevard, #5, Indio, CA 92201, (619) 347–2124

Free color product sheet and price list

Brilliantly colored felt figures to move around on flannelboard backgrounds are the specialty of this concern. No glueing, pinning, or taping is necessary. The durable, heavy-duty felt is washable and available in sets of thirteen butterflies, bees, and ladybugs for $4.25. Twenty animals and their babies are $3.50. Also offered are ten children from various ethnic groups, a family of seven plus their dog, twelve felt birds, dinosaurs, fifty-two pieces of the human organs, plus a basic food groups charts. Upper- and lower-case letters as well as numbers are also available.

Nine scenic flannelboard backgrounds are priced from $4.25 to $27.95.

■ Markline

P.O. Box 13807, Philadelphia, PA 19101-3807, (800) 922–8600

Free 40-page color catalog

Markline searches for well-made, well-designed products that are new, unique, and useful. Nine pages of this catalog are dedicated to young children and teens.

A Kawaski One-Man Jam Electric Digital Guitar by Remco is $99.95 and makes it easy to get great sounds: You play chords by touching twelve buttons that are programmed for major, minor and seventh chords.

For $49.95, an authentic-looking Huey helicopter flies 200 feet up in the air, and then its parachutist jumps out. It uses two "D" batteries and requires some assembly.

Your children need not despair over putting away their skateboards when the snow comes. For $49.95, they can have lightweight, high-impact plastic snowskates for speeding across the powder.

You can fly your own 4½-foot Goodyear Blimp filled with helium (sold separately here). The blimp is $39.95 and is maneuvered with two joysticks on a remote control box.

■ Naturally British Ltd.

13 New Row, Covent Garden, London WC2 N4LF

Write for current price of 7-page color catalog

Established in 1978, Naturally British of Covent Garden is justifiably renowned for their handmade rocking horses. The prices are staggering, but they seem to have plenty of buyers. The rockers run in price from $3,000.00 for a giant rocking horse to $735.00 for a small one on bows. They are each individually carved from the best laminated hardwoods and treated with a clear sealant to produce an original muscled effect. The tack is handmade in genuine leather and comes complete with noseband, bit, breast plate, and saddle with girth and stirrups. Manes and tails are genuine horsehair.

Naturally British also carries a whole range of hand-cut and hand-painted items based on *Alice in Wonderland* characters. Bookends of Alice, the Cards, the Queen, the Mad Hatter, and others can be made to order for $99.50.

Prices, steep as they are, are quoted in U.S. dollars.

■ The Penny Whistle

1283 Madison Avenue, New York, NY 10128, (212) 369–3868

Free 16-page color catalog

I was initially curious about this catalog just because the Penny Whistle toy stores are partly owned by Meredith (Tom's wife) Brokaw. Once I had it in hand, I admired it on its own merits because, as the covers says, it includes "classic toys carefully chosen."

A wonderful Rainbow Board from Kidderoo invites kids to attach 157 colorful, reusable vinyl Stickeroo play pieces to a portable board with Velcro fastenings. Kids can make up stories and scenarios with unlimited possibilities for $37.00. Inspiring building blocks are made from natural hard-rock maple in wonderful triangle, moon, cone, and rectangle shapes; thirty-six pieces in thirteen shapes are $52.50.

Order science and nature kits such as a Giant Ant Farm or a Rock and Mineral Hunt kit. Young fashion designers will enjoy a great duffy cap to decorate with glue, markers, and doodads ($11.00, supplies included). For the future jeweler, a Bead Machine from Battat features a simple bead-stringing mechanical system.

Each item has an age recommendation which, of course, is a wonderful aid to all gift-buyers.

■ PlayFair Toys

1690 28th Street, Boulder, CO 80301, (800) 824–7255

Free 24-page color catalog

PlayFair Toys claims to sell "nonsexist, nonviolent, educational toys for all ages." I must say, they have made some nice choices. One part of the catalog includes Toys To Enjoy Alone, and another is called Toys To Share With Others. They have many books, games, building toys, a weaving loom, rubber stamp sets, puzzles, some reusable sticker books, play tables and chairs, rocking horses, a log cabin playhouse, educational videos, and craft and science kits.

A 25-piece Design Your Own Clown set contains colorful plastic sections that fit together in several ways; imported from France, it sells for $36.98. A 16 x 24-inch hand-cut, 64-piece wooden puzzle of Santa's Workshop is $39.98 and recommended for ages 3 and up. A tabletop wooden easel with a wipe-off board and plastic tray collapses for storage ($49.98).

■ Play-Safe and Learn
745 State Circle, Box 1941, Ann Arbor, MI 48106,
(800) 521–2832; in Michigan, (313) 761–5690

Free 63-page color catalog

A division of Wolverine Sports, Play-Safe and Learn offers a wide variety of action toys and games for tots and teens. This catalog is directed to the schools and day care centers, so you will find good quality products at reasonable prices.

Big, lightweight nylon parachutes are a popular item for groups of kids, and five sizes are sold here. The smallest (6 feet in diameter) is reasonably priced at $19.50.

Your young child can ride and rock on a big plastic snail or giraffe that includes a storage area for other toys; the snail is $34.95, the giraffe is $49.95.

Floor puzzles, building blocks, bricks, foam forms, and hurdles are all available.

Lots of outdoor activity items provide an outlet for energy. Choose from pedal-powered coupe cars, play slides, and junior activity gyms.

■ Radio Flyer, Inc.
6515 W. Grand Avenue, Chicago, IL 60635, (800) 621–7613

Free 6-page color catalog

If you are feeling nostalgic (and your child needs a great toy), look here for the original little red wagon in eleven different models. With durable steel bodies and non-toxic paint, they still make them the way they did when the first Radio Flyer was introduced at Chicago's 1933 World's Fair. Appropriate age ranges for each wagon are suggested. The inventory now boasts a Radio Flyer Mini-Barrow, a Trike N'Trailer, a Scooter, Tiny Trike, Row Cart, Rolling Pony, and a rock maple chair and bench.

■ R.E.A.L. izms
921 Eastwind Drive, Suite 114, Westerville, OH 43081-5306, (800) 344–4144

Free 32-page color catalog

The explanation of this company's name is that "izms are Right-on, Essential And the Latest—R.E.A.L. izms."

This is indeed a catalog that was designed to be enticing for kids to thumb through, but when it comes time to check the "method of payment" box, they will most likely remember to include you. About a half-dozen skateboards and various accessories will please aficionados of the latest kids' craze. A Sno-Go sled, Stradas scooter, Skoot skate, pogo-stick, snow or water tube, unicycle, and roller racer are a few of the other modes of transportation offered, so do not despair if the $1,199.99 gas-powered Porsche racer costs a little more than you wanted to spend.

They also sell various remote-control toys, sweet-looking baby dolls with clothing collections, some interesting games, and musical keyboards for the rock stars of the future.

■ Richman Cotton Company

Charming toys of the traditional variety. See page 64 under **Clothing.**

■ Sears, Roebuck & Co.

Toy catalog with comprehensive selection of toys for all ages. Seasonal edition. See page 266 under **General Merchandise Catalogs.**

■ Sensational Beginnings

P.O. Box 2009, 430 N. Monroe, Monroe, MI 48161, (800) 444–2147

Free 32-page color catalog

The folks at Sensational Beginnings bill their publications as "the seeing, hearing, touching, baby catalog" and indeed, the biggest concentration of their products is for children from earliest infancy to five years. Eschewing products that need batteries or electricity, the company has made an effort to select stimulating toys that run on kidpower!

A nice selection of crib toys, mobiles, wooden and cloth rattles, teethers, stuffed animals, sheepskins, and even pillowcases have been assembled for the infant.

Toddles will enjoy stacking toys, spinning tops, shape sorters, simple construction sets, knobbed puzzles, push and pull toys, and a variety of hard and soft balls.

Lullaby audiocassettes will ease youngsters into sleep, and tapes of morning songs, hand rhymes, and songs for playtime will stimulate laughter and learning. Children's picture books include a poetry collection, bedtime stories, and first board books. Several titles of books and videos aimed at helping parents include breast-feeding guides, infant massage instruction, and baby care basics. Siblings and siblings-to-be can learn about babies through titles like *101 Things to do with a Baby* and *The New Baby at Your House.*

■ The Sesame Street Catalog

2515 East 43rd Street, Chattanooga, TN 37422, (800) 446–9415

Free 48-page color catalog

The whole Sesame Street gang is here with their likenesses on everything from slippers and bottles to sewing boxes and umbrellas. Little children *love* this public television show, and they delight in products that bear the faces of their television friends.

Now they can have a bedtime penlight with Oscar the Grouch on the side, tea sets with Big Bird, Bert, and Ernie on the plates, and a soft vinyl Cookie Monster that can float in the bathtub. Thirteen-inch Sesame Street Babies dressed in diapers and bonnets are priced at $14.95. A set of eight rolls of wrapping paper plus gift tags, all with colorful Sesame Street designs, sells for $9.95.

Other toys, puppets, stuffed animals, games, puzzles, learning aids, videos, books, and even software should please the preschoolers in your house.

■ Shaker Shops West

Five Inverness Way, Inverness, CA 94937, (415) 669–7256

$3.00 for 27-page color catalog

Although Shaker communities were not actually founded farther west than Indiana and Kentucky, Shaker Shop West hand-crafts toys and furnishings in the Shaker tradition.

Hand-crafted toys are modeled after early American designs and include a 6-inch calico bear with movable arms and legs, a 16-inch Shaker doll, a Jacob's Ladder tumbling toy, and a 9-piece furniture puzzle which can be used to furnish a dollhouse.

A child's version of the New Lebanon Rocking chair will become a beautiful family heirloom; it is available as a kit ($77.00), or it can be assembled and custom-finished for $149.00.

■ The Sharper Image

P.O. Box 7031, San Francisco, CA 94120-7031, (800) 344–4444

$2.00 for a 77-page color catalog

High tech toys for adults is the prevailing category here but some great kids' gadgets are sprinkled throughout the pages. A boombox is built like the back end of a '59 pink or black Cadillac. Open the trunk and you will find a quality stereo AM/FM radio and a recording cassette deck. A retractable antenna is styled just like the car's antenna. Your child can cruise with this 50s nostalgia for $199.00.

For $99.00, a talking parrot with a sound-recording microchip will repeat anything you say. Bytey Bird also uses lots of body language, flapping his wings and moving his head and body.

The Laser FX II Image Maker will sweep your walls and ceilings with multi-colored lights similar to the laser light effects at live concerts. Light beams respond to the beat and frequency of the music being played in the room; the unit plugs into a wall outlet and sells for $249.00.

■ Toys To Grow On

P.O. Box 17, 2695 E. Dominguez Street, Long Beach, CA 90801,
(800) 542–8338; in Los Angeles, (213) 603–8890

Free 48-page color catalog

These folks pride themselves on their 100 percent efficiency (your order shipped within 48 hours), 100 percent toll free ordering, and 100 percent guarantee (you may return any item).

This terrific catalog is certain to provide you and your child with some good ideas. They have lovely seasonal goods; a reusable wooden Advent calendar has twenty-four drawers, each containing a little ornament that you can hang on the knob of the drawer.

Grandma's Dress-Up Trunk has dress-up clothes for a little girl and a 12-inch doll that comes with all the same clothes that the little girl receives.

Look for kids' collections of horses, cars, stickers, and rubber bugs; check the inventory for costumes, puzzles, rubber stamps, books, art supplies, games, kid-safe makeup, marbles, blocks, and soft music cassettes.

■ Tully Toys, Inc.

4606 Warrenton Road, Vicksburg, MS 39180, (601) 638–1724

Free 4-page color catalog

A menagerie of children's rockers is amusing and reasonably priced. Your child can ride the range, prowl the plains, or swim in the sea on an elephant, giraffe, ostrich, ram, lion, shrimp, dinosaur, cow, and more. The hand grips of each rocker are appropriate to the species whenever possible. Kids hang onto the neck of a dinosaur or a giraffe and hold onto the curling horns of a ram. There are sixteen critters available, all handmade with a combination of natural-finish oak and ash.

■ USA Toys

P.O. Box 158, Cathedral Station, New York, NY 10025

Free 5-page color catalog

Created from the finest woods and sure to become beloved treasures, USA Toys have no sharp edges and all the finishes are non-toxic.

A folding ironing board and iron is $31.99. A solid wood teaching clock that can be hung on the wall is $14.99, and a solid pine tic-tac-toe board with balls marked X or O is $17.99.

Just a dozen items are offered. Children will enjoy a clown puzzle, an animal van, a pull dog, building blocks, a slide puzzle, a doll cradle, a jeep, a rocking horse, and a double-sided easel.

■ U. S. Chess Catalog

186 Route 9W, New Windsor, NY 12500-7698, (914) 562–3555

Free 24-page color catalog

This is the official catalog of the U.S. Chess Federation, serving members for more than fifty years. Dozens of chess sets and accessories are available, as are battery-operated clocks for perfect timing. A buttery-soft cowhide playing surface can be rolled up and used anywhere; it lists for $29.95.

Encyclopedias of chess game openings and closings show how to clinch the win. The Chessmaster video game cartridge lets you learn, practice, and play chess alone or with a friend on your Nintendo system.

■ The Wooden Soldier

Quality toys for young children. See page 68 under **Clothing.**

■ Wordsworth Ltd.

Box 410, Birmingham, MI 48012-0410, (313) 435–5573

$1.00 for a 50-page color catalog

Wordsworth Ltd. is the joint effort of a former child educator and a high school and college counselor. Offering primarily a collection of Discovery Playthings, the partners believe that a toy's play value is measured by the joy that comes from solving a problem or learning something new. Parents will find nursery rhyme puzzles, nesting dolls, water activity toys, rubber stamps, hand puppets, and more.

For babies, they offer the Infant Stim-Mobile ($13.95) to hang over the crib when your child is very young. The black and white faces and graphics offer engaging views from any angle, and the mobile can be packed flat for travel.

This is the first time I have seen a Paint, Peel & Stick Creativity Kit. Your child brushes the brilliantly colored paint onto a vinyl work surface. Once dry, the pictures peel off the mat and cling to any smooth surface; the children actually make their own stickers! Non-toxic and 100 percent biodegradable, the washable peel-off paint comes in five vivid colors, and the kit also contains five brushes, palette knife, work mat, and directions, all in a handy storage bucket; it is suggested for children four and up and sells for $14.95.

■ World Traveler/Orchard Toys

P.O. Box 550, Needham Heights, MA 02194, (617) 444–2296

Free 4-page color catalog

World Traveler sells games, giant floor puzzles, and tracing sets for children of all ages.

Alphabet, Fire Engine, and School Bus jigsaw puzzles have no more than 25 pieces and so will be fun for small children. Teddy Bears' Picnic, Scaredy Cat, Three Blind Mice, and Nursery Rhyme Cards all sound like fun first games. Many of the games for older children involve world geography, so fun and learning are combined.

Everything is very reasonably priced, with most products costing between $8.00 and $10.00.

■ World Wide Games

Colchester, CT 06415, (800) 243–9232

Free 36-page color catalog

World Wide Games has done a splendid job of producing outstanding quality in a wide variety of board games, puzzles, and activities like pick-up-sticks and dominoes.

If you enjoy this kind of entertainment, you should not miss this catalog. It has the standards like Yahtzee, Monopoly, Scrabble, Sorry, Cage Bingo, and Pictionary, but more importantly, it has wonderfully interesting wooden puzzles and games like Ta Ka Radi Tiles, Mexican Balero, Pic-E-U-Nee (table tennis for one), Shisima, Senet, and dozens more.

They also have several Sliding puzzles, Tavern puzzles, and a special section of fun and easy skill games for the younger children.

DOLLS—STANDARD SIZE

■ Amazing Grace Elephant Company, Ltd.

G.P.O. Box 12206, Hong Kong, Phone: 011-852-4541608

Free 39-page color catalog

Amazing Grace sells handcrafts, giftware, and jewelry from all over the Far East. The only items for children are dolls, and naturally, they are designed with an Oriental flair.

A mother doll, Ma Jong, carries her daughter Jong Yi in a floral-printed back carrier and they are both dressed in their finest red satin. Ma Jong is 15 inches tall and sells for $23.00. Jong Yi is 8 inches tall and sells separately for $11.00. Martial arts enthusiasts will enjoy the black-belted Kung Fu Charlie, while decidedly gentler, soft-bodied Chinese sisters are 14 inches tall and $23.00 each. Another softly stuffed doll is Mei Mei (little sister); she is 14 inches tall and sells for $14.50.

■ bea skydell's dolls and toys

476 Union Avenue, Middlesex, NJ 08846-9990,
(800) 843–3655; in New Jersey, (201) 356–5400

Free 40-page color catalog

This is the place to look if you would like to start a special doll collection for your favorite child. If you need dolls for everyday play, however, the prices here are too steep in most cases.

After ten years in the mail-order business, bea skydell has put together an amazing collection of lifelike, exquisitely made dolls. The finest brands and limited editions are here, with names like Götz, Madame Alexander, Dynasty, Dolls by Pauline, Wendy Lawton, Robin Woods, Walker Dolls, Carolle, Jerri, Royal House, Turner Vlasta, and more.

The Effanbee dolls are some of the few that are affordable as play friends. Prices on these range from $22.00 to $46.75.

Do you remember Ginny dolls? Well, they are here as well, and they are also affordable with prices from $20.00 for the Medical Ginny to $34.00 for the Ginny Cowgirl.

■ The Cotton Gin

P.O. Box 24, Deep Creek Farm, Jarrisburg, NC 27947-0024, (800) 637–2446

Free 24-page color catalog

The Cotton Gin has been providing handcrafted country gifts and accessories for your home and family for twenty years.

Old-fashioned handmade dolls will make lovely gifts for children. A See-Saw doll ($28.95) with yarn hair has a frowning face until you turn her upside down—hidden under her skirt is another half-doll, but this one has a smile. A wooden see-saw for the doll is $11.95.

Miriam High is a basketmaker doll, and she holds one of her miniature creations over her arm. Baskets are signed and dated by The Cotton Gin's local craftsmen.

Country rabbits are dear little long-eared, tea-colored dolls dressed in ribbons and calicos with contrasting aprons.

You will also find three sizes of tea party bears, the Valentines sisters doing their homework and pitting cherries, plantation dolls, and a porcelain Victorian bride doll dressed in ecru lace with mauve ribbons and roses.

■ The Country Loft

South Shore Park, Hingham, MA 02043, (800) 225–5408

Free 40-page color catalog

If you are a fan of American Country decor, you will enjoy thumbing through this catalog of traditional furniture and accessories which include some toys and dolls. Soft folk-art dolls are sold throughout these pages. A schoolteacher doll dressed in calico holds a daily lesson slate; you can buy her alone for $36.00, or with her school desk for $49.00. Tom and Kitty are the names of two silly-faced cat twins that sell for $20.00 each ($38.00 for the pair).

Mohair bears, a Besty Ross rabbit, and doll-sized chairs, benches, rocking horses, and a doll wagon are all suitable for children and look like they came straight from Grandma's attic.

■ Country Manor

Mail Order Dept., Rt. 211, P.O. Box 520, Sperryville, VA 22740-0520, (800) 344–8354

$2.00 for a 52-page black-and-white (some color) illustrated catalog

From the foothills of Virginia's Blue Ridge mountains, Country Manor brings you country collectibles and folk art dolls along with other traditional products for the whole family.

A charming collection of cloth folk dolls come in various sizes and are dressed in country fabrics. Black or white 5- and 6-inch dolls are $5.95 each. The 10-inch dolls are $11.95 and a 14-inch doll is $18.95. Cloth Amish dolls are 11 inches long and sell for $15.95 each. Still more dolls with names like Fat Alice with Pet Pig, Long Tall Sally, and Bootie Doll look like dolls that Grandma would have loved.

Several wooden toys are also available. A Noah's Ark with seven pairs of hand-carved wooden animals is $44.00. Wooden *Wizard of Oz* ornaments make imaginative toys as well as Christmas decorations. A handcrafted wooden rattle made in Vermont from a single piece of rock maple is 6 inches long and sells for $14.00.

■ Dollspart Supply Co., Inc.

Doll-making supplies, clothes, stands. Madame Alexander dolls.
See page 6 under **Arts and Crafts.**

■ Hearthside Quilts

Doll crib quilt kits. See page 9 under **Arts and Crafts.**

■ Kirchen Bros.

Doll-making supplies. See page 11 under **Arts and Crafts.**

■ Platypus

Kits for dolls and doll quilts. See page 13 under **Arts and Crafts.**

■ Pleasant Company

P.O. Box 190, Middleton, WI 53562-0190, (800) 845–0005

Free 46-page color catalog

Pleasant Company features The American Girls Collection of dolls, dollclothes, accessories, and books. The lives of three girls from three eras in American history are embodied in these lovely dolls. Kirsten represents a Swedish immigrant child living on the Minnesota frontier in 1854; Samantha is meant to be a young Victorian orphan living with her grandmother in New York City in 1904; Molly is modeled after a child from suburban Illinois during World War II.

The dolls are 18 inches tall, have soft cloth bodies, posable arms, legs, and heads of vinyl, and hair that can be brushed and braided. All of their clothes are historically accurate reproductions of period costumes and are finely finished garments with Velcro closures.

Each doll comes with a paperback book of her life story and one outfit. Several changes of clothes and many accessories for each doll are sold separately. Doll dishes, trunks, furniture, food, school books, and more are among the extras.

These dolls are a bit pricey, but not out of the norm for very good quality dolls (and they are *the* rage in the third grade). A doll and paperback book sells for $74; accessories and outfits range from $8 to about $22 each. Furniture is $25 and up.

Pleasant Company also sells a collection of books about the girls and a collection of activity and craft books that reflect the pastimes they might have enjoyed in each of the eras. Patterns for all of the doll clothes are also offered, as are children's clothes to match the doll clothes (in sizes 6X to 16).

■ Shoppe Full of Dolls

39 North Main Street, New Hope, PA 18938, (215) 862–5524

$2.00 for a 23-page color catalog

Dolls for all tastes and budgets are here at fair prices. The first page offers discontinued dolls that will be of special interest to collectors. After that, choose from brands like Madame Alexander, Ginny, Kewpie, Mattel Barbies, Royal House of Dolls, Suzanne Gibson, and Robin Woods. *Gone With the Wind* and *Wizard of Oz* dolls feature character dolls from these films. A 9-inch munchkin is $29.98 and an 11-inch Auntie Em is $36.00. You can also buy film and cartoon stars like The Three Stooges, Betty Boop, or a 3-inch vinyl Batman.

Career dolls are appropriately dressed for nursing, law enforcement, the executive suite, and the convent; another assortment is decked out in Christmas finery.

Prices range from under $5.00 for a tiny figure to a mid-range of $18.00 to $60.00; large dolls and collector's editions sell for as high as $342.00.

■ Standard Doll Co.

Doll-making kits, doll clothes, patterns, and doll furniture kits.
See page 15 **Arts and Crafts.**

■ Timbers Woodworking

Dollcradle patterns. See page 17 under **Arts and Crafts.**

■ USA Doll Company, Inc.

2005 Gentilly Boulevard, New Orleans, LA 70119, (800) USA–DOLL

$3.50 for a 31-page color catalog

USA Doll Company, Inc. is an authorized distributor of Gambina Doll products. A series of about fifty dolls are available with moving arms, legs, eyes, and heads and rooted hair that can be braided, teased, or curled. The dolls can be hand-washed, and most garments are designed for easy removal.

Gambina Doll, Tammy Traveler, Sally Rally, Marie Laveau, and Ninkie are the most popular models in this collection.

DOLLHOUSES AND ACCESSORIES

■ Annie's Attic

Needlework dollhouse furniture. See page 1 under **Arts and Crafts.**

■ Cherry Tree Toys

Dollhouse and dollhouse furniture kits. See page 2 under **Arts and Crafts.**

■ Doll Domiciles

P.O. Box 91026, Atlanta, GA 30364, (404) 766–5572

$1.00 for a 16-page black-and-white illustrated catalog

Doll Domiciles sells dollhouse plans for those lucky children who have a skilled craftsperson handy to complete the project. The plans for the houses are fully detailed drawings for architecturally and historically authentic dollhouses.

Of the eleven house plans, some are reproductions of actual historic homes (an adaptation of Josias Moody's house in Williamsburg, Virginia, sells for $7.50), others are composite designs, drawn to reflect the architectural details of a particular period (a grand, three-story Second Empire Victorian sells for $12.00).

■ Gail Wilson Duggan Designs, Inc.

Folk dolls, clothing, furniture, and miniature accessories.
See page 8 under **Arts and Crafts.**

■ HearthSong

Wooden dollhouses from Germany, dollhouse families and furniture.
See page 224 under **Toys**.

■ Lundby of Sweden AB

Box 303, S-443 01 Lerum, Sweden, Phone: 0302-223 55

Free 24-page color catalog

Lundby presents a lovely collection of dollhouses and dollhouse furnishings. Only four dollhouses are shown in this catalog, but lots of unusual and interesting furniture and dolls fill the pages. The Family Bakes section has stoves, sinks, three styles of dishwashers, a clothes dryer, a microwave, and several appliance combinations. Just choose a table and chair set and pots and pans for a complete kitchen set-up.

A couch that turns into a bed, bookcases, a piano, fireplace, chandeliers, dolls, and extra doll clothes all add up to a full house.

■ The Miniature Shop

RE: Miniature and Dollhouse Catalog, 1115 Fourth Avenue, Huntington, WV 25701, (304) 523–2418

$10.00 for a 412-page color catalog and price list

The Miniature and Dollhouse Catalog is truly the source book for this popular pastime.

This catalog is not an exclusive publication from The Miniature Shop, but is published by a distributor and used by several dollhouse retailers. You may be able to buy or borrow a copy from your local dollhouse store; if not, you can order a copy from The Miniature Shop.

Expand your dollhouse with traditional dormers, and dress up the windows with wooden cornices and matchstick or Venetian blinds. Install an old-fashioned weather vane on the roof, or keep the parlor tidy with a walnut waste-paper basket. All these plus dolls, dollhouses, and literally *thousands* of fascinating miniatures are sold through this remarkable resource.

■ My Uncle

133 Main Street, Fryeburg, ME 04037

Free 3-page brochure

My Uncle sells a dollhouse kit for a seventeenth-century New England Saltbox home. This careful reproduction includes all the materials necessary to complete the project (except simple tools). All of the siding, roofing, and trims are wood (no masonite or particle board).

The dollhouse is scaled 1 inch to 1 foot, and the kit sells for $325.00. Allow eight to ten weeks for delivery.

■ Rose's Doll House Store

5826 West Bluemound Road, Milwaukee, WI 53213, (414) 259–9965

Free 48-page color catalog

Rose's Doll House Store publishes a catalog filled with dollhouses, dollhouse furniture, dolls, toys, and miniatures. I counted six dollhouses in their eighth annual catalog and hundreds of items for the dollhouse aficionado. Dollhouse wallpapers are designed to suit every room in the dollhouse, and hundreds of miniatures have been crafted to fully decorate any style of house inside and out. Buy miniature framed pictures, tiny stuffed animals, carpet, curtains, tricycles, pillows, perfume sets, or a diamond pendant necklace to drape around the neck of one of the many tiny dolls they sell. You can even buy a miniature dollhouse to put inside your dollhouse!

Prices are reasonable and imaginative color layouts display all the items in rooms so you can get a sense of the objects you are ordering and good ideas on how to use them in your own dollhouse.

■ Suncoast Discount Arts & Crafts

Dollhouses and dollhouse wallpaper. See page 16 under **Arts and Crafts.**

■ The Wooden Soldier

Three-story dollhouse, doll furniture. See page 68 under **Clothing.**

KITES AND BOOMERANGS

■ Boomerang Man

1806 N. 3rd Street, Monroe, LA 71201-4222, (318) 325–8157

Free 4-page black-and-white illustrated catalog

E-Z toss, one-hand, behind-the-back. Your child will be doing it all with a 'rang from the Boomerang Man.

Models from the United States, Australia, England, Germany, and France are pictured with full descriptions.

All B's, as they call them, arrive with detailed throwing instructions.

■ Into The Wind

1408 Pearl Street, Boulder, CO 80302, (303) 449–5356

Free 48-page color catalog

This great catalog has dozens and dozens of fantastic kites, kite-making kits and materials, and even wind socks, whirligigs, and lightweight boomerangs.

Every kite is coded with a rating system that progresses from "very easy to fly" to "challenging, experience advised." A little black teddy bear silhouette appears next to the special kits for kids that are particularly easy to fly and have only a light pull.

Every kind of kite imaginable, in gorgeous colors, is listed here. Peter Powell stunt kites, TRLBY multiple kites, stunters, deltas, beautiful snowflake shapes, long Mylar dragons, and much more are available at reasonable prices, from $5.50 to $185.00.

OUTDOOR PLAY EQUIPMENT

■ Child Life Play Specialties, Inc.

55 Whitney Street, Holliston, MA 01746-8001, (800) 462–4445; in Massachusetts, (508) 429–4639

$1.00 for a 27-page color catalog

We have had a Child Life play set for three years, and it is still hanging in against the rugged New England weather. Child Life has been making durable, wooden play equipment for more than forty years, and you can count on them for a variety of quality products. Douglas fir, Alaskan yellow cedar, pine, and oak are used in every set, and pressure treated 2x3s and 2x4s provide a long life.

A basic swing set with a climbing tower, yellow climbing net, and three swings is $529.00. A smaller three-ladder frame with three swing places is $395.00. An optional 8-foot slide can be added to either set for $115.00.

The basic sets with three or four swing places can be customized with many combinations of the dozens of options Child Life sells. For instance, imagine the fun the kids would have with a Crow's Nest Tree House, a trapeze bar and rings, a deluxe baby swing, or a toddler's swing. All of these accessories and more can be added at any time.

Once you have customized your swing set, you can move on to a solid cedar children's picnic table ($175.00), a Fireman's Gym, a rope ladder, a knotted climbing rope, an adjustable seesaw, and a variety of sandboxes. Every part of every play set is fully guaranteed, and replacement swings, hardware, and paint are available.

■ Children's Playgrounds, Inc.

190 Concord Avenue, Cambridge, MA 02138, (617) 497–1588

Children's Playgrounds build large wooden structures for public playgrounds, and they also import Quadro play systems for indoor use in private homes. The Quadro systems are available in three basic kits.

■ English Garden Toys, Ltd.

Medrad Drive, Indianola, PA 15051, (800) 445–5675; in Pennsylvania, (412) 767–5332

$1.00 for a 40-page color catalog

This brand of outdoor play equipment is the kind that Princess Di uses to entertain the future King of England. English Garden Toys offers an extensive range of well-made activity structures, toys, and sports equipment. Jolly good fun can be had on trampolines, scooters, slides, treehouses, swings, sandboxes, seesaws, and a merry-go-round. Even a 26-foot roller coaster with 10-foot extension tracks is available. Most of the equipment is made from weatherproof galvanized steel and everything is fit for your own king . . . or queen.

■ Gym-N-I Playgrounds, Inc.

Box 96, Laurel Bend, New Braunfels, TX 78130, (512) 629–6000

Free 12-page color catalog

Gym-N-I makes outdoor wooden playscapes and accessories that are designed for expansion and modification as your children grow. Holes are even pre-drilled for future additions.

With strong, warp-resistant 4 x 4 redwood uprights used on all vertical pieces, these products are sturdy and built to last.

You can start with the basic swingscape, which consists of three swings, trapeze bars, two climbing ladders, and overhead monkey bars; it sells for $329.99. If you wish, add a slide and mini-deck, a gang plank and safety rope, a tent top, a first-level sandbox, or any of several exciting options.

■ Landscape Structures, Inc.

601 7th Street South, Delano, MN 55328, (800) 328–0035;
in Minnesota, (612) 479–2546

Free 25-page color catalog

Landscape Structures has been developing children's outdoor play equipment for twenty years and they do offer more than the typical wooden structure with three swings, a slide, and a climbing area.

Most of their colorful equipment looks like it was designed with the skill levels of toddlers to eight-year-olds specifically in mind. They have a collection of easily customized, multi-functional "learning centers." These modular, expandable systems can be changed and enlarged.

Units are made of heavy, galvanized tubular steel, with a baked-on polyester powder coating that resists corrosion and holds its luster indefinitely. This is not an inexpensive product, but you have so many choices of ladders, tunnels, panels, tables, bars, beams, and benches that the cost is quite flexible. An interesting structure could be devised for about $1,000.

■ Woodbuilt

P.O. Box 92, Janesville, WI 53547-0092, (608) 754–5050

Free 11-page color catalog

If the prices of quality wooden outdoor-activity sets are a threat to the family budget (many start near $1,000), welcome to Woodbuilt, where you can do-it-yourself for about one-fourth that cost.

Their kits include plans for playcenters of various sizes and shapes; hardware, instructions, and basic equipment such as swings and bars are part of each package. You provide the lumber—4 x 4 and 4 x 6 pieces are required for extra strength and reliability. Plans can easily be enlarged and modified.

The basic starter kit is the Scout, which comes with two swing seats and a trapeze bar. This kit is $99.50, and Woodbuilt estimates your lumber cost at $34.00.

■ Woodset

P.O. Box 2127, Waldorf, MD 20604, (301) 843–7767

Free 11-page color catalog

Woodset sells outdoor playsets with versatile modular components that allow buyers to arrange the pieces in a variety of designs. Play platforms, swing structures, and swing apparatus, as well as towers, slides, poles, ropes, ladders, and balance beams are among the optional equipment.

These durable units are made from high grade 4x4 and 4x6 southern yellow pine that has been treated with a special stain containing a water repellent and a fungicide.

PUZZLES

■ Bits & Pieces

1 Puzzle Place, B8016, Stevens Point, WI 54481-7199, (800) JIG–SAWS

Free 32-page color catalog

This catalog presents real treats for the jigsaw puzzle lover with all levels of skill represented.

For $16.95, you and your child can finish Mad King Ludwig's Dream by fitting together 1500 pieces to complete his marvelous Neuschanwanstein Castle. Three hundred large pieces form a world map, and children can glue the pieces together for a permanent reference map ($8.50). A set of six, 7x7-inch 100-piece jigsaw puzzles depict old-fashioned Christmas cards and are just the right size for stocking stuffers ($19.95 for set of six). Blank 80-piece jigsaw puzzles await your child's drawing or painting skills.

Most of the puzzles are too difficult for the younger child, but older kids will have hours of fun with dinosaur and animal puzzles.

Some toys are scattered through this lively catalog. A foolproof yo-yo will return to you automatically; it comes with a guide to famous yo-yo tricks and sells for $16.95. For cat lovers of all ages, they offer *The Cat Game Book* ($19.95) with more than three dozen cat games from around the world. The collection includes cat finger puppets, word games, a set of cat fortune-telling cards, five cat board games, and more. You will also find a bubble maker, kaleidoscope, a balloon magic kit, and a wooden nativity scene.

■ Every Buddies Garden

P.O. Box 778, Corvallis, OR 97339

Free 6-page color catalog

"Peaceful puzzles for peaceful play" is the motto here, and more than thirty colorful, handcrafted hardwood puzzles are for sale.

Beginners' puzzles are offered with small wooden knobs for gripping by little hands. An 11-piece pegged Vegie Garden puzzle shows a cross-section view of various vegetables growing above ground and their roots underneath the dirt. Alphabet, number, and even some 3-D, multi-layered puzzles are offered for small children.

All puzzle colors are non-toxic and coated with a tough, satin finish. Each puzzle comes with a handwritten signature and date; an information card is included to help you order a replacement piece should you ever lose part of the puzzle. You can also have a child's name cut into any one of six puzzles for a personal touch.

■ LibertyTree

Puzzles and games on our heritage and practice of liberty. See page 35 under **Books.**

■ Pacific Puzzle Company

378 Guemes Island Road, Anacortes, WA 98221, (206) 293–7034

Free, 5 pages of color information sheets

Pacific Puzzle Company is justifiably proud of their hand-cut hardwood map puzzles of the United States, the world, and individual continents, as well as of their alphabet, numbers, and geometric shape puzzles.

The standard United States puzzle is a best-seller and is available in three sizes. Each puzzle is designed with the use of current maps and includes state capitals, many cities, rivers, lakes, and mountains. A Beginners' United States puzzle (for children three and up) is 14x19 inches and sells for $39.00. Puzzles of the five continents sell for $16.00 or $19.00.

Puzzles of dinosaurs, whales, fishes, cats, and elephants are designed for younger children and can be ordered with knobs. Add $.20 per knob with a $3.00 minimum.

■ The Puzzle People

22719 Tree Farm Road, Colfax, CA 95713, (916) 637–4823

Free illustrated brochures, some in color.

"Our business is puzzling people" state the folks in charge here.

These handcrafted puzzles are made in the United States of select birch or California pine plywood. Only non-toxic stains and finishes are used, and replacement pieces are available.

Educational map puzzles of the United States and of each separate state are available; the state maps are cut into individual counties. Also available are maps of Europe, the world, or your choice of countries.

"Stand Ups" are, as the name implies, puzzles that are designed to stand upright when put together. A 10x12-inch 7-piece spouting whale is $10.00. A stegosaurus with nine pieces is $12.00, and a 3-piece Baby Bronto is just $2.50.

■ Stave Puzzles Inc.

Main Street, Norwich, VT 05055, (802) 295–5200

Free 32-page black-and-white catalog

Stave produces luxury, limited-edition, handcrafted puzzles that include special effects like irregular edges, stand-up pieces, split corners, drop-outs, and hidden edges.

Prices start at $200.00 and go to $2,500 for the most mind-bending designs. Only two of forty buyers have been able to solve their "It's a Clowder of Cats" puzzle. These beauties are designed and priced for true aficionados, but the kids may be able to help complete some of the simplest compositions.

TEDDY BEARS AND STUFFED TOYS

■ bear-in-mind

53 Bradford Street, W. Concord, MA 01742, (508) 369–1167

$1.00 for 40-page color catalog

Since its beginning in 1978, the bear-in-mind catalog has been a mecca of sorts for arctophiles (admirers of bears or anything bear related).

You will discover the very finest in stuffed-bear makers on these pages with the likes of Gund, North American, Hermann, Steiff, and Eden. The company guarantees that if for any reason you and your bear do not get along, you may return it within thirty days for a refund, and they will find another good home for it.

If you are bear hunting for more than just the stuffed variety, you will also find arctophile T-shirts ($11.00) or sweatshirts ($21.00) and a Mama Bear tea set by Otagiri. They sell teddy muffin pans made of heavy cast-iron with six different molds and a non-stick finish ($19.25). Teddy cast-iron doorstops with red bows are $19.25. Look here for books, a watch, nightshirts, and more T-shirts and sweatshirts.

■ CR's Crafts

Patterns for bears, dolls, and puppets. See page 4 under **Arts and Crafts**.

■ Cuddle Toys By Douglas

Douglas Co., Inc., P.O. Drawer D, Keene, NH 03431, (800) 992–9002,
in New Hampshire, (603) 352–3414

$2.00 for a 40-page color catalog, refundable with first order.

Straight from the factory come some of the most realistic, well-made stuffed animals
you will find anywhere. These are not imports, but are made with pride right in
New Hampshire. They even take the extra precaution of using heavy-duty washers
to make sure the eyes in their toys stay locked in securely!

A majestic Sentor Stag sells for $66.00, a 16-inch, howling Lobo Wolf is $53.00. A
very cuddly moose, a chipmunk, a Scotty dog, a snowy owl, a puffin, a whale, a
penguin, an otter, a harbor seal, a flamingo, and an "alley gator" flock across the
pages of this exceptionally well done catalog. Dozens more await your review and
you will be amazed how lifelike and lovable they all are.

■ Gail Wilson Duggan Design, Inc.

Felt bears, clothing, furniture, and miniature accessories.
See page 8 under **Arts and Crafts.**

■ Pillow Pals, Inc.

P.O. Box 291, Harvey, LA 70059, (504) 367–9814

Free 4-page catalog and price list

Now your child can hug a pillow that will (sort of) hug back. Available in white,
assorted pastel colors, and gingham, these cheerful bedfellows have faces on the
front side of the pillow and arms and legs that dangle from the sides and bottom.
You can select one of several characters and sizes. These pillow friends are great for
car rides and sleepovers. The small size is $7.95, medium is $10.95, and large is
$12.95.

■ Schwatlo Gm 6H

Zeilring 26, D-6239 Eppstein, West Germany, Phone: 0 61 98-32970

Write for current price of 16-page color catalog

This wonderful catalog shows the entire collection of adorable, lifelike, stuffed animals made by the renowned Steiff. Although the catalog is written in German, a
price list, a description of the toys, and instructions for ordering are included in
English, with prices quoted in U.S. dollars.

Of course, you will find lots of cuddly teddy bears, but you will also see pigs, zebras, lions, tigers, Husky dogs, leopards, hares, Dachshunds, lambs, ducks, Scotch terriers, West Highland terriers, frogs, and dinosaurs.

Eleven-inch glove puppets ($25.00 and $27.00) are available as a crocodile, a king, Punch, a police officer, and a devil. These animal toys are expensive, but remarkably realistic and beautifully made.

■ Shillcraft

Latchhook kits for teddy bears and stuffed animals.
See page 15 under **Arts and Crafts.**

■ Soundprints Corporation

165 Water Street, Norwalk, CT 06856, (800) 228–7839

Free 19-page color catalog

Soundprints provides top-quality plush toy animals along with beautiful storybooks and tapes that help bring the featured animals to life for young children. They feature The Smithsonian Wild Heritage Collection and their items are of the best quality.

A dear little 12-inch Alaskan moose calf comes with the book and audiocassette *Beezle's Bravery*; kids can enjoy the story of a moose calf who leaves his mother and lives on his own ($36.95 for the 3-piece set).

Soundprints has a wonderful selection of sea otters, beavers, Dinobaby Pop-Up Books, tassel-eared squirrels, a wild Alaska series, and more.

■ The Toy Works

Fiddler's Elbow Road, Middle Falls, NY 12848, (518) 692–9665

$2.00 for a 24-page color catalog

The Toy Works produces soft stuffed toys printed in full color on suede cloth. This collection contains faithful reproductions of characters from many children's classic stories. From *The Wind in the Willows* come very realistic renditions of Ratty, Mole, Toad, and Mr. Badger. Characters from Beatrix Potter, *Babar, Alphabears, Foxwood Tales,* Mother Goose, *Goldilocks and the Three Bears, The Velveteen Rabbit,* and more are all faithfully reproduced. Many of these toys are also available in sew-it-yourself kits.

Twins

■

■ A Baby Carriage

5935 W. Irving Park Road, Chicago, IL 60634,
(800) 228–TWIN; in Illinois, (312) 794–2742

Free black-and-white illustrated brochure

A Baby Carriage has made juvenile furniture since 1955, and they offer seven styles
of carriages for those parents blessed with more than one newborn. Manufacturers
such as Delta, Inglesina Biposta, Perego, and Maclaren produce strollers for twins;
two models will comfortably hold triplets, and yet another is designed for quads.
Parents of a toddler and a newborn will also find that a double stroller is a practical
solution for their family. You can also buy mosquito netting, clear rainshields, and
wire shopping baskets.

Prices run from $139.95 for a reclinable tandem to $595.00 for a quad style
imported from Italy by Inglesina Biposta.

■ Racing Strollers, Inc.

Heavy-duty twin strollers designed for use by joggers.
See page 143 under **Infant Products and Equipment.**

■ Twice As Nice

McGills, 4965 Center, Omaha, NE 68106, (402) 556–1861

Free color brochure

Twice As Nice features novelty items such as T-shirts, mugs, and hats that celebrate
twins. You can buy T-shirts that proclaim "Double Trouble" or "Double Pleasure,"
and balloons that wish "Happy Birthday Twins." A mug and a double-visored hat
ask "I'm their leader—which way did they go?" Car signs proclaim "Twins on
Board" or "Twins in Trunk." You will also find bumper stickers, twin birth
announcements, and birthday invitations.

■ Twozies Plus

P.O. Box 462, West Hempstead, NY 11552, (516) 486–6135

Free black-and-white illustrated product sheets

Sweatshirts proclaim "My Twin Did It," and T-shirts announce that the wearer is the sister, grandfather, or grandmother of twins. Key chains read "I love my twins."

For $9.95, you can have a license plate frame with your choice of eight sayings. My vote for most original goes to : "We Are Parents of Twingles (Twins and Singles)."

Look here for mugs, car window signs, hats, and a double-sided easel.

Video

■

■ American Camping Association, Inc.

Camping and nature videocassettes. See page 19 under **Books**.

■ A Baby's Secret Garden

Parenting videocassettes. See page 103 under **Gifts**.

■ Bennett Marine Video-Dept. C

730 Washington Street, Marina del Rey, CA 90292,
(800) 262–8862; in California, (213) 821–3329

Free 46-page black-and-white illustrated catalog

With more than 500 titles on boating, fishing, and diving, Bennett is one of the
largest suppliers of marine videos.

Young children will enjoy a special educational series called "Tell Me Why,"
which features a dozen 30-minute tapes on topics like Water and Weather,
Mammals, Fish, Shellfish and Other Underwater Life, Prehistoric Animals, Reptiles
and Amphibians; each tape sells for $19.95. Several titles from the Jacques Cousteau
Undersea World series are also suitable for the younger children and are available
here for $29.95 each.

Older kids interested in boating might enjoy videos like *Learn To Sail, The Boater's
Video, Wm. F. Buckley's Celestial Navigation Simplified, Yank it Back! The Story of
America's Cup, Learn to Sail, The Annapolis Book of Seamanship, Scuba Video Refresher
Course, Windsurfing Made Easy*, and *Look Mom I'm Fishing*.

■ Best Products Co., Inc.

Videos for the family. See page 263 under **General Merchandise Catalogs**.

■ Children's Book and Music Center

Extensive choice of classic and new videos. See page 24 under **Books**.

■ Discount Books and Video, Inc.
A variety of videos. See page 27 under **Books**.

■ The Disney Catalog
Disney videos. See page 105 under **Gifts**.

■ Diversions
Entertainment videos for the whole family. See page 28 under **Books**.

■ Educational Activities, Inc.
Early childhood videocassettes. See page 172 under **Records, Tapes, and CDs**.

■ ESPN Home Video
P.O. Box 2342, Chatsworth, CA 91313-2342, (800) 448–3776

Free 24-page color catalog

Brought to you from the sports cable channel, this catalog offers instructional tapes for almost every sport.

Young children will enjoy titles like *My First Skates* ($19.95), *Baseball Card Collecting* ($19.95), and *Magic Johnson: Put Magic In Your Game* ($19.95). *Get the Feeling: Winning* is a 55-minute inspirational tape produced by Sports Illustrated; it is sent to shoppers at no charge with the purchase of any three kids' tapes.

Coaches and parents may pick up some valuable tips from titles like *Teaching Kids Basketball* and *Teaching Kids Soccer*; each tape sells for $29.95.

■ Family Communications
Children's videos from the producers of "Mr. Rogers' Neighborhood." See page 30 under **Books**.

■ Gospel Light Publications
Christian education videos. See page 31 under **Books**.

■ J.A. Enterprises

Self Improvement Video Catalog, 3550 S. Harlan, Suite 260, Denver, CO 80235, (303) 980–1698

Free 25-page catalog

The few dozen titles offered here are designed to help you become healthier, have an easier childbirth, teach your children the alphabet, and make your dog heel.

Olympic champion Mary Lou Retton guides kids through a series of physical activities in *ABC Fun Fit* for $24.95. For $17.95 each, you can buy VHS tapes that are *All About Alphabets, Colors, Numbers, Shapes,* or *Sounds. Animal Alphabet* travels the world with The National Geographic Society to introduce children to exotic animals and colorful letters; each animal-and-letter segment features a song. Other titles include *A Child's Guide to Divorce, For Safety's Sake,* and *Home Alone: A Kid's Guide to Playing Safe When You're On Your Own.*

■ Kimbo Educational

Educational videos. See page 173 under **Records, Tapes, and CDs.**

■ Learn and Play for Kids

Educational videos. See page 227 under **Toys.**

■ Movies Unlimited

6736 Castor Avenue, Philadelphia, PA 19149, (800) 523–0823

$7.95 plus $2.00 shipping; the $7.95 is refundable if your order is $25.00 or more.

This may seem like a lot to pay, but consider that this catalog lists and briefly describes over 20,000 videocassette tapes. Sixty-one pages are devoted just to family titles. Look here also for sections on Concerts and Music, Action and Adventure, Comedy, Documentary, History and War, Musicals, Performing Arts, Religious, Science Fiction and Fantasy, Sports, and Television and Westerns, and you will start to see this as the good value it is.

All Movies Unlimited tapes are in VHS format.

■ Music for Little People

Carefully selected videos, including the Bolshoi Ballet's Nutcracker and the fanciful winter classic, The Snowman. See page 174 under **Records, Tapes, and CDs.**

■ National Geographic Society/Videos Educational Services

Washington, DC 20036, (800) 368–2728; in Maryland, (301) 921–1330

Free 42-page color catalog

Probably some of the most spectacular and educational film available is offered by The National Geographic Society.

From the World of Science they bring you titles such as *Mammals and Their Young, Secrets of Animal Survival,* and *Pets and Their Wild Relatives.* Under Social Studies you will find *Portrait of a Coal Miner, Families of the World,* and *Branches of Government.* All of the films are available on videocassette in VHS format.

General interest films that have been television specials are also available on 59-minute color videocassettes for $26.95. They include titles like *Lions of The African Night, Madagascar, Rain Forest, Egypt: Quest for Eternity, Dr. Leakey and The Dawn of Man, Siberia: the Endless Horizon,* and many more.

■ Piragis' Northwoods Company

Family Camping Video Series. See page 80 under **Clothing.**

■ PlayFair Toys

Educational videos. See page 230 under **Toys.**

■ Rand McNally & Company

Travel and animal videos including titles from National Geographic, National Parks Video, and Readers Digest. See page 39 under **Books.**

■ Sailors Bookshelf, Inc.

Nautical videos. *Annapolis Book of Seamanship* series is a highly regarded choice. See page 39 under **Books.**

■ Salad Days

Small selection of videos. See page 40 under **Books.**

■ Schoolmasters Video

745 State Circle, P.O.Box 1941, Ann Arbor, MI 48106-1941,
(800) 521–2832 (orders only); all other inquiries: (313) 761–5175

Free 96-page color catalog

Schoolmasters offers more than 275 videos for children, all carefully chosen for their educational and entertainment value.

This delightful, comprehensive catalog has something for every age and every taste. Small children will surely enjoy all the newest *Sesame Street* segments, classic tales like *The Elephant's Child*, Dr. Seuss titles, and *The Velveteen Rabbit*. *Charlie Brown* is well represented, as are *Golden Book Classics, My Little Pony,* and *Tell Me Why* video encyclopedias.

Personal development and educational titles abound; look for *What's Happening To Me: A Guide To Puberty, Divorce Can Happen to The Nicest People, Where Did I Come From?*, and several drug education films for various age levels.

■ Sears, Roebuck & Co.

Family entertainment videos. See page 266 under **General Merchandise Catalogs.**

■ Sensational Beginnings

Parenting videos. See page 232 under **Toys.**

■ The Sesame Street Catalog

Sesame Street videos for pre-schoolers. See page 233 under **Toys.**

■ Signals Catalog

274 Fillmore Avenue East, St. Paul, MN 55107, (800) 669–9696

Free 40-page color catalog

This terrific catalog is offered by Boston-based public television station WGBH and it is chockablock full of high-quality educational videos. You will find *Nova* specials, *Audubon VideoGuides, Natural States, National Geographic* films, *March of Time*, war histories, travelogues, and PBS series like *Victory Garden, Baby Basics,* and more.

The children will especially enjoy the *Sesame Street* home videos, David Attenborough's *Life on Earth*, Raffi, Ed Emberley, and several other offerings that Mom and Dad will enjoy as well.

■ Special Interest Video

3475 Oberlin Avenue South, Lakewood, NJ 08701-1062, (800) 522–0502

Free 32-page color catalog

When first-time parents throw their hands up in despair and say they wish that babies came with instructions, why not give them *Baby Basics?* For $39.95, you can offer 120 minutes of instruction on bathing, diapering, dressing, and feeding their newborn. They will also benefit from tips on health and safety, crying, and that all-important topic—sleeping!

Dr. Lee Salk's *Super Sitters* shows you how to find and train sitters. *Exploring The English Language* helps kids in grades two through eight sharpen their communication skills. For preschoolers, the *Growing Up Smarter* series contains 20-30-minute lessons on *Learning To Tell Time, Learning the Calendar, Learning About The Planets*, and more.

Children six to twelve will enjoy *Dinosaurs, Dinosaurs, Dinosaurs* for $29.95. With full-color animation, the film explores the mystery of the dinosaurs' existence.

■ Spoken Arts

Videos of children's classic literature. See page 47 under **Books.**

■ Stewart MacDonald's Guitar Shop Supply

Videos for repairing musical instruments. See page 161 under **Music.**

■ The Video Catalog

P.O. Box 64428, St. Paul, MN 55164-0428, (800) 733–6656

Free 32-page color catalog

This new catalog is brought to you by the public television folks that put out the excellent Signals Catalog.

The whole family will enjoy the fine programs and films available here; most are rarely carried in local video stores, and The Video Catalog aims to remedy the situation.

Check the listings for classics such as *The Wizard of Oz*, Irving Berlin's *Easter Parade*, Lawrence Olivier in *Henry V*, Shirley Temple's hits, *The Three Stooges*, and the pilot episode of *Star Trek*. Younger children will enjoy *Charlotte's Web, Mary Poppins, The Red Balloon, The Tales of Beatrix Potter*, Disney classics, and *Sesame Street* tapes.

Educational titles are in abundance, with the likes of *Return of the Great Whales*, David Attenborough's *Life on Earth*, and documentaries about Civil War Generals Jackson, Grant, and Lee.

■ Walden Video By Mail

P.O. Box 7002, La Vergne, TN 37086-7002, (800) 322–2000

Free 32-page color catalog

If you have been unable to find the film you are looking for, give Walden a call: They have access to more than 10,000 titles.

How the Grinch Stole Christmas, Frosty the Snowman, Batman: The Movie, Winnie the Pooh, Babar, and Disney's *Duck Tales* are some of the videos available here. Among the selections for the whole family are musicals, Shirley Temple films, *Anne of Green Gables,* travelogues, documentaries, *Nova* and *National Geographic* specials, and nonfiction movies.

■ Yellow Moon Press

Small selection of videos featuring imaginative and interesting stories.
See page 43 under **Books.**

General Merchandise Catalogs

■

■ Best Products Co., Inc.

Tele-Mail Center, P.O. Box C23091, Richmond, VA 23260-5031, (800) 950–2378;
TDD service for the Hearing Impaired: (800) 950–0678 (accepts Baudot and AscII)

Free 330-page color catalog

Because Best Products Company buys in bulk to serve 194 stores, they can bring you their products at very reasonable prices. Their inventory includes home, office, and recreational products such as household gadgets and appliances, electronic equipment, jewelry, cameras, camping equipment, bedding, and furnishings. Parents can equip baby's nursery with cribs, changing tables, crib linens, and other basics. Car seats, strollers, swings, and more are available as well.

A large part of the catalog is devoted to children's toys, games, and videos. Wooden puzzles, costumes, Nintendo, bed linens, books, hobby supplies, electronic games, a Big Foot Ski Board, and a 27-inch plastic giraffe bank are among the temptations for kids. Piñatas as low as $5.99 and a 12-inch desk globe for $19.99 are good bargains.

■ Co-op America Order Service

10 Farrell Street, South Burlington, VT 05403, (802) 658–5507

Free 55-page color catalog

Co-op America is a consumer membership association that guarantees the social responsibility, quality, and fair value of all their products.

About twenty percent of their catalog is devoted to children. WinterWear of Clancy, Montana, offers 100 percent cotton union suits, hand-dyed in outrageously warm colors and sold in sizes 2T through 12. Biodegradable paper diaper liners are available for use with waterproof cotton Nikky Diaper Covers.

A wonderful toy in the children's section features a rainbow of large colored arches that children assemble to build bridges, tunnels, domes, towers, and tipis. Both a puzzle and a construction toy, it is made from maple and birch hardwood and sells for $42.00. A small selection of books, most with a Native American theme, are $9.95 each.

I had to smile over the verse on their bestselling T-shirt:

"it will be a great day
when
our schools
get all the money
they need
and the air force
has to hold
a bake sale
to buy a
bomber."

■ J.C. Penney Co., Inc.

Circulation Department, Box 2056, Milwaukee, WI 53201-2056, (800) 222–6161

$4.00 (plus local sales tax) for a 1,299-page color catalog. You receive a $5.00 gift certificate. Specialty catalogs ($1.00 each by phone or free at catalog sales offices) of interest to kids and parents are: "Big Kids/Fashions for Larger Size Children," a 16-page color catalog, and "Baby and You," a 48-page color catalog.

Like Sears, this company is a virtual supermarket of merchandise that families need or want at family-friendly prices. One of the largest stores in the world, Penney's sells clothes from newborn to adult sizes. Camping equipment, draperies and bedding, furniture, health care products, maternity clothing, pet supplies, shoes, sporting goods, stereos, telephones, televisions, word processors, and word processing supplies are all offered here.

■ The Mast General Store

Highway 194, Valle Crucis, NC 28691-0714, (800) 633–6278

Free 36-page color catalog

Take a step back in time with The Mast General Store, in operation for more than 100 years. Browse through pages of basic goods with an old-time flavor. Choose from hammocks, old advertising signs, picnic baskets, balms and salves, Americana collectibles, folk remedy books, kitchen gadgets, and more.

About five pages are devoted to children's items with such nostalgic offerings as cast-iron animal banks that are replicas of turn-of-the-century molds. They are painted and unbreakable, and they range in price from $8.00 for a pig bank to $16.00 for a white hen bank with a red comb.

A nice selection of old-fashioned wooden toys are also available at reasonable prices. Children may also enjoy such products as kaleidoscopes, bird feeders, wildflower seeds, lace collars, and books.

They offer a few clothing items for kids, all of the practical nature of striped railroad overalls by Liberty and OshKosh and those wonderful Rockford Red Heel Work Socks. These are also called Monkeysocks because they are the socks that Americans have made into monkeys, elephants, and bears for generations. Instructions for toymaking are included with each pair of socks.

■ Mothercare Home Shopping

P.O. Box 145, Watford WD2 5SH England, Phone: 0923 240365, Faxline: 0923 240944

Write for current price of 211-page color catalog

When I gave birth to my first child, a friend who had been living in England gave me her copy of Mothercare with the advice that everything I would ever need was within its pages. She was right.

From maternity and children's clothes to all kinds of baby equipment, this company is right on target with up-to-the-minute styles and features. You will find prams, bedding, sleeping bags, baby travel items, strollers, portable cribs, baby carriers, car seats, and home safety products. Toys, special gifts, books, and videos are all at your fingertips in this attractively photographed catalog.

Unfortunately, prices are listed in British pounds, so you should have an idea of the pound-to-dollar exchange rate before you order. If you put your order on a major credit card, they will, of course, do the exact conversion for you.

■ Neiman Marcus

Mail Order Division, P.O. Box 2968, Dallas, TX 75221-2968, (800) 634–6267

Free 129-page color catalog
$5.00 for the color Christmas Catalog

Neiman's glamorous Christmas catalog is justifiably famous for the extravagance of its gifts; for example, you can order a week at The Greenhouse spa for your mother for $2,975.00. But while these are the gifts that garner the most press copy, they also have seven pages of children's (and even pets') items.

For your precious small dog or cat, a designer bent-willow bed with floral printed cotton chintz pad is $180.00. "My Dream Trunk," with three completely accessorized outfits for little girls, allows your child to dress like a can-can dancer, a waitress, and a bride. You can indulge these fantasies for $235.00.

A hardwood rocker of a cow jumping (rocking?) over the moon is $100.00. A slick, red convertible is pedal-powered and includes a steering wheel and an air horn; it sells for $110.00.

■ Sears, Roebuck & Co.

P.O. Box 780593, Wichita, KS 67278-0593, (800) 366–3000

$5.00 for 1,082-page color Home Catalog, plus 427-page color Style Catalog. They come with a $6.00 gift certificate. Free 48-page color Focus catalog (The Complete Baby Store)

You certainly get a lot for your money here. The gigantic Home catalog contains coordinated bedroom fashions just for kids, brand-name electronics, design-it-your-self storage systems, furniture, computers, word processors, telephones, CD's, stereos, tape players, and more.

The Style catalog features a complete line of products for kids of all ages, with dozens of coordinating items to mix and match for baby's nursery. You will find cribs, high chairs, and children's clothes, as well as maternity fashions and nursing bras.

Focus, The Complete Baby Store, carries, as its name implies, all kinds of infants' furniture and supplies, including clothes for newborns to toddlers. You will find strollers, car seats, infant seats, crib mattresses, layette sets, towels, sheets, diapers, lamps, comforters, bumper pads, baby carriers and backpacks, safety gates, and much more.

The catalogs also contain outdoor play equipment, children's beds and bedding, toys, child-sized furniture, camping equipment, sporting goods, bicycles, scooters, radio-controlled cars, log cabin playhouses, video game systems, telescopes and other scientific toys, musical instruments, dolls, art supplies, dancewear, pet gear, and much more. A Holiday catalog is a veritable treasure trove of reasonably priced goods and gifts for the whole family.

■ Spiegel

P.O. Box 6340, Chicago, IL 60680-6340, (800) 345–4500

$3.00 for 580-page color catalog includes a $3.00 merchandise certificate good toward any order.

Spiegel has discontinued its children's clothes and toy lines, but they do carry home furnishings of interest to parents.

You will find a good selection of tape players, televisions, typewriters, lamps, luggage, desks, twin-sized bedding and beds, linens and curtains in child-friendly motifs, and storage solutions. The Holiday catalog does still offer gifts for children; you will find dolls, toys, pajamas, ornaments, and special treasures like music boxes, snow globes, telescopes, and more.

■ Vermont Country Store

Mail Order Office, P.O. Box 3000, Manchester Center, VT 05255-3000, (802) 362–2400

Free 112-page illustrated catalog

This catalog, called "Voice of the Mountains," is a nostalgic peek into an old-fashioned country store. Founded in 1946, they feature a wide variety of indoor and outdoor home needs, cleaning products, natural fiber clothes and undergarments, bedding, health and beauty products, and a limited selection of toys for children. Seasonal catalogs are mailed throughout the year; the Christmas edition includes a wider range of items especially for kids.

My latest catalog included such kids' fare as red flannel sleepwear; nightgowns and rib-knit long johns are colorfast in sizes 2T, 3T, and 4T for $21.95 and $19.95; children's sizes 4 through 7 are $22.95. Mother-daughter tartan flannel jumpers are $39.50 for Mom and $26.50 for daughter.

Toys include the original 1956 Ant Farm for $21.95, a pogo stick for $33.95, and an electric train set for $49.95.

Company Index

Interest Index

■